Sacred Prayers Drawn from the Psalms of David

The Peter Martyr Library
Volume Three

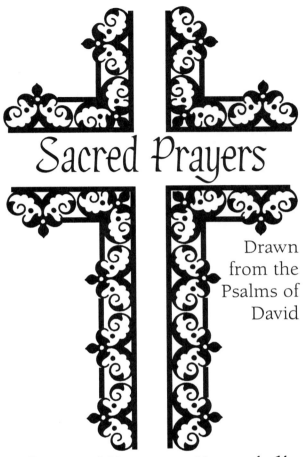

Sacred Prayers

Drawn
from the
Psalms of
David

Peter Martyr Vermigli

Translated and Edited
by John Patrick Donnelly, S.J.

VOLUME XXXIV
SIXTEENTH CENTURY ESSAYS & STUDIES
KIRKSVILLE, MISSOURI USA ◆ 1996

This book has been brought to publication with the generous support of
Truman (formerly Northeast Missouri) State University,
Marquette University, and the Jesuit Community of Marquette
and is published jointly by
The Thomas Jefferson University Press
and Sixteenth Century Journal Publishers, Inc.
Kirksville, Missouri, U.S.A.

Library of Congress Cataloging-in-Publication Data

Vermigli, Pietro Martire, 1499–1562.
    [Preces sacrae de Psalmis Davidis desumptae. English]
    Sacred prayers drawn from the Psalms of David / Peter Martyr Ver-
migli ; translated and edited by John Patrick Donnelly.
        p.   cm. — (Sixteenth century essays & studies : v. 34) (The Peter
Martyr library. Series one ; v. 3)
    Includes bibliographical references and index
    ISBN 0-940474-36-0 (alk. paper)
        1. Prayers—Early works to 1800. 2 Bible. O.T. Psalms—Devotional
use—Early works to 1800. I. Title. II. Series. III. Series: Vermigli, Pietro
Martine, 1499-1562. Works. English. 1994 : v. 3.

BR350.V37   1994 vol. 3
[BV245]
242—dc20   95-44461
                                                                          CIP

Composed at Truman (formerly Northeast Missouri) State University
Kirksville, Missouri 63501

Cover Art and Title Page by Teresa Wheeler, Truman State University Designer
Manufactured by Edwards Brothers, Ann Arbor, Michigan
Text is set in Galliard Oldstyle 10/13; display in Hadfield

Contents

General Editors' Preface

THE PETER MARTYR LIBRARY presents a series of English translations of the chief works of Peter Martyr Vermigli (1499–1562). This influential Reformer, neglected until the recent revival of scholarly interest, was a major player in the sixteenth-century Reform movement in Italy and northern Europe. His stature rivaled that of John Calvin among those known as Calvinists; his teaching is reflected from the Heidelberg Catechism to covenant theology; Puritans admired him and brought his works with them to North American. Yet he is not himself easily labeled, as simply Calvinist or—more controversial—as Reformed Aristotelian, or by his former colleagues in his believed Italy, as heretic. He regarded himself as primarily a biblical commentator, and indeed most of his works are just that, laced with numerous scholia which disciples gathered after his death into the famous commonplace book, *Loci Communes*. This gathering of topics gave later generations the impression that he wrote it himself in scholastic manner. In fact he handled topics suggested by the biblical narrative he was treating. The *Loci,* arranged in four sections, bears comparison with Calvin's more familiar *Institutio,* the model which Robert Masson had before him when preparing the first edition of the *Loci* in 1576. In turn, Calvin can be read best with Martyr as foil, as John T. McNeill and Ford Lewis Battles recognized in their modern edition of the *Institutes.* If our PMV Library series helps correct the image of Martyr as scholastic, and if our work introduces the variety of topics so well considered by this most erudite of Reformers, our aims will have been accomplished.

The third volume of the Peter Martyr Library shows Martyr as he leads his students at the Strasbourg Academy in prayer before his lectures on the Pentateuch. Their prayer had a special urgency because war and the possible religious persecution were threatening. These prayers were discovered after Martyr's death by his friend Josiah Simler and published in 1564 at Zurich. They must have struck a responsive chord in many Protestant communities since they were republished more often than any of Martyr's individual works and were translated from Latin into English, French, German, and Czech.

John Patrick Donnelly, S.J. and Joseph C. McLelland
General Editors

About the Translator

John Patrick Donnelly, S.J., received his Ph.D. in history from the University of Wisconsin–Madison in 1972, where he wrote a dissertation on Peter Martyr Vermigli under the direction of Robert M. Kingdon. Since 1971, he has taught at Marquette University in Milwaukee, where he is professor of history. His research has centered mainly on the Jesuits and on Peter Martyr Vermigli. In addition to six articles and chapters in books dealing with Vermigli, he has published *Calvinism and Scholasticism in Vermigli's Doctrine of Man and Grace* (Leiden: Brill, 1976), and with Robert M. Kingdon, *A Bibliography of the Works of Peter Martyr Vermigli,* Sixteenth Century Essays and Studies, XII (Kirksville, Mo.), 1990. He has previously translated from Latin various works of Thomas More (1982), Robert Bellarmine (1989), and Girolamo Savonarola (1994). He has held various offices in professional societies, including President of the Sixteenth Century Studies Conference (1977) and President of the Society for Reformation Research (1990–1991). He currently serves on the editorial boards of *The Sixteenth Century Journal* and *Archive for Reformation Research*. He is co-general editor of the Peter Martyr Library.

Translator's Preface

THIS IS THE SECOND VOLUME that I have prepared for The Peter Martyr Library. The first was an edition and translation of Peter Martyr Vermigli's *Dialogus de utraque in Christo natura,* which was published as volume 2 in 1995. The contrast between that work and this translation of Martyr's *Preces sacrae de Psalmis Davidis desumptae (Sacred Prayers Drawn from the Psalms of David)* is striking. The *Dialogus* was a work of enormous erudition, rich in references to Scripture, ancient philosophers, medieval scholastics, and especially to the Church Fathers. The *Dialogus* contains 689 footnotes for the text, not counting the introduction. The *Preces* contains only fourteen notes, mostly dealing with readings of the Latin text. In this respect and many others the *Preces* stands apart from Vermigli's other works and therefore deserves a place in The Peter Martyr Library. All of Vermigli's other major works take two literary forms: they are commentaries, usually on Scripture but also one commentary on Aristotle, or they are polemical works. The *Preces* precisely as prayers might seem to give us a glimpse into Martyr's heart and his intimate dealings with God, but we must be cautious. The *Preces* were written to be read at the end of lectures and strive for an elevated, formal tone that lacks the personal touch that might bare Vermigli's soul. What they lose thereby as biographical source, they gain as prayers that can still be of use to Christians in all ages. The translator is a Jesuit priest who disagrees with many points of Vermigli's theology and lives in a world very different from his, but he did not find any sentiment in these prayers from the Psalms that he could not address to God. The more the study of the Reformation moves away from theology and especially from polemics into treatises on spirituality and into devotional works, the more the common Christian heritage comes to the fore. Several years ago I published a translation of Saint Robert Bellarmine's *The Mind's Ascent to God.* Three of the four previous English translations of that work were made by Protestants.

In preparing this translation, I had help from many sources, most importantly from the series co-editor, Joseph C. McLelland, and from the publisher, Robert V. Schnucker of Truman (formerly Northeast Missouri) State University. Without their encouragement I would not have taken on the project. My research assistant at Marquette University, Andrea Brown, helped me weed out errors from the first draft of the manuscript. Thomas Caldwell, S.J., of Marquette's Department of Theology reviewed the Introduction. John Treloar, S.J., of Marquette's Department of Philosophy checked over the whole of the second draft and suggested modifications. Roland Teske, S.J., of the same Department helped me with several sticky passages. Lowell Zuck of Eden Seminary, Ulrich Kopp of the Herzog Augustus Bibliothek Wolfenbüttel, and Oliver Olson of Marquette's Department of Theology helped me in checking Latin editions for alternative readings different from my base text. The photograph of the *Preces* title page is printed with the permission of the Zentralbibliothek of Zurich.

John Patrick Donnelly, S.J.

Marquette University

Introduction

The Psalms
and Reformation Piety

No BOOK OF THE OLD TESTAMENT approaches the importance of the Psalms for Christianity. The Psalter has been called the microcosm of the whole of the Old Testament.[1] Since the Middle Ages the Divine Office, which monks and friars recited daily in choir, was drawn mainly from the Psalms and until recently usually involved the recitation of the whole Psalter each week. The reason for the prominence of the Psalms in Christian worship is obvious enough. They make up not only the longest book in the Bible, but they are easily the largest collection of prayers in the Scriptures. There are many other prayers scattered through the Scriptures, most notably various canticles and the Lord's Prayer, but all of the other prayers of the Bible combined fall far short of Psalms in length.

The Reformation, with its emphasis on scripture alone, involved a considerable shift in the prayer and piety of Protestant Christians. Because many old Catholic prayers and religious practices were no long acceptable, the Psalter took on still greater importance in the prayer of Protestants. Both Luther and Calvin wrote commentaries on the Psalms. Many leading Protestant theologians, several of whom were Peter Martyr Vermigli's friends, such as Ulrich Zwingli, Martin Bucer, John Calvin, and Immanuel Tremellius,

[1]Leopold Sabourin, *The Psalms: Their Origin and Meaning* (New York: Alba House, 1974), 4.

published their own Latin translations of the Psalms. Partly this was because the translation of the Psalms was perhaps the least satisfactory part of the whole Vulgate Latin Bible. The most famous Psalter of the Reformation was undoubtedly the French verse translation of Theodore Beza, who became Vermigli's close collaborator and friend at the Colloquy of Poissy in 1561. Beza's translation of the Psalms became the most popular hymnal in French Protestant churches, and Huguenot armies spontaneously chanted them before going into battle during the French Wars of Religion.[2]

The country whose use of the Psalms for prayers has been examined most closely and recently is England. Rivkah Zim's *English Metrical Psalms: Poetry as Praise and Prayer, 1535-1601* studies ninety English translations of the Psalms from the time of Henry VIII's break from Rome until the death of Elizabeth I. Although Zim's emphasis is on metrical translations, often by famous poets and churchmen such as Philip Sydney, Edmund Spenser, and Matthew Parker, he gives details on a number of largely forgotten collections of prayers and meditations based on the Psalms that parallel Vermigli's *Preces sacrae*.[3] A similarly careful examination of Psalm translations and paraphrases in continental countries where Protestantism was strong would undoubtedly yield results similar to Zim's examination of England. It is hoped that this translation of Vermigli's *Preces* based on the Psalms will give modern readers a handy example of this very considerable literature, most of which is available only in rare book collections.

PETER MARTYR VERMIGLI AND THE PSALMS

During his more than twenty years as an Augustinian Canon Regular Peter Martyr sang the daily Divine Office in choir along with the other Augustinians. Given his retentive memory, he probably came to know most or all of the Psalms by heart. In Martyr's last years in Italy, 1540 to 1542, he was a semi-Nicodemite, increasingly Protestant in his inward convictions but compelled

---

[2]Garrett Mattingly, *The Armada* (Boston: Houghton Mifflin, 1959), 156, describes how at the outset of the Battle of Coutras, when the Huguenot army started to sing Beza's metrical version of Psalm 118, a young Catholic took it as a sign of cowardice. A veteran corrected him: "When the Huguenots make those noises, they are ready to fight hard."

[3]The authors whose works came close to Vermigli's *Preces* were Robert Fylles and John Bull. Bull's work in fact contains sections translated from Vermigli's *Preces*; see Rivkah Zim, *English Metrical Psalms: Poetry and Prayer, 1535-1601* (Cambridge: Cambridge University Press, 1987), 236–237. The verse translation by Matthew Parker, Elizabeth I's second Archbishop of Canterbury, contains a short verse argument at the beginning of the translations and a prose prayer at the end. See items no. 14, 44, 46, 52, 58, 59, 61, 63, and 66 in Zim's appendix, pp. 220–247, for examples of prayers based on the Psalms.

by his duties as a canon and later as prior at San Frediano's in Lucca to celebrate the Roman Catholic liturgy. The text of the Mass, with its many references to the Mass as a sacrifice, must have weighed heavily upon his conscience, but omitting or changing texts during public Masses would instantly have given rise to suspicions. Singing the Divine Office would have been less a burden since the texts were overwhelmingly drawn from Scripture and the Church Fathers, and the Psalms may have been a keen source of consolation for Martyr since he could sing them with a sincere heart.

Martyr fled Italy late in August of 1542 and went to Zurich, where he was warmly received, but there was no appropriate position for him in Zurich. The death of Wolfgang Capito left the post of professor of Old Testament open at Strasbourg, and Vermigli took up the position in December 1542. He obviously made a strong impression on Martin Bucer and the other leaders of the Strasbourg church since he was entrusted with such an important post within months of his open conversion to Protestantism. Martyr continued to teach at Strasbourg until his departure for England in October 1547. As will be argued later, Martyr wrote or at least began the *Preces* toward the end of his first stay at the Strasbourg Academy. While at Strasbourg he lectured on Lamentations, the minor prophets, Genesis, Exodus, and part of Leviticus.[4] We know less about the events of Martyr's first years in Strasbourg (1542–1547) than about the other three periods of his career as a Protestant theologian.[5] His reputation as a scholar was spreading only gradually, and initially he was overshadowed by Martin Bucer, who lectured on the New Testament. Unlike the later periods of his life, he did not become involved in theological controversy, an activity that often produced biographical material. He was diligent in preparing his lectures on the Old Testament, but most of them from this period have not survived. We have only his Genesis commentary (which breaks off abruptly at Gen. 42:25), some theses for his students to dispute based on his lectures on Genesis, Exodus, and Leviticus, the fairly short commentary on Lamentations, and the *Preces*. There are also some letters and a short explanation of the creed in Italian, the only work that Martyr published

---

[4]The sequence of Martyr's early Strasbourg lecture's is given by Josiah Simler in his biography of Martyr: see J.C. McLelland and G.E. Duffield, eds., *The Life, Early Letters and Eucharistic Writings of Peter Martyr* (Appleford, Oxford: Sutton Courtenay Press, 1989), 52.

[5]Martyr was in England, where he held the chair of Regius Professor of Divinity at Oxford, from November 1547 to October 1553. He returned to Strasbourg after the accession of Mary Tudor to resume teaching from November 1553 until July 1556. Disagreements with the Lutheran pastors in Strasbourg led to his departure for Zurich, where he lectured from July 1556 until his death in November 1562.

(1544) during these years. All the other works from this period were published posthumously from his notes.

Even though he was a foreigner and learning the ropes (his Genesis commentary from this period is probably the least distinguished of his major biblical commentaries), Martyr gradually eclipsed the great Martin Bucer in his popularity as a teacher. He was clearer, better organized, and less prolix than Bucer. Josiah Simler, who was Martyr's friend, biographer, successor as professor at Zurich, and editor of the *Preces*, tells us that Martyr "pleased the minds of his hearers, not only for the gravity of the things themselves but also for the sweetness and elegance of his style." Simler goes on to note, possibly with reference to the *Preces*, that his lectures "sometimes exhorted to godly life, ... stirred up repentance ..." and joined excellent doctrine and eloquence "with singular piety."[6]

When were the *Preces* written? The prayers make only vague allusions to contemporary events and contain no direct evidence for dating their composition. The best evidence is from the prefatory letter to the *Preces* provided by their editor, Josiah Simler. In the years immediately after his death nobody knew more about Martyr's whole life than Simler, except Martyr's longtime personal servant Giulio Santerenziano, and Simler was in a position to question Santerenziano. In his prefatory letter to the *Preces*, which begins this edition, Simler tells us three things about their composition: "when the Council of Trent had just begun and a serious and internecine war had broken out in Germany over religion, Martyr read these prayers at the end of his lectures at the Strasbourg Academy." Since Simler gives three coordinates, fixing the date might seem an easy task. But Vermigli had two sojourns in Strasbourg, there were two Schmalkaldic Wars in Germany over religion, and two of the three periods of the Council of Trent took place during Vermigli's lifetime. Three earlier scholars have addressed themselves in passing to the question of when the *Preces* were written. They do not agree. Charles Schmidt does not list the *Preces* among the works written during Vermigli's first stay at Strasbourg, but later he definitely links them to the First Schmalkaldic War, which broke out in 1546.[7] Klaus Sturm also suggests that the *Preces* were written during Martyr's first sojourn in Strasbourg but says that "The dating is questionable."[8] Marvin Anderson puts the composition of the *Preces* during Vermigli's second

---

[6]McLelland and Duffield, *Life ... of Martyr*, 53.

[7]Charles Schmidt, *Peter Martyr Vermigli: Leben und ausgewählte Schriften* (Elberfeld: R.L. Friederichs, 1858), 58, 72.

[8]Klaus Sturm, *Die Theologie Peter Martyr Vermiglis während seines ersten Aufenthalts in Strassburg 1542-1547* (Neukirchen: Neukirchener Verlag, 1971), 275.

term as professor at Strasbourg.[9] I am convinced that the *Preces* must be dated toward the end of Vermigli's first stay in Strasbourg, December 1542 to October 1547. Simler says that the *Preces* were written shortly after the Council of Trent had begun. The Council met at Trent itself from December 1545 to March 1547, then was transferred to Bologna from March 1547 to February 1548. That fits perfectly. Moreover, the First Schmalkaldic War started in 1546 and reached its climax in a crushing defeat of the Protestant forces by Charles V at Mühlberg on April 24, 1547. The *Preces* contain a few passing references to war and ubiquitous lamentations over the calamities afflicting God's Church. Martyr returned to Strasbourg in November 1553 and stayed till July 1556. The Second Schmalkaldic War was 1552 till 1556, but the renewed warfare went in the Protestants' favor from the beginning, largely because they had Henry II of France as an ally. It would be difficult to square the doleful tone of the *Preces* with the course of the Second Schmalkaldic War. Moreover, the second set of sessions at Trent, May 1551 to April 1552, does not coincide at all with Vermigli's second sojourn in Strasbourg. When all that is taken into account, a difficulty remains: Simler says that Vermigli read the prayers at the end of his lectures, but the *Preces* contain 297 prayers (counting the nineteen parts of the prayer on Psalm 119 as only one prayer). It may be doubted that Vermigli gave 297 lectures between the opening of Trent and his departure for England. He may well have written them then and used many of them later or simply put them aside.

STRUCTURE AND CONTENT OF THE *PRECES*:

The *Preces* contain 297 prayers based on 149 of the Psalms.[10] There is no prayer for Psalm 87; if Vermigli wrote one, which seems likely, it is lost. The prayer for Psalm 119 does not fit the usual pattern; at first glance Vermigli wrote only one prayer for it, but that prayer is broken into nineteen parts, each of which is in fact an independent prayer and is subtitled by two letters of the Hebrew alphabet. The majority of the Psalms have either two prayers (79 Psalms) or one prayer (39 Psalms) based on them. Psalms 68 and 78 have four prayers, and Psalms 18 and 105 have five. The others have three prayers. Most of the prayers run about a page in the Latin text of the three first editions.

---

[9]Marvin W. Anderson, *Peter Martyr Vermigli, A Reformer in Exile (1542-1562): A Chronology of Biblical Writings in England and Europe* (Nieuwkoop: De Graaf, 1975), 285, 300.

[10]At the end of the *Preces* proper Simler appended a prayer of Vermigli against "Bread worshipers." This prayer does not seem related to the *Preces* and does not come into consideration here.

It is not clear why Vermigli chose to write more prayers on some Psalms than on others. Generally the longer Psalms get more treatment. Psalm 119 is by far the longest Psalm and receives by far the longest treatment from Martyr. Psalm 68 (four prayers) has thirty-five verses; Psalm 78 (four prayers) has seventy-eight verses; Psalm 105 (five prayers) has forty-five verses. But there is no simple correlation between the length of a Psalm and the number of prayers Vermigli devoted to it; thus Psalm 18 has five prayers but only twenty-one verses, while Psalm 15 has only one prayer but thirty-five verses. Neither does the content of a Psalm seemed to have controlled the number of prayers devoted to it. By far the longest treatment is given to Psalm 119, a pedestrian glorification of the Law, not the subject closest to the hearts of Protestant theologians, but Psalm 119 could have fitted in nicely with Martyr's lectures on Exodus or Leviticus. Psalm 139 has a depth of intimate communion with God and a poetic vision rarely matched in the Psalter, yet Vermigli based only one prayer on it.

There seems to be no way of knowing with certainty in what order Martyr wrote or used his prayers drawn from the Psalms. Simler in his prefatory letter tells us that as he was checking over Vermigli's writings after his death and while "gathering together in his library some tiny sheets of paper written in his own hand, I chanced upon pages that had been misplaced and scattered. On them were some sacred prayers written in his own hand." It may be that Simler ordered the prayers in the simplest way—by the order of the Psalms on which they were based. While it is possible that Vermigli wrote them in a different sequence, his was a very orderly mind, and the odds are that Vermigli himself wrote the prayers starting with Psalm 1 and working through to Psalm 150.

Anyone who reads these prayers starting at the beginning and moving ahead rapidly will find them very repetitious. They might be compared to listening to a dozen concerti by Antonio Vivaldi in sequence: it is all very well done, but have we not heard this before? The sameness has three sources. The first is that the Psalms themselves are repetitious. The great expert on the Psalms, Sigmund Mowinckel, noted long ago that uniformity and formality pervade the Psalms so that individuality fades into the background and the imagery is stereotyped and traditional. Unlike the outpourings of the Romantic poets, which tend to express individuality, the Psalms arise out of ritual, cultic background and express the experience and moods of the cultic community.[11] The second reason is that although many of the Psalms do use concrete

---

[11]Sigmund Mowinckel, *Psalmenstudien* (Oslo, 1921), 1:30.

images that stay in the memory and strike a lyrical note, they seem faded in Vermigli's prayers based on the Psalms. Vermigli's strengths as a writer were clarity, organization, and erudition. He is sober, solid, stolid, and sensible. One can read a thousand of his pages without finding a trace of humor. The final reason is the specific conditions under which Vermigli was writing: war was going on, and the forces of what he saw as the Antichrist were having the best of it. All that he loved and cherished seemed about to go down to destruction unless God intervened decisively in the human arena. This pessimism, at least as regards the immediate situation of Protestantism in Germany, was surely a major factor in his decision in October 1547 to go to Edwardian England, where prospects were brighter. Vermigli was not driven out of Strasbourg but left well before the Augsburg and Leipzig Interims tried to reimpose Catholic practices; Martin Bucer managed to hold on at Strasbourg until 1549 before joining Vermigli in England.

Most of Martyr's prayers on the Psalms touch on the same themes in roughly the same order. They almost always begin with an invocation of God the Father, and almost always address God in the first person plural. The prayers then usually place before God the afflictions of his people. The troubles of the Church flow from the sins of the people, which God is rightly punishing. A sense of personal and collective sinfulness pervades the prayers.[12] But because God is good, he will deliver his people and protect them from their enemies. Then his people will praise him joyously forever. The prayers end with "Through Jesus Christ, our Lord. Amen" or with a minor variant on that conclusion. Sometimes various phrases in the prayer are closely tied to expressions in the Psalm, but not always.

If the sense of guilt and affliction most strikes modern readers of the *Preces*, it must be remembered not only that they were written in a time of real crisis but also that they voice an abiding confidence and trust in God's power and goodwill to deliver his people from their present woes and carry them to victory both in this life and the next. During the Reformation era political and religious turmoil and war nurtured in many people an apocalyptic mentality which many recent scholars have explored. Panic over an imminent doomsday obsessed not only a relative handful of Anabaptists at Münster but was also

---

[12]Jean Delumeau, *Sin and Fear: The Emergence of a Western Guilt Culture, 13th-18th Centuries*, trans. Eric Nicholson (New York: St. Martin's, 1990), makes no reference to Vermigli's *Preces*, but they would have provided excellent evidence for his main thesis: that early modern Europe was pervaded with a sense of guilt and fear. Delumeau, p. 538, does make one passing reference to Martyr with regard to his request that Theodore Beza add a commentary to his *Tabula praedestinationis*.

widespread among mainstream Protestants and Catholics.[13] One will look in vain among the *Preces* for a truly apocalyptic note: that the end times are at hand.[14] If there is a sense of crisis in many of the prayers, there is also an ultimate confidence and even serenity: we may be sinful and do not have the resources to escape our afflictions on our own, but God loves us, and he remains the master of political and military events and will deliver us in the end. He sends us troubles and afflictions to punish our sins and drive us to amend our sinful ways. When we are properly repentant, he will give us the victory, and once he has decided for us, our enemies will be unable to stand against us. This providential view of events was rooted in the Bible, not least in the Psalter, and was the common conviction of Vermigli's age.[15]

The prayers contain many references to the Antichrist or Antichrists, and while there is little doubt that Vermigli had the Pope and Roman Catholic forces mainly in mind, he does not make that explicit, nor does he attack the papacy and Catholics with anything approaching the vehemence found in Luther's last writings, which appeared a few years before the *Preces*. As far as the text of the *Preces* goes, Antichrist is simply those forces that oppose Christ and his Church, not the persons of Paul III and his ally Charles V.

THE POPULARITY OF MARTYR'S *PRECES*:

Aside from the *Loci Communes*, which Robert Masson, pastor of the French Congregation in London, compiled from Vermigli's theological work in 1576, the *Preces* proved the most popular of all Martyr's works. It appeared in ten editions in all and was translated from Latin into four vernacular

[13]Norman Cohn, *The Pursuit of the Millennium* (Oxford: Oxford University Press, 1970); Robin Barnes, *Prophecy and Gnosis: Apocalypticism in the Wake of the Lutheran Reformation* (Stanford: Stanford University Press, 1988); Katharine R. Firth, *The Apocalyptic Tradition in Reformation Britain, 1530-1645* (Oxford: Oxford University Press, 1979); Denis Crouzet, *Les guerriers de Dieu. La violence au temps des troubles de religion (vers 1525-vers 1610)* (Seyssel: Editions Champ Vallon, 1990).

[14]Philip McNair, *Peter Martyr in Italy: An Anatomy of Apostasy* (Oxford: Clarendon Press, 1967), 68–69, lays out how little foundation there is for the claims of earlier historians who have seen a strong influence of Savonarola on Vermigli. The lack of an apocalyptic note in the *Preces* only reinforces McNair's argument.

[15]The reaction of the Spanish Jesuit Pedro de Ribadeneira to the defeat of the Spanish Armada has many parallels with Vermigli's reaction to the First Schmalkaldic War. His *Treatise on Tribulation* was written to provide Spaniards with consolation for "those general calamities of these our days." God uses events to punish not just individuals but cities and nations. Although the Spanish Armada set out "to defend the cause of God" with "so many prayers, supplications and penances of his faithful servants…, no one can deny that it was a severe punishment and chastisement from the hand of the Most High." The *Treatise on Tribulation* is described by Robert Bireley, *Anti-Machiavellianism or Catholic Statecraft in Early Modern Europe* (Chapel Hill: University of North Carolina Press, 1990) 114-115.

languages: English, French, German, and Czech. The next most popular of Vermigli's works were the *Tractatio* on the Eucharist and the *Dialogus* with seven editions each and his commentary on the Epistle to the Romans with eight editions. The first edition of the *Preces*, as has been noted, was edited by Martyr's friend Josiah Simler from pages he discovered in Martyr's library after his death. It was issued by Martyr's favorite publisher, Christopher Froschauer of Zurich, in 1564, two years after the author's death. Froschauer published identical editions in 1566 and 1578. It appeared again in the third volume of Vermigli's *Locorum Communium* published by the distinguished Peter Perna Press in 1582. The title page of the last Latin edition (Zurich: Johann Wolf, 1604) proudly states "Nunc vero ex autographis correctae," but it contains only a few corrections of typographical slips. The notes in this present translation points out when it follows the 1604 corrections. This last Latin edition adds a new prefatory letter, dated March 6, 1604 (not found in earlier editions) from R. Simler, who taught philosophy at Zurich, to his colleague, the theologian Johann Wilhelm Stucki. Since the letter adds no new information about either Martyr or the *Preces*, it is not translated here.

The first translations of the *Preces* were into English. Henry Bull's *Christian Prayers and Holy Meditations as Well for Private as Public Exercise* (London: Middleton, 1568) printed Vermigli's first five prayers at the end of his volume, praising Martyr's book and stating: "which if it may please any of the godly learned to translate into the English tongue, he shall doubtless do great service to God and to his congregation: and we trust that godly zeal shall stir up the hearts of some to take this worthy enterprise in hand."[16] His invitation was soon taken up by Charles Glemhan, whose translation was published by William Seres at London in 1569 under the title *Most Godly Prayers Compiled out of Davids Psalmes*. There were two French editions published, one in Geneva by Jean Durant in 1577, and one at La Rocelle by Pierre Hautin in 1581. Both of these were in sexidecimo for easy handling. Froschauer published a German translation in 1589 at Zurich in a duodecimo format. The rarest of all editions is the Czech translation by Johann Sudlicius (Jana Sudlicya). The sole known copy is at the State Library in Prague. The year of its publication in 1620 is significant, for in that year the Czech Protestants were defeated by Ferdinand II in the Battle of White Mountain. Their situation in late 1620 had many parallels with that of Vermigli and Strasbourg in 1547 after the defeat of Protestant forces by Charles V.

---

[16]I use the edition reprinted for the Parker Society (Cambridge: Cambridge University Press, 1844), 205.

About This Translation

This translation simplifies the Latin to help it sound like modern English. Most of Vermigli's sentences begin with a connective: *unde, itaque, sane, quidem, verum, igitur, tandem* — and a dozen others. That is not how English is written today, so the translation drops most of these connectives at the beginning of sentences. Many of Vermigli's long sentences, which tend to run six or seven lines, have been broken into several shorter sentences. It is a rare adjective that Vermigli does not put in the superlative; these have usually been scaled down to the positive degree. Thus his most common way of addressing God, "Deus Opt. Max " (a classical expression, used by the Romans to address Jupiter), is here rendered as "O great and good God." The translator has used an occasional turn of phrase from Charles Glemhan's 1569 English translation. Glemhan is very good at catching the meaning of the Latin, but he belongs to the "aureate" school of Tudor translators and embroiders the original with many words which are not found in the original. The result is a translation that is much longer than the original. Vermigli's text in the first three Latin editions runs 365 sexidecimo pages; Glemhan's translation runs 527 pages in octavo. Vermigli's vocabulary is very large, but his ideas in this work are simple and repetitious. Vermigli only rarely uses a technical vocabulary, so the translator has not tried to be consistent in translating a given word. A good but pesky example is *pius* and its cognates such as *pietas, impietas, impius*: sometimes *pius* is translated as *godly* or *devout* or *religious*; when applied to God it becomes *paternal*. Another common term is *animus*, which means soul in a technical context, but *animus* in the *Preces* usually means the affective side of human nature and has often been translated as *heart*.

The tone of Vermigli's prayers is elevated, ornate, and reminiscent of the prayers of the *Missale Romanum*, which Vermigli would have known well. In trying to reproduce the tonality of Vermigli's prayers, this translation employs some semi-archaic terms such as *deign* and *wont*. For stylistic reasons the translator has often put petitions which Vermigli has in the subjunctive into the imperative. For example: "May you help us, O Lord," becomes, "Help us, O Lord." Latin uses the passive voice far more than does modern English; here many sentences Vermigli wrote in the passive have been turned into active voice. Despite these modifications, the translator has generally tried to produce a rather literal translation.

The base text used by the translator was the second edition published by Froschauer of Zurich in 1566. The first three Latin editions, all by Froschauer and dated 1564, 1566, and 1578, are identical in foliation. The translator has inserted in square brackets the foliation numbers. Thus [34r] means that folio 34 recto begins at this point; [56v] means that folio 56 verso begins here. These insertions will make it easy for anybody to compare the text with the three first Latin editions. These editions are the source of the English and French translations. The German translation of 1589 probably used the same Latin text but may have been based on the text printed in the *Locorum Communium*, vol. 2 (Basel: Petrus Perna, 1582). As noted earlier, the last Latin edition (Zurich: J. Wolf, 1604) claims that its text has been corrected from Vermigli's autograph, but the corrections are minimal.

Since the *Preces* almost never refer to any text outside the specific Psalm on which a given prayer is based, it made no sense to put down a footnote after the heading of each prayer, "From Psalm 34" referring readers to Psalm 34. Although this volume, unlike others in the Peter Martyr Library, does not contain a Scripture index, for all practical purposes the Table of Contents to the volume serves as a Scripture index since it provides the page numbers on which the prayers for each Psalm are to be found. The brief index in this volume is to the introduction.

PRECE3

EX PSALMO IX.

SI caufam noftram fufceperis,ô Deus,
nosq; ab hoftibus tui nominis & hu-
manæ falutis vendicaueris,ex toto corde
& fumma lætitia narrabimus celebrabi.
musq; tua eximia gefta. Noftra quidem
culpa tentationibus & huiufmodi preffu
ris affligimur, fed te per tuam bonitatem
atque mifericordiam obteftamur, vt qui
oppreſsis ad te confugientibus confueui
ſti afylum effe ne nos deferas , nêue has
preces , quas tibi fedulò effundimus , vi-
dearis obliuioni tradidiffe. Miferere no.
ftri,ô Deus, & à portis mortis eximas, ne
illis abforbeamur. Abs te adiuti,laudes
tuas in Ecclefia deprædicabimus, quod
nimirum in te haud incaffum fperaueri-
mus.Exurgas igitur,ne impietas, iniufti-
tia & peccata in nos præualeant,ac largi-
re,vt probè memores conditionis noftrę,
modefto demiffoq; animo tuæ voluntati
perpetuò fubijciamur, per Iefum Chri-
ftum dominum noftrum,Amen.

EX EODEM.

FAɔtum eft fæpius patrum tempefta-
te,Deus omnipotens,vt perfufus fue
                                        rit

Page from the prayer on Psalm 9 from *Preces Sacrae ex Psalmis Davidis primum per Petrum Martyrem collectae* … (Zurich: J. Wolf, 1604). 12°, approx 8 x 13.5 cm

Holy Prayers.

and looke vppon vs, and thofe whome thou haft made little inferiour vnto Aun-gels, make them partakers of thy owne nature. Finallye, feing that thou hafte in lawfull wife made vs Lordes ouer all thy creatures, graunt that we maye vfe them to the praife and glorie of thy name, fo, as thy facred worde and Gofpell maye be fpreade abroade amongft all Nations, through Iefus Chrift our Lorde. Amen.

¶ A prayer out of the ninth Pfalme.

F thou (O good God) wilt take our caufe in hâd, ¢ reuenge vs vpô the enimies of thy glorious name ¢ of mans faluation, we will (from the bottome of our hart, and with an exceeding great gladneffe) fhewe forth and celebrate thy wôderous and excellent actes: who be afflicted in deede with temptations ¢ other like oppreffions (by reafon of our heynous finnes) but we befeeche thee O highe and mightie God (for thy goodneffe and mer-cies fake) that as thou haft accuftomed to be a Sanctuarie and fure defence for the oppreffed which flie vnto thee for fuccour,

Page from the prayer on Psalm 9 from *Most Godly prayers compiled out of Davids Psalms* ...... (London: William Seres, 1569). 8°, approx. 9 x 14 cm

SACRAE. 16

rit populus tuus admirabili gaudio, ac to
tus lætabundus, nomé tuum cantibus ex-
tulerit, & fummis laudibus celebrarit, id-
que ex toto corde, eò quod te protegen-
te hoftes ipfis in prælio terga dederint,
impegerint, & perierint à facie tua. Neq;
femel iudicafti pro fanctis tuis, aut illo-
rum caufam afferuifti, frequenter gentes
increpuifti & perdidifti, qui extrema va-
ftitate vrbes præclaras populi tui fecú fta
tuerant euertere, ac ita deleuifti huiufmo
di improbos, vt nomen quoq; illorú fue-
rit abolitum. Cum itaq; æternum regnes,
& femper tribunal paratum habeas, vt de
effufo fanguine fanctorum quæftiones in
ftituas, in præfentia, ô Deus, ne fpernas,
aut obliuifcaris precum noftrarú. Scimus
quidem nos peccaffe, & plurimis modis
offendiffe maieftaté tuam, quod nunc, &
dolemus ex animo, & apertè fatemur, ta-
mé pro fiducia, quam erga te gerimus, ex
his concepta, quæ patribus noftris, etiam
immeritis contulifti, accedimus te, ac ora
mus, vt miferearis Ecclefiæ tuæ : refpice
quæfumus illius afflictioné, eamq; eripi-
as à portis mortis, quo laudes tuas indies

Page (*continued*) from the prayer on Psalm 9 from *Preces Sacrae ex Psalmis Davidis primum per Petrum Martyrem collectae ...*

Holy Prayers.

so now forsake vs not, nepther sceme to be forgetful of the prayers that we vnseinedlye poure out before thy diuine Maiestye. Haue mercy vpon vs (O good God) deliuer and rescue vs from the Gates of death, least we be swallowed vp therewith : being aided and holpen by thee, we shal shew forth thy worthy praises in the congregation, namely, bycause our trust hath not bene reposed in thee in baine. Arise therefore, and suffer not impietie, vnrighteousnesse, and sinne to preuayle agaynst vs, but graunt also, that we bearing well in minde oure owne estate and condition, maye with a modest and lowlye minde, be alwayes obedient to thy will and pleasure, through Jesus Christ oure Lorde, Amen,

Another prayer out of the same psalme.

I T happened verie often in our fathers dayes (O most mightie God) that thy people were filled with a wonderful & vnspeakable gladnes, who being replenished with exceeding great ioye, did set forth thy glorious name with songs, and celebrated

Page (*continued*) from the prayer on Psalm 9 from *Most Godly prayers compiled out of Davids Psalms* ...... (London: William Seres, 1569)

PETER MARTYR VERMIGLI (1499–1562)
From *Icones, id est, Verae imagines virorvm doctrina simvl et pietate illvstrivm,* by
Theodore Beza (Geneva, 1580)

PRAYERS

FROM THE PSALMS OF DAVID BY D. PETER MARTYR VERMIGLI

Florentine

TRANSLATED BY
JOHN PATRICK DONNELLY, S.J.

PRECES

SACRAE EX

PSALMIS DAVIDIS

DESVMPTAE PER D.Ph♣
TRVM MARTYREM VERMI-
lium Florentinum, facrarum lite-
rarum in fchola Tigurina
profefforem.

TIGVRI.
Excudebat Chriftophorus Frofchouerus,
Anno M. D. LXVI.

·S·m ·oa· ! ¡ of·droi ·¡¡
ᴌᴝ

Title page from the *Preces Sacrae ex Pslamis Davidis desumptae …*, printed
at Zurich by C. Froschauer in 1566. Title page used by permission of the
Zurich Zentralasbibliothek

$\mathcal{J}$OSIAH SIMLER sends abundant greetings to Hermann Folkersheimer of Frisia, a man much respected and his close friend:

Dear Hermann:

Last year when I was checking over the writings of our teacher, that good and learned man Peter Martyr, and was gathering together in his library some tiny sheets of paper written in his own hand, I chanced upon pages that had been misplaced and scattered. On them were some sacred prayers written in his own hand. After I had gone through them rather carefully, I judged that they were worthy of being published, even though I knew that they were not written by him with this in mind. Several considerations have led me to do this. The first is that in that time, when the Council of Trent had just begun and a serious and internecine war had broken out in Germany over religion, Martyr read these prayers in public at the end of his lectures at the Strasbourg Academy. It is appropriate to publish them now at this time when we need to beseech God with ardent prayer that no similar conflagration break out now that the Council of Trent has been concluded.[1] Secondly, the prayers in this little book [2v] are clear and depart only a little from the words of the Psalms—this is something I judge very important in prayers. These prayers partly explain briefly and clearly the theme of many Psalms and partly explain many obscure and difficult passages with a lucid paraphrase. So I have no doubt that, in the judgment of many, zealous persons will derive great profit from reading this short book.

I have dedicated this book to you, gracious Hermann, that you may have a remembrance [μνημόσυνον] both of our Martyr and of me. For you honored and esteemed Martyr when he was alive like a parent. Moreover you have hitherto extended to me so much love that forever I must rightly count you in the number of my dearest friends. I believe that it will please you to have me send you this book, small as it may be, inscribed with the name of you both. Every time that you look into this book, and given your piety you will look rather often, you will be looking at a reminder, not wholly unpleasant, I hope, of your old friends. Martyr's death could not destroy our memory of

---

[1] The Council of Trent opened 13 December 1545 and continued, with several prolonged breaks, until 4 December 1563. The First Schmalkaldic War began in the autumn of 1546.

him. The distance between our towns will neither separate the close relation-
ship of us who are alive nor keep us from preserving through letters and the
fond recollection of old memories the friendship that we began long ago.

Farewell from Zurich,
June 20 in the year of our salvation 1564.

[3r]Sacred Prayers Drawn from the Psalms of David written by Peter Martyr

FROM PSALM 1:

Take away from us, O great and good God, wicked plans and their attendant sins. Do not let us fall into an evil and shameful life. Likewise keep our souls far from contemning piety and scorning virtues. Instead of these plagues grant that we may constantly meditate on your law and your sacred writings. Then we will not, like the wicked, be carried about by every wind of impulse and doctrine as are light flakes of dust and worthless rubbish. Rather like trees planted by streams of water, endowed with faith and the life of the spirit, may we also bear the outward fruit of good works, and may whatever we do prosper and give praise and glory to your name and [3v] add to our salvation. Finally may we, in accord with your mercy, both stand up and be absolved before the court of your judgment after the wicked have already fallen. Through our Lord Jesus Christ. Amen.

FROM THE SAME PSALM:

Almighty God, we already understand quite clearly how serious troubles and woeful disasters so afflict the Church because we have often yielded to the counsels of the wicked when we should have turned away from the moment we recognized them. We have in no way turned aside from the path of sinners but have followed their path closely with our constant transgressions against your commandments. Moreover, for a long time we have contemned sound admonitions and healthy practices. We have neglected with considerable laziness and even insolence and have derided whatever your word offered to us. It is no wonder that now we have to undergo every heavy, irksome, and bitter experience instead of the happiness and tranquil peace that for so long we have, alas, misused. But now, O God, we flee to you as suppliants, confessing the evil deeds we have done, and we ask with urgent and ardent prayers that [4r] you be kind and forgive us the sins that we have committed in our stupidity and wickedness. Make our souls as devoted as possible to your law so that

5

we may ponder in our hearts day and night nothing except the words of your Holy Scriptures. That way we shall bring forth in due season sweet fruit, employing our faith in your word, and we will not be robbed of the gifts of the Holy Spirit. Indeed, our efforts will always have a blessed outcome. But now we are hard pressed by our sins and are not unlike husks blown up and down by the winds of tribulation. At least, good Father, grant this: that our life may not be wasted in evil like the wicked. Rather, like the cause of the just, may you defend our life with the highest care and protection so that we may stand at the judgment and gathering of the just and that we may not fail in our cause. Through Jesus Christ our Lord. Amen.

FROM THE SAME PSALM:

Since it has already been explained to us, O almighty God, that our happiness while we live here depends in large measure on how we beware of evil advice and profligate behavior and flee the company of those who [4v] spurn and deride everything and on how such plagues are replaced by wondrous zeal for the divine law on which we meditate and reflect night and day. Since we realize we have strayed far from this goal of our salvation, indeed have sinned grievously against this, we ask you that in your mercy you forgive our failures and deign to make us henceforward fruitful plants by the continual study and use of your word. May we not only bear fruit in your Church while we live, but may we also be able to pass successfully our judgment in the other world before you, who knows perfectly the way of the just. Through Jesus Christ, our Lord. Amen.

FROM PSALM 2:

In this time, O great and good God, we feel that not only the Antichrist but all the power and force of the world has conspired against you and your Christ—namely those who think that the Gospel and the reformation of the Church are intolerable chains and a heavy yoke, so that they try by every device to break apart communities of believers and reject all discipline. But since you [5r] dwell in heaven and since the plotting of the devil and sinful flesh are not hidden from you, you laugh at their useless schemes, render vain their efforts, and make them instead the joke and laughingstock of your elect. Make them realize your anger, and may they at last be filled with terror by the fury of your wrath so that they cannot destroy your Church. You have put Jesus Christ, our only savior, over the Church so that he may reign in it mighty and invincible by his word and spirit. Graciously grant to us, your children, even though we are unworthy and disloyal, enough faith and constancy that we may have him as our only king and confess the same. May we have no doubts that we are his nation, people, and heritage. May we rightly understand that he is endowed with such strength and power that he punishes those he wishes with a power stronger than iron and brings them low like clay pots. O God, convert the kings of the earth to yourself so that they may understand and acknowledge and embrace and kiss your Son lest, his wrath being kindled, they perish on the spot. When it seems good to you, make blessed forever those who have really committed themselves to your faith. Through Christ our Lord. Amen.

[*5v*] FROM THE SAME PSALM:

Regardless of how much the devil rages, O great and good God, or the worldly powers rise up daily, or the flesh conspires with its slaves against the kingdom of your only begotten Son, our Lord Jesus Christ, still we know and hold firmly as part of our steadfast faith that you mock and scorn all such things—you who are mighty to crush them in your wrath and anger as soon as it pleases you. Since we are sometimes weak in our faith, so that driven by various fears we obey your commandments less than we ought, we beseech you that in your goodness you show us your favor so that we may be firmly convinced that your Son is our king and redeemer and holds complete power at your side over all things. When you begot him, you handed over all the nations for him to rule rightfully as his heritage. Grant us now finally to realize that and learn it so well that by serving you with all fear and honor we may not be smashed on the last day like a clay pot by the rod of your anger. Through Jesus Christ, our Lord. Amen.

[*6r*] FROM PSALM 3:

O great and good God, the forces of those who have risen up against your Church have grown beyond measure. Many already dare to attack her and cruelly rebel against her, relying on this one idea which they have decided upon among themselves, that we could no longer hope for salvation from you, as if you had completely abandoned your people and stripped them of every protector and defense. We do not indeed deny, when we look upon the sins with which we have offended you, that we fully merit being deprived of your help and being exposed to insults, reproaches, and injuries from the enemies of your name. Nonetheless, because of the faith which through your mercy survives in us, we dare to approach you and ask that you deign to supply us amid the reproaches of our enemies with enough of the Spirit and with enough constancy that we may not doubt that you will be the only protection, honor, and vindication of your people. If we have begged your help in prayers, we will be strengthened by that trust, and you will undoubtedly look favorably on us from your heavenly dwelling. When we are safe under your protection, our fear will leave us so completely that, even though [*6v*] vast hosts of enemies besiege us, we will take our sleep and get up as usual while we courageously rely on you alone. Arise then, O God, in accord with this beginning of our trust, and as you were wont to do in times past, smash the teeth of those who pit themselves against you lest they be able to wound your Church at their whim. Show us that salvation comes from you and that in your goodness you are still able to help your people in their extreme distress. Through Jesus Christ our Lord. Amen.

FROM THE SAME PSALM:
O almighty God, day by day the forces of Satan and of all the powers opposing us seem to be growing, and they are trying to overturn upon us the kingdom of your Son. They try to drive us to despair, as if we could no longer find salvation in you.

Nonetheless, even though we feel ourselves terribly burdened by our sins, we lift up our heads and our hands to you, who are our shield and our glory. We beseech you, because you are merciful, forgive what we have done wrongly and answer graciously the prayers and vows that we pour forth before you. Then, having been called away from dead works and [*7r*] relying strongly on your graciousness, we will not fear the infinite hosts of the enemies of your name since our faith teaches us that you have already struck and smashed their jaws. Grant us, good Father, to recognize how abundant is your blessing upon us, and may we be utterly convinced that our salvation depends upon you alone. Through Jesus Christ, our Lord. Amen.

FROM PSALM 4:
We call upon you, almighty God, hard pressed by troubles and dangers, so that, helped by your aid, we may finally attain a free and happy escape from our present sufferings. We admit that we are unworthy of your help since we have turned away from you frequently and painfully. But we beg you to deign to examine not our individual actions but the worthiness of our cause. Since you are wont to vindicate the justice of your words, may you now protect powerfully your worship and Gospel, after having also corrected and punished us as you wish. We now weep before you because the mighty of this world have united for a supreme effort to drag down the glory of the Gospel and your worship into shame, [*7v*] indeed into nothingness, because of the mindless enthusiasms and false hopes which they have set their hearts on. We

hope that you, O God, will reveal and show to them the nature of the true Church, which you have chosen for yourself and which you listen to when full of faith it calls upon you with its prayers and cries. Perhaps they may gain understanding and even be moved and take heed not to sin against that Church. May they take thought, even in their beds, how they should regard the Church, and perhaps they will grow quiet and can be led to offer sacrifices of true justice with her. But now they are blinded and want nothing so much as to discharge their rage against her; they regard destroying her as the highest good. But every time we worship you in spirit and in truth, O God, we have prayed repeatedly to you for the salvation of our enemies. We heartily rejoiced when good and happy things happened to them. Grant then in your mercy that they may finally allow us to live in peace and tranquillity; grant, I say, that we may find rest in you alone and that we may dwell with you in safety, putting our confidence in you. Through Jesus Christ, our Lord. Amen.

FROM THE SAME PSALM:

O God, in you is all our justice; since [*8r*] you are good, you have always been wont to hear those who call upon you and to lead them from their troubles to a better fortune. We beseech you not to be deaf to those who beg your help and not to allow our glory, which is our true devotion, to be reduced to shame by any overwhelming power of this world. We have indeed sinned against you, and very seriously, but in your kindness prevent vanity and untruthfulness from overcoming us. But since you have chosen for yourself those you wish to save, make the grace and favor of your countenance so shine upon us that we may rejoice even in the good fortune of our enemies. Grant, best of fathers, that upheld by a stout faith we may find rest in you alone and that we may be gathered to a safe refuge by you alone. Through Jesus Christ, our Lord. Amen.

FROM PSALM 5:

We fly to you, almighty God, in our daily prayers, and we put before you each morning our requests, not unmindful of how you hate iniquities and detest sin to an astonishing degree. Although we do not deny that our sins have us in their grip (for we feel very keenly how they pull us down), [*8v*] still we approach you relying on the abundance of your great goodness. We beseech you that you forgive all the ways we have sinned against you and that henceforward you lead us in your justice and innocence lest the enemies of our salvation, in whom there is nothing upright and every vice, prevail against us. May their designs come to naught, may their might and efforts come to ruin, so that trusting in you we may enjoy a solid happiness while you protect, favor, and surround us with your goodwill like a shield. Through Jesus Christ, our Lord. Amen.

FROM PSALM 6:

We undoubtedly deserve, O almighty God, to be punished severely for the evils that we have done and for our infinite sins, but we beseech you, relying on your great mercy, that you do not punish us in your wrath and anger. Good Father, we are shaken and are almost crushed in spirit when we think about our sins and your justice. We beg you not to thrust us down into hell as we have merited by our evil deeds, seeing that there we will not be able to sing unto you nor offer you praise, as our enemies in wondrous wise desire to happen. [9r] O God, look upon the tears of those who trust in you and make the authors of iniquity draw back from us. Lastly, hear us so that all who work against our salvation and your glory may be brought to shame and cast down. Through Jesus Christ, our Lord. Amen.

FROM PSALM 7:

You have known, O great and good God, how eagerly the enemies of our salvation attack us day and night. They desire, unless you assist us, to turn us over for eternal destruction, after having cruelly torn us and devoured us like wild beasts. But as we trust in you alone, so we beg that you may wish to stand by us. We do not try to justify our cause in your presence, as though we had done nothing of the things they charge us with, but we are convinced that they have been forgiven us by your mercy, through the intercession of our mediator, Jesus Christ. Therefore we pray that you arise and direct our help and defend us like a strong shield so that these same evils may recoil upon the authors of these temptations, deceit and malice. But we exalt you and proclaim your name in elegant praises. Through Jesus Christ, our Lord. Amen.

[9v] FROM THE SAME PSALM:

It is indeed an outstanding gift to live in the observance of your commandments, O almighty God, but one that cannot in the least happen to those from whose eyes you do not withdraw the veil of darkness, for otherwise the secrets of your law are completely invisible to the eyes of those gripped by blindness. We therefore beg help and light from you for our weakness and ignorance so that while we spend this life as pilgrims you do not hide from us the pure and rightful understanding of your commandments. It is through our own fault that we have so far been too little educated in that understanding; we therefore have fallen into these reproaches, into this contempt, and into these detractions. On top of the dangers and afflictions that now disquiet and burden your Church, there have been added insults against doctrine, curses against true devotion, and terrible blasphemies against your name. Pardon your people and forgive, O God, what they have committed against you and raise up the fallen by your word and promises. Every single day we boldly plead our case before you. We beg that you hear us and immediately strengthen our failing faith and hope with new benefits. [*10r*] Do not put to shame those who call upon you, so that once more at peace and more than fully restored we may run full speed in the path of your commandments. Through Jesus Christ, our Lord. Amen.

FROM PSALM 8:

O great and good God, everything that you have created in heaven and on earth for our help and great advantage attests clearly how wondrous and magnificent is your name. Granted that your goodness reaches out to and is revealed in all things, we nonetheless grow in this conviction because on this topic we can promise ourselves nothing that is not splendid; you desire to nourish us and devote yourself to favor us with the greatest kindness right from the infancy of human offspring. For while infants are being nourished and are beginning to talk, they give us clear proof of your goodness. The wicked are put to shame by these miracles every time they denigrate your goodness and providence. The heavens could be seen as a work worthy of your artistry, but a great and wonderful sign of your goodness is seen in the fact that you are so willing to come down to take care of a frail mortal with so much solicitude. [*10v*] Hence we are stirred rightly and repeatedly, even though we have sinned and lived unworthily of you and of our calling, to beseech you with the greatest confidence that you do not permit your Church to be overwhelmed by her present woes. If you have lifted up man, otherwise so lowly in his nature, so that he is a little less than the angels, I beg you to be even more mindful of those whom you have already gathered to yourself as your children and to whom you have willed in your mercy to make subject and subservient all the works of your hands, so that you do not allow them to be ground under heel by the wicked. You have always been accustomed to watch over the children of men with your care; now come to us too with your help when we need it so badly. Deliver us, we pray, so that all may thereby acknowledge your name to be as wonderful as it really is and as deserving every kind of respect. Through Jesus Christ, our Lord. Amen.

FROM THE SAME PSALM:

From the things which have come to be both in heaven and on earth through your power and providence, O almighty God, your magnificence and glory manifest themselves not just well but excellently. Your [*11r*] power reveals itself even better and stirs the souls (which are heavier than lead) in children and babies. We are wretched and cast off, not because of the effort and care with which you fashioned us, but because of our own sins and infinite guilt which we ourselves have accumulated. We pray nonetheless that you be not angry with us over them but rather that you come to us frequently, as you used to do, and make those whom you wanted to be a little less than the angels sharers in your own divine nature. And since you have set us up as rightful lords over all your creatures, grant that we may use them to the praise and glory of your name so that your word and Gospel may be spread to all mortals. Through Jesus Christ, our Lord. Amen.

FROM PSALM 9:

If you, O God, uphold our cause and defend us from the enemies of your name and of human salvation, we shall recount and proclaim your magnificent deeds with our whole hearts and the greatest joy. Due to our own fault we are afflicted by temptations and similar troubles, but through your goodness and mercy we implore you that as [*11v*] you used to be the refuge of those who flee to you in their sufferings, so you may neither desert us nor seem to have pushed off into oblivion these prayers which we earnestly pour forth to you.   Have mercy on us, O God, and take us far from the gates of death lest they swallow us. With your aid we shall proclaim your praise in the Church because it was not in vain that we placed our hopes in you. Arise then lest wickedness, injustice, and sin prevail against us. Grant that rightly mindful of our condition we may always be subject to your will with a modest and humble heart. Through Jesus Christ. Amen.

FROM THE SAME PSALM:

It often happened in the age of our fathers, O almighty God, that your people were filled with wondrous gladness and, rejoicing to the full, extolled your name in song, celebrated it with the highest praises, and did so with their whole heart because thanks to your protection their enemies turned their backs in battle, fell and perished before your face. More than once you decided in favor of your saints or upheld their cause. Many times you rebuked and destroyed the Gentiles who had agreed among themselves to turn the lovely cities of your people over to utter destruction, [*12r*] and you destroyed wicked men of that sort so that even their name was wiped out. Therefore since you reign forever and keep your tribunal always open so that you can investigate the spilling of the blood of your saints, do not at this time, O God, spurn us or forget our petitions. We know well that we have sinned and offended your majesty in many ways. We are now sorrowful in our hearts and confess our sins openly, but because of the confidence we have in you, which has grown out of the unmerited gifts you have conferred upon our fathers, we come to you and beg you to have mercy on your Church. We beseech you to look upon her affliction and rescue her from the gates of death so that she may grow more fervent day by day in celebrating your praise. Show your wrath against those who are unmindful of you. May they perish by their own evil tricks and devices, and may those who eagerly and violently seek the destruction of your people be caught up in their own snares. But may we, who are poor and afflicted, still continue living under your protection. Arise, O God, and do not permit miserable men to prevail against you and your holy Gospel. Strike terror into your enemies so they may realize what it is to attack piety and religion. [*12v*] Through Jesus Christ, our Lord. Amen.

FROM PSALM 10:

Because we believe, O great and good God, that you are not only the highest good but also goodness itself, we are aflame with the desire that you do not turn your favor away from us, even though that sometimes seems the case. Although we do not doubt that our sins have merited such punishment, still we pray that, because you are good and merciful, you will forgive us our sins. We pray that you will still favor our cause, even though we do not merit it, for the glory of your name so that the wicked will realize that they were wrong in deciding that you do not exist and that you would never trace back to their hands the crimes they have mapped out. They are entrapping, oppressing, slaying, and horribly destroying holy men, for they have already convinced themselves that you are unconcerned about human affairs. Come to those who call upon you and mercifully hear to their prayers so that after you have set holy men free they may teach the proud and violent to act with restraint since it will be clear that you watch over the Church with utmost care. Through our Lord Jesus Christ. Amen.

[*13r*] FROM THE SAME PSALM:

Gracious Father, it might seem that in these dreadful days you have put an enormous distance between yourself and your people so that you have closed your eyes and averted your gaze from what the wicked Antichrists in their consummate pride and total perversity are doing to your people, seeing that everything they attempt enjoys great success. As a result, they treat your people according to their whim, they hurl insults against you and have even come to the firm conviction that God does not exist. Since you seem to have exempted them from any punishment, they think that they will never be shaken. They promise themselves continuous successes so that they take no account at all of their perjuries, deceits, injuries, and wickedness, and they kill off your faithful people in public and in secret. They attack, afflict, and crush your Church. O God, they think you do not care about her. We have now fully merited your averting your eyes from our troubles and have sinned seriously so that you should not take account of our sufferings. We have been utterly ungrateful for your precious benefits and have misused your calling, Gospel, and sacraments, [*13v*] spurning the opportunity you have given us, even though we should devote ourselves to serving you according to your word—we acknowledge all this and the other countless outrages we have committed against you. Now we earnestly beg and beseech pardon for them so that at last you may rise up and with your hand hold back the sinner from the curses that he has launched against you and your teaching. In our misery we commend ourselves to you who are wont to assist those who are otherwise helpless and orphans. Break at last the strength of the wicked, give ear to the pleas of the afflicted, and avenge at last the oppressed so that freed from all these fears they may give you in your Church the thanks which they owe because of your mercy. Through Jesus Christ, our Lord. Amen.

FROM PSALM 11:
In you, O great and good God, we put all our trust and protection, and therefore when our flesh, human prudence, and wicked men work against us, when our cause is already lost, and when we have no hope of defending true doctrine and the holy Gospel, we still do not thereupon conclude that we should despair of your mercy and might. We see how [*14r*] the enemies of your name have bent the bow of their strength and have prepared their arrows to pierce us. We acknowledge, moreover, that we have lived in such a way as to have merited every one of these troubles and disasters. We have not followed you, as obedient children should have. Alas, so far we have always been in rebellion against your commandments. But now we humbly beg pardon for our sins. We dare to make this prayer because we rely on your goodness and mercy since you are the one who has his court and most holy throne in heaven. From there you are wont to observe everything that is done on earth; accordingly you can now look into the justice of this cause and see the

wickedness and violence of our enemies. Since you have quite often been wont to cast fire, sulphur, and burning thunderbolts on the sinful, at least put a check to the persecutors of your Church so that everyone may acknowledge that you favor a just cause and desire to defend us who are zealously working for your glory and name. Through Jesus Christ, our Lord. Amen. [*14v*]

FROM THE SAME PSALM:
Since we trust with all our strength in you, O great and good God, the inclinations of our flesh, sinful men, and the snares of the demons are at work night and day to drive us to give up on piety, as if were going to be completely destroyed by the bows, arrows, and violence of our enemies if we keep on trying to live for you. But even if we are buried in sins and iniquities, we still rely on your mercy and pray that you take away sins, especially the sins of those who confess them before you. Henceforward turn your face with favor from your sacred courts to help us. Since you test both causes with impartial judgment, may the enemies of religion suffer the punishment they have earned. May they in turn experience, through the gift of your salvation, that you are the defender of right and justice. Through Jesus Christ, our Lord. Amen.

FROM PSALM 12:
Because there are so few good and devout men, O great and good God, you alone remain our fortress. We therefore seek refuge in you with our daily prayers, [*15r*] begging that at last you now pay heed to our troubled affairs. For if you do not defend the Church, who can make her safe amidst enemies of this sort, who have no regard for truthfulness and are always trying to trick simple folk with empty lies and false flattery and never believe in their hearts what they profess in their words? Do not, good Father, hand us over to their mistreatment, even though we deserve it because of our iniquities and sins. Here take heed of the glory of your name, the propagation of the Gospel, and the truth of your promises. For the reason just given, look favorably upon us. Do not put up with those who are only trying to increase their own power and pay you not the least attention since they are opposed to piety. Pay heed to the affliction and groans of your Church. Arise now and assist us as you have promised. Your words are bright and purer than even the finest silver. Defend your Church for the sake of your mercy and trustworthiness from the attacks and oppression of those wicked men, each of whom is striving for the pinnacle of power. Through Jesus Christ, our Lord. Amen.

FROM THE SAME PSALM:

. Heavenly Father, [*15v*] while we live in this world there is among mortals a complete lack of devout, truthful, and trustworthy men but an enormous supply of lying, flattering, and boasting rascals. Hence we rightly pour out our prayers to you, our refuge, that you disregard the wrongful deeds we have committed against you whereby you allow us, as we have merited, to be oppressed or smashed by the caprice and wrath of sinners. Rather, because your mercy is enormous and abundant, arouse yourself and snatch by your saving power those who trust in you from the snares, deceits, and tricks which the enemies of all religion are ceaselessly devising against them. That way, when you have saved them from a depraved and disease bearing generation, everybody will understand that your promises and your statements are distinguished by their utter truthfulness and have no stain of deceit. Through Jesus Christ, our Lord. Amen.

FROM PSALM 13:

When the devout see themselves oppressed by heavy afflictions and tossed about by harsh misfortunes, O almighty God, [*16r*] they are afraid that you are unmindful or have turned your favor away from them. Keep us from entertaining this sort of thought or suspicion in our heart. Because of our great guilt, we deserve being ignored by you, but do not, O God, because of the honor of your name allow the insolent enemies of religion either to prevail or lord it over your faithful like conquerors. We beg you to enlighten the eyes of our mind with your spirit so that, seeing and approving what is right, we may not go astray in worshipping you nor be made slothful in right living. That way our opponents will have lost their reason for rejoicing, and we will render you the eternal thanks you deserve. Through Jesus Christ, our Lord. Amen.

FROM PSALM 14:

Turn away from your children, O almighty God, those evil plans and foolish thoughts which lead us to imagine in our minds that you do not exist. Nor has it escaped your notice that we have rather often strayed from the narrow, straight path of justice. [*16v*] Thereby we have fully deserved to be eaten and devoured like bread and delicate food by the sinful and wrathful enemies of religion; nonetheless we suppliantly beseech you that, as you have promised that you want to stand by that generation and those who trust in you, you do not desert us who are so crushed and afflicted. May your help from the heavenly Zion appear so that the universal Church may both be restored and rejoice when you have reclaimed us from the captivity of sin, the devil and death. Through Jesus Christ, our Lord. Amen.

FROM PSALM 15:

Only those can have a place, O almighty God, in eternal happiness and in your heavenly kingdom who are cleansed of sin and are not contaminated by the stain of crimes and who have so devoted and dedicated their heart, tongue, and outward deeds to your worship that they do not fail to carry out any of your commandments either through carelessness or malice. From this we already know that if a matter were dealt with on the basis of our merits or the dignity of our works, we would fall so far short as to almost have despaired of our salvation. But relying on your goodness, we boldly demand that [*17r*] the merits of our actions be disregarded and that your promises remain firm and unshaken, just as we have believed. Deign to enrich us whom you have received into your grace so that hereafter, resplendent with the trappings of justice, truth, and charity, we may never be torn from the dwelling place of your happiness. Through Jesus Christ, our Lord. Amen.

FROM PSALM 16:

Since we are so poor, good Father in heaven, and you are so rich in all things and in abundant works, there is indeed nothing given to us with which we can either endow or increase your happiness. But as we still hope in you, may we be beggars before your majesty so that you may protect us from the evils that surround us on every side. Remitting the sins that you see we are burdened with, grant that as you have become our inheritance, we may always take delight in you alone and always find it pleasant and beautiful to preach and esteem you alone. May you teach us, give us advice, and stand always before our eyes lest we ever turn aside from the straight path so that, happy during our life here, we may rejoice in you. [*17v*] May we enjoy after our blessed resurrection those solid delights which we believe lie within your hand alone. Through Jesus Christ, our Lord.

FROM PSALM 17:

Your Church prays, O almighty God, that you now look favorably upon her most just cause. Every day she lifts up to you her cries; so hear the prayers which she pours forth in your sight in a trustful spirit. We indeed acknowledge that we are burdened with countless other sins so that every day we ask you to pardon them. But we find nothing within us of the sins of which our enemies accuse us. So were our case to come under judgment even with you as judge, we know that nothing can be found that can be condemned on the basis of your word. We seek only this, that the reformation of religion and piety go forward toward the fulfillment of your commandments and toward the sincere observance of your law. Our care for this has put us in extreme danger, even of our complete destruction, unless you prevent it. We pray that you strengthen with great constancy our steps, otherwise so prone to slip, along your paths so that in these difficulties we neither waver nor incur injury. [*18r*] Here, O God, you can exercise your wonderful goodness. If you save those who trust in you from the unexpected, you will avenge by a single stroke not only us but yourself since it is mainly against you that they have arisen. Protect us under the shadow of your wings, and when things seem to be going best for them, so that they seem about to pounce on our necks like a lion, anticipate their fury and snatch from them the life of your faithful people. Grant that the faithful by their confessing you may be far happier both in this life and the next than their enemies, who delight too much in their present good fortune. Through Jesus Christ, our Lord. Amen.

FROM THE SAME PSALM:

We beg you now, O almighty God, that we may not be slow to believe that you will hear our prayers. We pour them forth before you, not out of hypocrisy or deceit but from a sincere heart since we want to be tried by you as our judge and not by men. Grant that when we are tested and undergo troubles, nothing will be found in us by which we should be condemned as guilty of eternal destruction. But because we are by our nature evil, how [*18v*] will this happen? May you yourself support our steps and so support them with your grace and spirit that your mercy may shine forth marvelously from our salvation. Protect us then from all those who resist the power of the Gospel and devote their whole strength to opposing your will. You see how our enemies look upon us, like a lion they want to make us their prey. They are like the sword, O God, and the hand and instruments of your wrath, but may you nevertheless defend us from them under the shadow and protection of your wings so that as long as we live here we may rejoice in your favor and that in the blessed resurrection we may enjoy the supreme happiness of your presence. Through Jesus Christ, our Lord. Amen.

FROM PSALM 18:

We acknowledge, O almighty God, that you are our one salvation, shield, protection, strength, and safe refuge. Accordingly, we experience great love for you and we want to praise you forever. But we are now so hard pressed by our enemies together with our sinful inclinations that we are almost lifeless and undergo the pains of death. Hence we [*19r*] seem to have no protection left except to call upon you and to lift up our voices in earnest prayers to you.   When mountains, the earth, the heavens, lightning, winds, clouds, rain, hail, and storms threaten suddenly, it will be very easy for you to snatch us from our enemies, however powerful. We pray, O God, that you deign to be generous to the prayers of your Church, taking no account of our evil merits, first because of your goodness and secondly because of the justice of the cause itself, so that you treat those you have made holy with your holiness and that instead you treat the wicked with harshness. Save your afflicted people, as you are accustomed to do, and in such great darkness light the lamp of faith and wisdom for them so that they may recognize no other shield and defender but you. Grant, good Father, we may walk without offense so that our feet may never slip amidst such great dangers to our faith. Prepare your people for war. May those who try to resist you, O God, be confounded, so that thereby your name may be celebrated among all the nations because you have marvelously brought about the salvation of your Church. Through Jesus Christ, our Lord. Amen.

FROM THE SAME PSALM:
Since we are very weak by nature [*19v*] and surrounded on all sides by dense darkness, we come to you, O almighty God, and ask you to light the lamp of your spirit in our soul so that we may grasp your pure teachings and the chaste statements of the Holy Scriptures which clearly promise that you will be the protector of all who hope in you. The sins that we have committed obviously do not merit that we should request and obtain from you so much favor and help, but we hope that this will happen to us through the glory of your great name. Since there is no other god to match you in power or goodness, may you yourself confer on us holiness and gird us with the strength by which we are first led safe from threatening dangers and then made triumphant over the enemies of our salvation and your glory. Through Jesus Christ, our Lord. Amen.

FROM THE SAME PSALM:
We cannot help loving you keenly, O great and good God, because by the faith you have given us we clearly see that you alone are our refuge, foundation, and liberator. Our sins have often brought upon us deadly sorrows and mighty and violent enemies [*20r*] who like rushing streams surround us with tribulations, traps, and even death itself. But it is you, O God, who have

complete control of all things and are acknowledged as having a throne in heaven. Therefore in your mercy, which is infinite, look upon us. When you have forgiven our sins, bring it about that we be delivered from your wrath and from the extreme punishment which you are wont to visit upon the wicked. Grant that, when we call upon you, our cry and prayers may not be poured forth in vain. Through Jesus Christ, our Lord. Amen.

FROM THE SAME PSALM:

You know, O great and good God, how numerous and how powerful are the enemies that we endure from within and without. Since they cannot brook your name and glory, they also harbor a bitter hatred toward our salvation. Not without reason then do we come to you as suppliants, since you have many times delivered us from damnation and the downfall of eternal destruction; so even now, despite the grave sins we have committed against you and of which we now repent in our hearts, please defend us with your protection so that we may conquer and overcome whatever sets itself against your kingdom [*20v*]. Then finally we can praise and glorify you as our only protector and savior in the enormous gathering of the human race. Through Jesus Christ, our Lord. Amen.

FROM THE SAME PSALM:

Since we are in countless perils as long as we live here, O heavenly Father, we direct our petitions and prayers to you so that you may reach out to us your helping hand and not allow the powerful enemies of our salvation to prevail. Declare yourself, O God, our protector at the moment when we are grievously afflicted by them. We have no justice or holiness based on works that we can boast about in your sight; indeed we frankly confess that we have wandered far from your paths. But because of your mercy overlook the evils we have committed and deign to enrich us with your grace that we may live hereafter as your elect, holy and innocent; then we in turn may experience you as electing, holy and innocent regarding us. Through Jesus Christ, our Lord. Amen. [*21r*]

FROM PSALM 19:

The wondrous power, wisdom, and goodness with which your nature is most abundantly endowed, O almighty God, everywhere strikes us in the things you have created. Heaven with all its jewels, the change of seasons, the brightness of the stars, and the mighty sun are so many voices and a lesson common to all peoples by which these heralds of your majesty are celebrated.

Hence we confess that we cannot pretend to have any excuse for our feeble confidence and failing love toward you. The witness of these things really ought to have persuaded us that we should cling inseparably to you alone as the author of so many good things. But, alas, spurning these warnings we have followed the desires of our flesh and the unhealthy lucubrations and fantasies of our mind, deserting you, the creator of all things. Thus have we rightly merited the sufferings that we are enduring. We have spurned not only the works of nature that draw us to you, but your word as well, that is, we have listened to the Holy Scripture and the Gospel of your Son with cold hearts and with no effect at all. [*21v*] From the things we should have used to refresh our mind and take in wisdom, light, joy, and uprightness, we have provoked your wrath against us. But now, even though for these reasons we seem unworthy of your mercy, we still pray urgently that you forgive us and that you be unwilling to afflict your Church on account of our deeds. Grant that henceforward we may admire creatures, which we are, in a saving way and may your words be for us sweeter, not just than honey, but than any human pleasure. Keep sin far from us and show that you are truly both the protector and redeemer of your people. Through Jesus Christ, our Lord. Amen.

FROM PSALM 19:[2]

We know, O almighty God, that your supreme goodness has arranged that a knowledge of you can be engendered in our hearts by the beautiful appearance, arrangement, and adornment of your creatures. The spheres of the heavens, the eternal alternation of day and night, and the supreme brightness of the sun witness to you and teach us in no unclear terms to acknowledge and admire you as their most wise author. Added to these are [*22r*] your holy laws which confer on us mortals true wisdom, testimony to your will, solid enjoyment, and heavenly delights. But because we are so wretched, we never stop misusing both of these faithful teachers. Hence we pray that you deign to forgive us any sins we have committed against you and contrary to the precepts of these powerful warnings. Grant that henceforward we may contemplate the structure of the world with profit so that we may be zealous upholders of your laws. Through Jesus Christ, our Lord. Amen.

FROM PSALM 20:

We pray daily, O almighty God, that the kingdom of our Lord Jesus Christ may increase and may at last emerge in full. We now also urgently

---

[2]Sic. The typesetter should have written: From the Same Psalm.

request precisely that in our petitions and prayers. Be constantly mindful, O God, of the rich and pleasing holocaust that he offered for us on the altar of the cross, and grant we may receive from his triumph both salvation and joyous pleasure. We will not be discouraged even though this would happen beyond the merits of us [*22v*] who have offended you in manifold and infinite ways with our sinfulness. Nonetheless in your gracious goodness you will put to shame those who put their trust in chariots and horses and human might. Lift up to salvation us who have made up our minds that we depend completely on you. Direct your kindness toward the prayers by which we petition you for the increase of the kingdom of Jesus Christ our Lord. Through the same Jesus Christ our Lord. Amen.

FROM PSALM 21:

O almighty God, we profess that our King Jesus Christ lives with you, endowed through his resurrection with supreme joy, power and honor. Since he has already attained and possesses to the full all that can be sought or desired for supreme happiness, it is impossible for it all not to be communicated also to us his members and greatly overflow from his salvation, good deeds and glory. Although we acknowledge our unworthiness for such good fortune and singular benefit because of the sinfulness our lives and practices, still since we regret our sinfulness we by no means are discouraged about his helping us. Indeed, we maintain the steadfast hope that [*23r*] he will at last both overcome and strike down all those who set themselves against his kingdom. Grant we beseech you, O good Father, that their diseased plans may be put to nought and that your lofty and splendid power may finally at some time be acknowledged so that we may glorify your praises and virtues forever. Through the same Jesus Christ, our Lord. Amen.

FROM PSALM 22:

You were able to bring it about, O almighty God, that your Son, our Lord Jesus Christ, suffered on the cross for the sins of men so much that he seemed to have been deserted and deprived of all help. You, who are wont to bring aid to your saints when they call upon you, seemed to spurn the prayers of our Savior, as if he were a worm and no man, the dregs of the people and the shame of humankind. You bore this even until he was killed in a most shameful death by angry Jews who circled about him not unlike rabid dogs, ferocious bulls, and roaring lions. But later you summoned him back from death so glorious that his faithful members forever praise and glorify your name on that account. [*23v*] Therefore through that abundant mercy of yours, which led you to hand over your only Son to such great sufferings, we pray and beseech you not to allow the cause of your suffering Church to perish. We confess that our sins are horrible; because of them we have earned not just temporal but eternal death. O God, do not look upon us as we are in ourselves, but as members of your only begotten Son. Protect effectually and defend powerfully our evangelical cause, which is your own cause and which the enemies of religion think you have deserted. Through Jesus Christ, our Lord. Amen.

FROM THE SAME PSALM:

O almighty God, your Son, our Lord Jesus Christ, has suffered for the sake of our redemption so that he was able to appear as rejected and deserted by you. For he was overwhelmed by the floods of a most bitter death on the cross, was finally killed, and having been made the innocent victim, paid the penalty that we ourselves had merited. But after three days he was raised from the dead, stood in the gathering of the disciples, [*24r*] and bore witness to your name and glory, just as he used to shortly before, when he was living among them. Therefore since we acknowledge and confess that we have misused your great mercy and infinite kindness, we seek refuge in you, begging that you deign to stir us to seek holiness with our whole strength, since you have inserted us into and given us new life in such a great mediator, who is the author and preserver of our salvation. May all of us living now, as well as all future mortals, be drawn to adore and worship you alone with devout and pure hearts. Through the same Jesus Christ, our Lord. Amen.

FROM THE SAME PSALM:

O great and good God, Jesus Christ, your Son and our Lord, underwent bitter punishments and harsh tortures for the salvation of the human race. Since he had taken upon himself all of the world's sins, it was necessary for him to be torn apart in such a frightful and cruel way that he could fully supply just punishment for all men. At last mounted upon the cross he poured out his sweet life for us and thereby merited for us the remission of sins, [*24v*] your friendship, and life everlasting, provided that we steadfastly believe in his teaching and Gospel. But, alas, because we are weak in faith we easily forget his great benefits; worse still, we live a life unworthy of the redemption that cost our innocent Lord so much. Hence we weep before you, heavenly Father, over this disaster and beg and beseech you not to allow us to be bereft of the fruit of the cross and death of our Lord Jesus Christ, who lives and reigns with you forever and ever. Amen.

FROM PSALM 23:

All who have you for their shepherd, O almighty God, spend their lives in great happiness like those who are provided with the food of heavenly doctrine and with the fertile irrigation of the Holy Spirit. They are restored and given heart whenever they have been hard pressed by the vicissitudes of this world or worn down by blows of persecution. Although we acknowledge that we are unworthy of having you care for us and watch over us like a shepherd, since we have often spurned you and your word and [25r] have deserved to be driven out of your blessed sheepfolds because of our grave and innumerable sins, still we rely on that mercy and goodness which are innate and deep-seated in your nature, and we pray that you deign to gather us to yourself like lost sheep. Do not allow us to wander away from you into the byways and ravines of this world. You see that we are now at the point of death, so come to us that we may put aside all our fear. Now we need you to strengthen us and console us with the rod and crook of your authority. If only you wish it, you can refresh us with enlightenment from the banquet of your teaching and sacraments and give us to drink deeply from the chalice of your spirit and grace, even while the enemies of your name look on. We beg that we may always remain in the embrace of your kindness and paternal care, which you are wont to have for your own people, so that they may be allowed to persevere in the Church, which is your house, and in the faith and glory of the Gospel, by the merits and favor of our Lord, Jesus Christ, who lives and reigns with you forever and ever. Amen.

FROM THE SAME PSALM:

O almighty God, you are accustomed to preserve those you have adopted as your children with no less care and watchfulness [25v] than if they were sheep whom you, their loving shepherd, are always leading forward to their salvation and true happiness. So long as they make use of you as their teacher they will not lack for the food and drink of saving doctrine. It is clear that if we are exhausted by hunger and thirst without the true good during the journey of this miserable life, this results from our turning away from you and following other shepherds. This is the source of our dangers and of our souls' misfortunes. So we pray to you, our faithful shepherd, to recall us from our wanderings to the path. Correct the vices of your wandering and foolish flock with the rod and crook of your uprightness so that we may at last find proper, pure, and chaste nourishment from the saving food of your word and sacrament. Thereby we shall gain strength for our head, heart, and all the forces of our soul, and thus we shall always find our support in your mercy so that in your house on the last day we shall enjoy the supreme delights of eternity. Through Jesus Christ, our Lord. Amen.

FROM PSALM 24:

You are not only the author, O almighty God, of the earth and everything contained within it, but you yourself also created [*26r*] man as its cultivator and deigned to warn mortals through the teaching of the law and the Gospel how they could again join themselves to you from whom they have gone forth into this light, that is, to establish themselves on the sacred mountain of the Church, where you dwell. But you demand from them that they be spotless in their deeds and clean of heart, not devoted to vain and passing goods nor given over to frauds or deceit. You promise that they will share in your mercy and kindness. It has therefore been our endeavor that for these reasons we seek after you. But we have miserably turned away from this narrow path of truth and justice and have wandered away from you through the sharp cliffs of vice and pleasures. It is then no surprise if we have fallen upon such hard times and into confusing situations. Now you see how things stand for your Church, which is almost deserted and destroyed. We beseech you to desire not the punishment that our wicked deeds merit. Rather, for the glory of your name, since you are a mighty king renowned for strength, who holds all armies and potentates in your hand, manifest by protecting your Church your mighty strength and your supreme goodwill toward believers. [*26v*] Through Jesus Christ, our Lord. Amen.

FROM THE SAME PSALM:

O great and good God, since you are the sole creator and author who has given existence to all things, we have concluded as something certain and beyond question that both the earth and these who cultivate it belong exclusively to you. But you are also deemed, truly and not falsely, to be he whom men cannot attain as goal and summit of our happiness (for you are the Lord of all things) unless they have a pure heart, innocent hands, and an abiding fidelity toward their neighbor. When we have not developed these qualities, but rather have been debased by vices which completely fight against these virtues, there is this resource: we beg for your mercy in our prayers, for since you are extolled as the king of glory, you are proclaimed powerful and mighty, victorious and triumphant in war, so in your goodness may you far surpass and overcome our evil deeds and grant that we may attain, even though we are unworthy, blessing and justice from you, for we have put our trust and hope in Jesus Christ, your Son, who lives and reigns with you forever and ever. Amen.

[*27r*] FROM PSALM 25:

We lift up our hearts, prayers, speech, and hands to you, O almighty God, with this petition especially, that since we rely on you, do not let us be put to shame so that the opponents of your name and the enemies of pure and sincere teaching may thereby take pleasure and be well pleased with themselves over their impiety. We do not make this request as if it were owed to our merits, for we acknowledge how much we have gone astray from your law and will. That we freely and openly confess, and we endeavor to win pardon from you by these our daily prayers. Henceforward, since you are good and merciful, explain to us efficaciously your ways and accustom us to the ways and practices which you have sought to bind us to observe. It is impossible for anybody whom you yourself have taught not to abide steadfastly by your covenant. His heart unquestionably enjoys lasting goods and his feet shall be freed from the tightest snare. Look now, O God, on how your Church is afflicted by troubles and burdens. Her salvation depends on you alone. Redeem her then, O God of Israel, lest she fall under the raging hatred [*27v*] of Antichrist and the devil. Through Jesus Christ, our Lord. Amen.

FROM THE SAME PSALM:

We come to you daily, O almighty God, with our petitions and prayers to beg your mercy, lest you allow us to be put to shame in the struggle in which we are involved with the enemies of human salvation. In your mercy may you wash away the sins and stains of our weakness, and although we are completely unworthy of your favor through our own fault, we still desire and pray again and again to you that you teach, direct, guide, and finally show us to your paths, which we know have been laid out with utmost kindness and unfailing truth. Look down, kindly Father, on the dangers and disasters in which we are caught up so that we may be not so oppressed. Deliver us and destroy our sins as well. It is for you alone to redeem your Church not only from the external afflictions which have torn her asunder, but even more from that stain which defiles your worship so that it is not manifested pure and chaste as it should have been. Through Jesus Christ, our Lord. Amen.

[*28r*] FROM PSALM 26:

O almighty God, had we grounded our lives in innocence, we would not be so shaken by the terrors of this time for, as we have discovered, they cannot waver who sincerely cling to you. Indeed, we submit our whole selves with willing hearts to your testing and probing. But because we trusted you too little, we have handed ourselves over to worthless men and the support of the flesh; we have not drawn back from the gathering of sinners and have befouled your Gospel with impure acts and dirty hands and practices so that we now live in great danger of losing our life and our soul like those vicious and bloodthirsty men. So we ask you to have mercy on us now, and as your name was invoked by us, please forgive the wicked deeds we have done up to now. May the goodness of our cause gain for us from you what we have not merited. Here we are praying not only for our own salvation, but also for your unsullied teaching and pure worship. Do not, then hand over the Church to the tricks and deceits of the Antichrist. Rescue her from the destruction which the devil himself and his adherents are preparing for her, so that henceforward we may live for you in holiness and innocence [*28v*] and proclaim your deeds and marvelous works in sacred gatherings. Through Jesus Christ, our Lord. Amen.

FROM THE SAME PSALM:

May a strong desire take hold of us, O almighty God, to live out our life in innocence before you. May we not turn aside from the straight path—something we have so far not done at all since we have dallied with different temptations and have put too little faith and likewise little solid trust in you. Therefore take pity on us and be willing to forgive what is sinful. For were we to enjoy your favor and benevolence, we would never forget your mercy and truth. Grant, good Father, that we may live in innocence among the innocent and detest with utter hatred trickery and vanity so that we may devote ourselves with our whole heart to your praise and the glorification of your name. Do not allow us to spend the end of our lives with wicked and irreligious men. Rather may the blessed entrance stand open to the house of that everlasting happiness for which we aspire every day. Through Jesus Christ, our Lord. Amen.

[*29r*] FROM PSALM 27:

Since we have made you alone, O heavenly Father, the pillar and pinnacle of our safety, light, strength, and solidity, we ought to conduct ourselves with good heart and fearless constancy in our pursuit of holiness regardless of the machinations of the world against us, regardless of the hostility that threatens from the devil, and finally regardless of any calamity men stir up against us. We should courageously hold all these in contempt because you are our protector and because you hide us in your tabernacle. It is because we are weak in faith and our trust in you often wavers that we are so timid and fearful. Strengthen us, O God, with your wonderful grace and your gift giving

Spirit so that we may live upright, holy, and chaste lives in the sacred gathering, which is your true home. Do not, we beg, turn your countenance away from us—this alone we desire. Grant that we may bear up manfully and grow strong so that we may await your help with unbroken spirits. Through Jesus Christ, Our Lord. Amen.

[*29v*] FROM PSALM 28:

If you, O almighty God, turn away and neglect to come to our aid in these afflictions, not only do we fall away from true piety but also we can soon easily busy ourselves in digging out and filling up a ditch. Hear, then, our prayers and cries, who, as you see, place no trust in any except your only Son and our Savior, Jesus Christ. As for ourselves, we have acted so badly and lived such evil and wicked lives that when we look at ourselves we see nothing remaining for us except death and eternal damnation. Therefore out of your pure goodness do not reckon us with the immoral, the deceitful, and the criminal as we deserve, but deal with your enemies and those of the holy Church in accord with their deeds, and may the machinations which they have devised against us believers recoil on themselves. When they fail to pay attention to your words and works, may their cruel and clever plans come to naught so that you yourself may be proclaimed with praises because you have heard the voices and prayers of your people. O God, be our strength and shield. Rescue from these dangers your people whom you have chosen as your heirs, heap up for them salvation and blessings, feed them [*30r*] while they live here, and finally carry them off to eternal life. Through Jesus Christ, our Lord. Amen.

FROM THE SAME PSALM:

We hope to obtain, O heavenly Father, your favor and goodwill in the day that we pour forth our prayers and petitions to you. Kindly hear them because of your goodness. For if you choose to deal with us as our uprightness has merited, we shall undergo infinite sufferings and disasters from all sides. There are no machinations that the opponents and enemies of our salvation and your honor have not devised so that they can tear asunder your servants and piety and sincere devotion to upright living. Be then our strength and shield against them. If we are your people and inheritance, as you have promised and we firmly believe, save us, feed us, favor us and lead us continuously to the final good toward which we are hastening. Through Jesus Christ, our Lord. Amen.

FROM PSALM 29:

May all of us, O heavenly Father, who have been brought to the point of being called and really being sons of God, never hold lightly [*30v*] or in contempt an opportunity to glorify you in the effects which we see as proceeding from you in nature. They are so excellent and marvelous that they furnish evidence of your glory and dignity to those who examine them. When it seems right you send showers, clouds, lightning, earthquakes, and rainstorms so mighty that there is no mountain, no tree, however lofty, and also no animal which is not violently shaken. We alone, O God, are blind and deaf and heedless to these mighty powers of yours. In your goodness, then, have mercy on our great ignorance, which can arise only from our sins, and grant that when we are finally freed from them we may acknowledge you in your wonderful works and worthily sing our praises to you forever. Through Jesus Christ, our Lord.

FROM PSALM 30:

We ought to celebrate and exalt you, O almighty God, with extraordinary praises because you are so ready to save those who call upon your name with faith. We openly acknowledge and freely confess that [*31r*] our sins are both serious and countless, and because of them we should be condemned to eternal destruction and perpetual death. But we pray that you exercise toward us that mercy with which you are accustomed to treat your elect. For you are wont to rebuke them with short and momentary anger, which you quickly change to supreme and lasting kindness. So save us from present evils and threatening dangers so that safe and sound we may confess you, and as both trustworthy and proven witnesses of the truth of your promises we may everywhere state and proclaim that we should rely on you alone. Through Jesus Christ, our Lord. Amen.

FROM THE SAME PSALM:

Your Church prays, O almighty God, that you lift her up from these troubles that are dragging her down. Do not permit the enemies of your name to rejoice over her destruction. It is your practice, O God, to hear those who call upon you and help them with immediate support. It lies within your hand to bring back from hell and revive those who have already almost fallen into the pit. Stir up in our hearts the friendly feelings of your praise, [*31v*] and proclaim that you have been angry with us, but only momentarily; despite that you have not broken off your infinite love for us, since through it we live in you and shall live forever. Take care, we beg, that our tears and sighs may quickly change to happiness and rejoicing. May you not take into account what we have merited but what befits you. Because of our sins we deserve deadly hatred and the extreme punishment, but so long as everything was going well and according to our plans, we foolishly thought that we could carry everything through by our own efforts. But now, since you have turned your face away from us for a short time and our present troubles have arisen, we are so downcast and terrified that we can barely stand on our feet. See, O God, what your mercy and promises demand: namely that you do not suffer those who call upon you to perish. When we are dead, there is no way that our enemies will praise you. Put, at last, an end to our sorrow so that with the spirit of rejoicing restored to us we may return our thanks and praises to you, both now and forever in the next world. Through Jesus Christ, our Lord. Amen.

FROM PSALM 31:
Since you, O almighty God, are our rock and citadel, for the sake of your name there is now need [*32r*] for you to lead those who trust in you to safety, so that in no way the trust by which we rely on you may be put to shame. You see how those who regard your teaching and the holy Gospel with hatred have secretly set nets and have stretched snares for us. Since we do not see how we can be saved by any other force, we now commend our souls to the protection of your hands and power. We put no trust in exotic and evil charms; we rely on you alone, O God, and pray that you look upon the afflictions amid which we live. Do not allow us to fall into the hands of the wicked. As we know, our sins press a very serious charge against us in your judgment; they are so heavy upon us that we cannot rightly escape them. But we beg you in your own goodness to take pity on us and not allow your Church to serve as a joke and sport for bystanders and enemies. May your face smile upon her, we beg you. Let the wicked be put to shame. Shut up their lying lips the moment when, filled with pride, they fabricate horrible charges against her. Granted that by fleshly standards we may think that we have been thrown down and cast out from the sweep of your eyes, in the Spirit we nonetheless still hope that you will help our prayers. Make the good men who love you realize that you guard your faithful and strengthen [*32v*] all those who worship and receive you in their hearts. Through Jesus Christ, our Lord. Amen.

FROM THE SAME PSALM:
We pray that the favor of your countenance may shine upon us, O almighty God, for from it all solace, happiness, and joy flow forth upon your

faithful. As long as we steadfastly beseech your help, the machinations, tricks, deceits, and snares of the hostile powers come to naught. Great, indeed, and splendid and joyous is the sweetness of your goodness which you have reserved for those who trust in you. May the sins then that we have committed not exclude us from it; we beseech you that we may be washed and cleansed by your grace. For if we have attained this cleansing, we do not doubt that we shall be hidden within the tabernacle and fortress of your protection and defended from all threatening evils so that, persevering manfully and stead-fastly in your love, we shall at length be carried unto you, the height of our happiness. Through Jesus Christ, our Lord. Amen.

[*33r*] FROM THE SAME PSALM:
The confidence which the devout put in you, O almighty God, has this special and singular characteristic: that the no one's just desire be put to shame or frustrated. Therefore this confidence moves us to beg for your help so that we may always have you for our strength, protection, leader, and provider. Otherwise because our sins fully merit it, we know that snares, ambushes, and tricks have been set for us on all sides by those who are enemies of your name and of our salvation. So we entrust to you both our spirit and our life and put them in your hands for protection. Because you see our countless infirmities, so that we are always surrounded by hostile powers, take pity on our lot, be present at our side, and since both life and death is in your hands for us who are your people, grant us to live forever with you. Through Jesus Christ, our Lord. Amen.

FROM PSALM 32:
You have warned us, O great and good God, that the happiness of your people lies in this: that [*33v*] their sins be forgiven, covered over and not imputed to them by your judgment. If there ever was a time that we needed to attain this, we seem to need it most urgently now when our present disasters put our sins right before our eyes. We feel the weight of your hand upon your Church, so we have thought to confess openly before you and not to hide our sins. We do not lose confidence that the punishments owed us can be immediately passed over and forgiven us through the goodness with which you are endowed. Therefore we, who are your people, beseech you now when we have no doubt that you are going to intervene, that you do not permit your people to be overwhelmed by the wicked who threaten like floodwaters. Be our hiding place and shelter in these afflictions. May you instruct and teach us in the ways of salvation. May you restrain with the spiked collar and bridle

of your Spirit all our brute and beastly desires which still remain, so that they may not cause us to be cast down into eternal destruction. May sufferings and disasters pour down at last on the enemies of your glory. May those who trust in you be walled round and fortified by your singular kindness so that those who are zealous for your name and are of upright heart may rejoice in you [*34r*] and exult in perfect gladness. Through Jesus Christ, our Lord. Amen.

FROM THE SAME PSALM:

Blessed beyond doubt are those, O great and good God, whose sins you have deigned in your mercy to forgive and not lay against them but rather to cover over and forgive everything evil and wicked which has stained them up to now. We acknowledge openly that such a great benefit could not happen to us unless we really had seen clearly our evils and brought before you and poured into your lap the sins which we have viciously and shamefully committed against your law. Therefore we confess to you, heavenly Father, that our injustice is enormous and that our souls are terribly burdened with the weight of our impiety. Help us now with your mercy; we pray that you may kindly and gently blot out anything left of our crimes. Deliver us from threatening disasters, provide us with a sound mind and guide us with your watchful care so that our evil inclinations do not make us lower ourselves to beastly stupidities. Instead, wrapped in your goodness, may we delight before you in upright joy and [*34v*] solid happiness. Through Jesus Christ, our Lord. Amen.

FROM PSALM 33:

All who have obtained justification by faith, O almighty God, rightly understand how much you are worthy of praise and commendation because of your marvelous works. There is nothing in the world that does not bear witness that you are good. The heavens studded with all their adornments exist by your command; the waters of the sea and of the abyss are contained within their places by only one force, your Spirit and your power. Our task then is and has been to worship and fear you alone, as you deserve. But alas there is nothing we have done less during our whole life. This is why we have fully earned the troubles and dangers into which we have fallen. But because your infinite goodness cannot be exhausted by men's evil deeds, however countless they be, we are asking you to pardon all of them that we have committed. We pray that since you are so merciful you bring to naught the plans and plots by which the enemies of religion strive to overturn the Church. May your attitude stand firm, O God, and your plans remain unchanged toward the nation which has you as its God and its lawful inheritance. [*35r*] You look down from heaven on the hearts of men which you have established from the beginning; you know perfectly well what the Antichrists have already wrought against your people. So we beg you, deign to save us at this time. We need no king, no horse, no human strength–these are useless for saving us. We run to you alone to free our souls; we beg that your mercy be at our side, even as we believe and hope without any doubt that it will be. Through Jesus Christ, our Lord. Amen.

FROM THE SAME PSALM:
For many reasons your name, O almighty God, deserves to be extolled with the highest praises and celebrated by the supreme effort and total strength of the pious because all your statements and all your commands and deeds are nothing except fidelity, uprightness, fairness, and goodness. Everything possessing beauty and splendor in the universe of creatures, everything having usefulness and convenience, all have you alone wrought. You alone undo the perverse plots of the wicked and [35v] render their evil endeavors utterly futile. Your decrees are indeed most sure and solid in their unshakable constancy. This is why the people who chose you for their God and who direct their pure and exclusive worship to you as their wondrous inheritance are happy and blessed. Since you are so good and great and are our maker and creator, you are not unmindful of how often and how grossly we have sinned against your law. We beg you to forgive us and not allow us to trust in any created power. Rather grant that having experienced your marvelous mercy, we may take enduring happiness and upright joy in it. Through Jesus Christ, our Lord. Amen.

FROM PSALM 34:
O almighty God, your singular and outstanding benefits toward us require that, regardless of the fortune in store for us, whether favorable or unfavorable, we glorify your name with praises. You are always present to those who call upon you in sincerity, and you snatch the suffering from the troubles and the disasters which are pressing upon them. You fortify and hedge round with the guardianship of the angels those who fly to your protection. We then who are burdened with the heavy baggage of sins will be led to utter ruin unless you come to help. [36r] So we beg and pray that you lift up the prostrate and teach us, whom you have received into your grace, sincere fear, worship, and piety so that we may have a pure heart as soon as possible. Bridle our tongue that it may not prattle things unworthy of you and our holiness. May we turn our actions away from vices; may we carry out the upright

actions that you enjoin; and may we become as eager as possible in seeking your peace. Just as you have wished to redeem our souls for no ordinary price, so may you deign to grant them eternal salvation freely and abundantly. Through Jesus Christ, our Lord. Amen.

FROM PSALM 35:
Since you, O great and good God, have invincible strength and a ready will in bringing help to your people when they call upon you in good faith, we now pray and request with all our petitions that you deign to be our help when we are continually so oppressed by hostile powers while we live here. For Satan is driven by an immense hatred to keep us from salvation. Therefore pay no heed to the evil deeds we have committed against you. After you in your mercy have forgiven our grievous faults, which [*36v*] in our misery we realize burden us, drive back from us the assaults of the devil and all his minions. By your power and by the strength of the holy angels, may their efforts not help them, and may our souls sweetly rejoice in your favor and prompt help, and may they proclaim that they can find no other god like you, who can rescue his people from every disaster. The [devils] mock and make fun of our weakness. But, good Father, you see our dangers; we pray that you lay claim to us for your own and deign to protect us from eternal damnation. Through Jesus Christ, our Lord. Amen.

FROM THE SAME PSALM:
Long and hard have we desired to glorify you, O great and good God, in the largest possible throng of devout people. We shall indeed do so with ready and happy hearts when you shall have delivered us by your power from the Devil and the minions of his wrath. It is no secret to you how deceitfully, untruthfully, and horribly he afflicts your faithful. So we pray with all the devotion we can muster that first you deign to forgive anything we have shamefully committed against your law [*37r*] and that secondly you make yourself conspicuous in defending and protecting our cause, lest your enemies mock your people by making them victims of their caprice. Rather may shame and confusion overtake them when they dare to set themselves against your glory and our salvation. On the contrary, may we who are seeking for your justice and honor be suffused with joy and happiness and proclaim with eager hearts your praise and majesty. Through Jesus Christ, our Lord. Amen.

FROM PSALM 36:

We realize, O almighty God, that the power of evil is so great that the person burdened by it is untouched and unmoved by fear or reverence for your name. Indeed that person takes so much pleasure in evildoing that he ends up making his deeds equally notorious and hateful to everybody. Everything he says is vicious, and he cannot be brought to let himself become involved in doing good. Even at night he harbors sin in his soul and so hardens himself in sin that he regards nothing as evil which he proposes to himself in his soul. Out of your mercy, your singular trustworthiness, and your incorruptible justice and judgment, O God, which [*37v*] fill the heavens and the ether, which overcome the broad mountains, which exceed the vast abyss and bring life and health not only to humans but to all the animals as well, we beseech you that, having wiped clean and forgiven the sins by which we wretches have offended you, you do not permit our souls to be stained by wickedness. Rather grant that finding support under the faith and protection of your wings, we may be suffused with the mighty spirit and eternal delights from your heavenly court. By the gift of your light may we contemplate the lamp of eternal happiness after having drunk deeply from the fount of life that is with you. May those who oppose our salvation be unable to turn us from it, but rather may they fall so flat that they cannot rise again unless they cease what they have begun. Through Jesus Christ, our Lord. Amen.

FROM PSALM 37:

Since your Church, O almighty God, has many weak members who might take serious offense when they see the great success enjoyed by evildoers and sinners, strengthen them with your Spirit so that they can rightly understand that the happiness which the enemies of the Gospel are now enjoying is not firm and solid but is set to wither and dry [*38r*] very quickly like languid blades and thin grass. May you deign to pour your grace upon us so that we may rely only on you and constantly strive for the kindness and love which will fully convince us that all pleasure and enjoyment is to be sought from you as from a unique and inexhaustible fountain. Grant moreover that with serene and patient hearts we may allow you to direct our affairs as seems best to your goodness. May we wait with courage when it happens that you put off saving us, that we do not become furious over our current difficulties, realizing that we deserve much worse punishments because of our grave sins. So greatly have we sinned against you, O God, that our evil deserts surpass any punishment. But regardless of all these obstacles, do you who are most kind deign to direct our steps and so favor those who trust in you that everybody may realize that, although we have fallen back, we are by no means wholly cast down because we are kindly and gently supported by your hand. May all confess that you have in no way deserted your upright people. May as many as possible dare to commit themselves to your faith so that you may help them and snatch them with prompt support from the hands of the wicked. [*38v*] Through Jesus Christ, our Lord. Amen.

FROM THE SAME PSALM:

O great and good God, may the successes of the wicked not influence us so that we deviate from worshiping with a totally pure religion, since you warn us that their good fortune is as brief and passing as growing grass and the flowers of the field. We beseech you to lift from our consciences as soon as possible the burden of sin that will easily make us fall into destruction unless we are held up by your favor. Because the hope on which we completely depend is in you and because we have entrusted ourselves to your faithfulness, we do not doubt that we will be given what we are seeking: that is, that we may place all our pleasure and delight in you alone and cast aside and spurn worldly success. For just as those who rely on it will be overthrown in a flash, so those who are quiet, gentle, and serene of heart will enjoy an eternal inheritance in peace and tranquillity. There is nothing to fear from the grumbling, straining and machinations of the wicked one against the saints, because his depraved efforts will recoil on himself. But may you, O God, [*39r*] pardon and approve both our accomplishments and our actions so that an eternal inheritance may await us who daily glorify your name with praise. Through Jesus Christ, our Lord. Amen.

FROM THE SAME PSALM:

You are acknowledged, O almighty God, as the leader and companion who keeps the devout from straying from the path of justice and as their support if they happened to have the misfortune to fall. Till now your promises have been so certain that a just man has yet to be found who has been deprived of your favor and has lacked the food needed for life. Hence we pray, relying on faith in you, that you do not punish us according to the sins we have committed against you. Rather in your mercy forgive the sins of those who fly unto you. Deign to grant those who trust in you to have your will and your laws imprinted on their hearts so that they unceasingly reflect upon and speak of them and that they may not be wavering and inconstant in carrying them out. May the striking and splendid good fortune of the wicked who nourish an implacable hostility against your people not turn us from the right path.

Rather may you enlighten our hearts by your Spirit so that we may realize [*39v*] that they will quickly perish and undergo extreme and unending punishment. May you give strength and salvation to us in the measure we have trusted in your promises, and may you snatch us from impending disasters and from the enemies of our salvation. Through Jesus Christ, our Lord. Amen.

FROM PSALM 38:

You accuse and punish us like sons, O great and good God, but may you avert your wrath and anger from our current difficulties. We feel your hand and acknowledge that the dangers in which we are caught up admit of no human escape. This has befallen us because we have indeed deserved it. We are weighed down and oppressed beyond our ability to endure because we are overwhelmed from all sides by sins and iniquities. This is why we go about sad and are almost broken up by heartfelt anxiety. We see that our friends and neighbors are far away and our enemies are setting their snares and hatching all kind of schemes so that we may be overthrown at last. Do you, O God, by the mercy with which you are endowed [*40r*] first reconcile us to yourself by forgiving the foul sins we have committed against you, then hasten to help us. We await you as our only refuge, for you are wont to stand by those who call upon you and answer their prayers. You are not unaware how the Antichrists are triumphing over us while we are so stricken and wavering. Each day they who unjustly hate us grow in strength and number. So we beseech you, good Father, do not put us off in our great afflictions, for you yourself are our salvation. We beg you to come quickly, bring aid to your Church, and support her in her extreme danger. Through Jesus Christ, our Lord. Amen.

FROM THE SAME PSALM:

We are experiencing such a heavy burden, O great and good God, and such a weight of the sins we have committed against you that we are now unequal to carrying them. We therefore come forward to invoke your fidelity in not punishing us with your wrath and anger because of them. May your warning be fatherly, as you are accustomed to use toward your children. See how our heart is almost thrown into confusion by our concern over our evil deeds. [*40v*] Everything in us is rotten and corrupt. Unless you help us, we go about sad, afflicted, and somehow deprived of light. There is nothing we can entrust to friends or neighbors, for our sins have made all things opposed and hostile to us. When, O God, we pour our iniquities into your lap, and are so eager to obtain your pardon, do not depart from your innate favor and mercy;

rather as you are approachable and gentle, deign to provide fast and firm help for our woes. Through Jesus Christ, our Lord. Amen.

FROM PSALM 39:

When we are so harassed in these hard times, O almighty God, by present disasters and crushed underneath such heavy afflictions, we take refuge in you so that by your Spirit you may check our mouth and tongue from uttering anything unworthy of your majesty or of our witness. Since we cannot complain that these troubles surpass our sins or that we are being punished undeservedly, make us block out the shouts of those who are complaining about you. [*41r*] May our breasts rather be moved by a rightful sorrow over the sins we have committed. May our souls grow warm and our hearts be inflamed by real contrition. Grant, kindly Father, that we may rightly understand the situation of our ongoing lives every hour since our whole existence here is mere vanity and our worried shouts and meager resources fall far short of being able to help us. Therefore it behooves us to wait for you alone, O Lord, for if you first relieve us from our sins and iniquities, we are confident that we will not be the laughingstock of the wicked. For you are wont to stop the blows against those you have washed and cleansed from their sins lest they be destroyed by the stroke of your mighty and invincible hand. If your hand continues to inflict sufferings on men, as they deserve, it will consume and destroy them no less than a moth eats away clothing. Hear our prayers then, O God, and since you see that on earth we can hardly obtain lasting rest, grant that we may at last live close to you in faith and dwell in safety. Through Jesus Christ, our Lord. Amen.

[*41v*] FROM THE SAME PSALM:

We are experiencing how severe your judgment can be, O almighty God, but your Spirit restrains us from questioning your goodness and justice. Still we are led by the greatness of our sufferings and by the consciousness of our sins to consider how life has soured on us. So when we confess to you that we have sinned and done evil before you in many ways, in your goodness and mercy be favorable to us. You see how short and empty is our lifetime, like a shadow which possesses nothing firm, solid, and true. We pass by in a moment, and whatever time is given here for our life, through our own fault we live the whole of it in violent, unruly, and vicious emotions. So we pray that you may now take pity on us; may our prayers and sighs reach your ears. Within us your own Spirit sends them forth from our hearts, and while we

wander like pilgrims in this world, be pleased to refresh our hearts from time
to time with your favor. Through Jesus Christ, our Lord. Amen.

[*42r*] FROM PSALM 40:
As you are gentle and kind, you listen at length to the prayers of those
who find so much support in their hope, O almighty God, that they look to
you amidst their present and pressing troubles, and in no way discouraged
they lift up their heart to you. You hear their cries from the watery depths, and
with your mighty help you lift up those who are lying stuck in filth and muck.
This is why the liberated have your praises always in their mouths and sing
those praises with new hymns in public and private to stir up everybody's
faith, hope and fear in you. Grant us now so much happiness that we make
you alone our fortress and that we pay no heed to the proud and deceitful who
rise up against your Church, since we know full well that you are the author
of all wonders. For you hold in the treasury of your providence those plans
and designs which no one can rightly relate and describe because they surpass
in their number and greatness all force of words and power of eloquence.
Since we have till now gravely offended you by our sins, [*42v*] and cannot
cleanse ourselves with any sacrifice of our own, give us an obedient faith that
we may be everywhere prompt to do your will, which you have deigned to
reveal to us in the book of the Law. Grant that faith may be so impressed in
our hearts that we can freely and spontaneously put it into practice. Just as you
never hold back anything from us in your mercy and goodness, so in turn your
faithful people give testimony in both word and deed to your faithfulness, justice and veracity. You see how we are weighed down with our sins so that we
are buried in troubles and feel forsaken in heart and soul. Take to heart our salvation; hasten to help us. Confound and put to shame your enemies instead;
but may we who seek you be restored and experience that it is not in vain that
you are proclaimed the very salvation and help of the suffering and poor.
Through Jesus Christ, our Lord. Amen.

FROM THE SAME PSALM:
Those who bear up under the delay of your help with a calm and patient
heart, O almighty God, will in the end realize that you do hear their prayers.
And while they experience that they have been set free by their good faith, not
only do they themselves [*43r*] celebrate your name with fitting praise but they
afford ample reason for other devout men to do the same. This task therefore
remains: since you are not moved by outward sacrifices, we strive to win you
over with our prayers so that, as day by day we become more and more loving

and eager in carrying out your will, we may exalt your truth and mercy toward us with frequent, even constant, public commendations. But meanwhile, because you are merciful and good, may you grant us forgiveness for all the shameful and disgraceful actions we have committed. Do not allow us to be buried by the penalties and disasters which our sins have fully merited. May those who seek to shame you and destroy us be themselves put to shame, but may those who are zealous for your name be flooded with true and enduring happiness. Since you are not unaware of how we are despised and deprived of earthly help, come quickly to our protection as our defender and champion. Through Jesus Christ, our Lord. Amen.

FROM PSALM 41:

It is no mean act of your goodness, O almighty God, when you test both the sick and the devout generally, whom [*43v*] you sometimes visit with ill fortune, for just as you chastise with a fatherly heart, you will also easily rescue them, give them life, and at last make them blessed in your presence. Relying on that hope while we are now being horribly afflicted, we also pray here together that you take pity on us and deliver us from the sins by which we have seriously offended you. You indeed know that the enemies of the holy Gospel are eager to do us wrong. You know what they are plotting and proposing together for our destruction. They plot nothing less than the destruction of your Church. These have been joined by those who we had thought were linked to us both by religion and by many other titles and duties.[3] May you be touched, O God, on our behalf by the mercy through which you are wont not only to raise up the prostrate but also to destroy their enemies. Do not allow the enemies of religion and piety to rejoice over the death of your servants. But if you deliver us from our present disasters and confirm us by your Spirit, your name will be praised openly by all the pious. We pray that this happen continuously and without ceasing. Through Jesus Christ, our Lord. Amen.

[*44r*] FROM THE SAME PSALM:

Magnificent rewards, O great and good God, await those who take pity on the downtrodden, for those who have mercy on the suffering and the afflicted imitate your singular goodness. For you are wont to be so present at

---

[3]This seems a veiled reference to Duke Maurice of Saxony and the other Lutherans who fought on the side of Charles V and the Catholics in the First Schmalkaldic War. As a reward Charles V transferred considerable territory and the title of Elector from John Frederick of Saxony, Luther's protector, to Maurice in October 1546.

the bed of your sick servant that you seem to be changing the bedding in order that he can lie more comfortably after being drained by sickness. Neither do we account it something singular when you do not deal indulgently with your people when you judge there is an opportunity to help them. Thus when we rightly understand that we have fallen into dangerous and severe troubles because of our sins, we fly to you alone and beg that you deign to forgive us for the transgressions we have committed and that you do not allow the enemies of our salvation to take delight in our perishing. That you help us in such critical affairs by itself manifests how extremely dear to you we are. Help us, we beg, and show that you have taken us to your heart, that we may celebrate the praises of your name, as is fitting. Through Jesus Christ, our Lord. Amen.

[*44v*] FROM PSALM 42:
There is none, O almighty God, who has really studied your goodness who does not pant and aspire for you night and day, like a stag who is dying from thirst. How could it happen that anyone endowed with true faith should not hasten to the living God? But so far that eagerness has been very slack in us, nor have we sought you, as was right, by good faith in holy assemblies. Because of our sadness and trouble, tears have become for us our food and drink in these difficult times, and enemies far and wide mock the Church and say, "Where is their God?" But we beg you, O God, since you are merciful and kind, to put aside your anger which you have rightly conceived against us, and mindful of your promises, grant that we may be made firm in a solid hope and faith, although we have not merited it, so our soul may not be unduly downcast. Although it seems that all the waves, storms and abysses of temptations have been poured upon your Church, may you be appeased by the goodness of your mercy and grace so that the solid joys of heart and conscience may not be taken away from us. Make it happen that stirred by the Holy Spirit [*45r*] we may continually encourage ourselves to hope and trust in your help, because henceforward we are going to glorify your name and give thanks for being restored to salvation and tranquillity. Through Jesus Christ, our Lord. Amen.

FROM THE SAME PSALM:
We desire with all our heart to join ourselves to you, O great and good God. Day and night we hunger and thirst for this, since, when you seem to have deserted us, we cannot hear without great pain the insults both of our own hearts and of our enemies, with which they mock our nascent devotion and faith, namely by deriding the hardships, troubles and disasters under which we seem to lie completely crushed because of our growing weight of

sins. We beg you to forgive us for them because of your mercy, O God, so that we can strengthen ourselves. May you mold our hearts so that they may be constant, and when evil inclinations and the weighty fear of punishment disturbs us, may we be strengthened by your promise; may we console and convince our own downcast souls with the hope that, as they rely on you alone, they will soon [*45v*] glorify your name, because for them there will exist both true salvation and a true God. Through Jesus Christ, our Lord. Amen.

FROM PSALM 43:

May you, O great and good God, undertake at last to judge with your authority and power our cause which, although it strives to offer you true worship and a purified religion and is therefore good, has been deserted and attacked by everybody. Hence we urgently need you yourself to rescue us from deceitful and depraved men. You alone remain as the consolation, strength, and foundation of the Church. For the most part we have lived unworthily of your name, profession, and teaching, but your mercy is such that it forgives all the iniquities and hidden sins of those who repent and return to you, and it does not impute against believers the shameful deeds they have done. Therefore we pray that as you have taken pity on us, so you make us partakers in your light and truth so that here we may give you pure worship in the holy assemblies and that hereafter we may be led to the holy dwelling place of eternal life. Now our soul is sad and downcast, we are repeatedly disturbed [*46r*] by fearful thoughts, and our stomachs churn inside us with terrors. Still we pray to you, good Father, to give us strength to hope for the best, because hereafter we shall also be glorifying you and rejoicing over the salvation we have attained, since you shall have proclaimed yourself our God, as you truly are. Through Jesus Christ, our Lord. Amen.

FROM THE SAME PSALM:

In this supreme crisis and in the great dangers of this life, we entrust our cause, O almighty God, to your protection and defense. Granted that while we carry on this miserable life there is no strength and solidity in ourselves that we can rely on because we have been pulled down by original sin and the infinite sins we have unhappily added to it, still we beseech you that the brightness of your favor may shine on us so that the dark corners of our mind may be enlightened. If that happens to us because of your mercy, we shall be flooded with supreme happiness and incredible joy, and we shall command our heart, otherwise downcast, to be of good hope. We beseech you, grant just one thing, that we put all our hope in you alone since [*46v*] you alone exist as our salvation and true God. Through Jesus Christ, our Lord. Amen.

FROM PSALM 44:[4]

In your supreme goodness, O almighty God, you have gathered yourself from many nations a Church which has not been planted by human powers but by your own hand. By your favor and Spirit she has been washed clean of sins and has escaped so far the cruel assaults of the devil since you have helped and strongly defended her. You have always saved her from her enemies and heaped shame and ignominy on those who pursued her out of hatred. We therefore ought to have gloried in you alone and extolled your name alone, but alas we have been utterly ungrateful for all these benefits and have trusted in flesh and human strength and have brought into disgrace your teaching, which we profess, by our unjust lives and wicked behavior. Hence you are now driving us away and heaping us with shame; already we have almost become prey for the Antichrist and are a reproach for our neighbors. Now your Gospel is a joke for the Gentiles, a laughing stock for the people, and a sport for the masses. All these things have happened to us quite rightly, we admit, because of our sins. [*47r*] But please, good Father, reconcile us again to yourself by the kindness with which you are endowed, and be willing to forgive all the evil and stupid things we have done. Grant that we may by no means be unmindful of you nor become traitors to your covenant. Even though we are downtrodden and the shadow of death covers us all round, may our heart never stray or depart from your paths. May we not do something that would result in our being counted like sheep for the slaughter, in our being forgetful of your name, or being turned toward disgusting forms of worship. Awaken, we beseech you, O God, and sleep no more. Do not hide your face from our afflictions. Arise and help the downcast whom we are certain you have chosen for yourself because of your kindness. Through Jesus Christ, our Lord. Amen.

FROM THE SAME PSALM:

The sacred histories tell us marvelous stories about your mercy and your conquering might which you manifested during ages past in protecting, saving and increasing your faithful. When we hear these stories, we are convinced that we should put our hope in you alone and not in our own strength, resources, and power. Now [*47v*] when we are crushed by the heavy weight of

---

[4]The Zurich edition has an obvious misprint, "Ex Psalmo LIIII."

our sins we feel the punishment of your wrath which we deserve, and because of our bad consciences we fear harsher punishment and severe penalties. Forgive and pass over, we pray, all the sins we have committed against you, because you are so rich in goodness. Moreover, if you have destined us to undergo disasters and hardships, grant that we may not for that reason fall short in the devotion and piety that we owe you. Do not let us run seeking counsel from anybody except you. May you rise up therefore and hasten to help us; as long as you put off supporting us, you seem to have turned your back to us. To give splendor to the mercy and goodness you are endowed with, deign to rescue us from the dangers that encircle us. Through Jesus Christ, our Lord. Amen.

FROM PSALM 45:

O great and good God, we have Christ for our only king, most rich in every kind of good. Just as he has supreme power, so the throne of his majesty has been made firm forever. His invincible power prevails, he is splendid in his supreme justice, he enjoys your [*48r*] boundless blessings, and he is conspicuous for his infinite wisdom. The Church is his bride, like a most honored queen, so that she may bear him an innumerable and holy progeny. Therefore we, who should have eagerly served such a great king, have foully defiled his name and his sacred reign by our vices. We now confess them and acknowledge them before you, good Father, and humbly ask you to forgive us so that, after we have been received back into your favor, we may at last realize the benefits of our king. Although we do not deserve it, we still pray that he may rise up in our present anguish, gird on his sword, and deliver the Church, his bride, from the attacks and insults of the Antichrist. Now may he hurl the sharpened spear of the word and Spirit, may he use the rod of justice and fairness which he is wont to employ in governing his kingdom. May he now show himself as one who loves truth and utterly detests iniquity. Through the same Jesus Christ, our Lord. Amen.

[*48v*] FROM THE SAME PSALM:

O great and good God, your only begotten Son, our Lord Jesus Christ, is truly worthy of being praised in every way. He has shown himself in the world before all as pure and as conspicuous by his virtuous bearing and by the splendor of his holiness. He employed a gracious way of speaking in teaching and encouraging men, and he brought all things under his power and sway by the sword of his speech and the effect of his power. He swore to be forever a lover of justice and a bitter enemy of vice. But we wretched people, who are destined to be married as a chaste spouse to one so great and excellent, have defiled ourselves with the many different stains of our vices. Accordingly we pray that we may be cleansed by repentance and by your Spirit so that, having forgotten the evil inclinations that are born within us, we may aspire after the love of this most excellent bridegroom. When our labors are laid aside, may many faithful children be born to take the place of their fathers who have already been gathered to Christ. May we extol forever with these children his honor and praises. Through the same Jesus Christ, our Lord. Amen.

[*49r*] FROM PSALM 46:
Your help was always at hand, O great and good God, for those in affliction who believe truly that you are their only protection and strength. Your faithful are therefore delivered from fear, even if the whole earth is shaken, the mountains waver, the waves and surging of the sea pound the shore so strongly that it seems that everything is about to collapse into the water and float away. Your people in contrast are gifted with supreme confidence because in the midst of their troubles you refresh them with pleasant streams of consolation by your fruitful Spirit and by putting forth rare and wonderful proofs of your help. We rely on your goodness and, despite our countless sins by which we confess that we have seriously offended you, we pray that the nations and kingdoms, which you see attacking your Church with great force and sly plots, may themselves waver and grow weak. May you cry out with that voice of yours which is wont to shake and break up the earth and all creatures. May you, our God, stand by us like a fortified citadel. Take away wars; may spears, horses, chariots, and all kinds of weapons [*49v*] grow weak without you so that those who are attacking us may finally give up their efforts. May you appear sublime and exalted before all creatures, after you have been acclaimed for providing us better protection than all the armies and all the power of this world. Through Jesus Christ, our Lord. Amen.

FROM THE SAME PSALM:
Whatever sudden and horrible misfortune troubles us, O almighty God, we will not lose hope nor be stricken at heart because we have already made you our only fortress. Even though the uproar of the world flares up, attacks of the flesh swell up, and the whole devil with all his entourage seems to be shattering all our possessions, we rest assured in your indescribable goodness and invincible power. Our sins deserve all these troubles and adversities, but out of your goodness forgive us for them, take pity on our present disasters, and grant salvation, peace, and tranquillity to those who call upon you. For it

is very easy for you to destroy the swords, bows, artillery, [*sor*] and all the devil's cunning devices, not only by your mighty word but even by a nod or your mere will. We desire, O God, that you would undertake the task of having us contemplate the deeds you do for your people so that all may realize that you stand by us and have destined yourself to be always the helper of your faithful people. Through Jesus Christ, our Lord. Amen.

FROM PSALM 47:

You have deigned, O almighty God, to gather to yourself a Church on earth and to establish it, not in stone buildings or marble temples but in living human hearts, which you adorn with wonderful gifts and refine with Holy Spirit. It is befitting for all the faithful who have been given so great a gift to break out in their festive rejoicing and joyous applause. But the deadly sins we have committed greatly overshadow the thanksgivings and joyful songs, and the punishments they have merited weigh heavily upon us. Since we admit that up to now we have gone astray, and you now see how we are undergoing sufferings commensurate with our sins, forgive your people since you are mercy itself, and [*sov*] do not destroy us as we have fully deserved because you are the most high and you rule far and near. Good Father, grant that our sins may not impede your kingdom. Continue to conquer new peoples for the faith and make nations, which so far have been without the faith, obey your word. You have chosen for yourself the Church as a choice and special inheritance; may you be greatly glorified in her forever by exquisite melodies and hymns so that all people may possess you, praise you, and sing to you as their king. But may you enlighten with your Spirit and rule with your Spirit your own people, who now seem the most abject of all, so that every one may see that they are governed by your command. May the monarchies and all the powers of the earth finally join themselves to you that you may be their God, just as you were of old to the faithful Abraham. Make kings and all princes, who because of their office should serve as protectors for their subjects, acknowledge you so that in them your majesty and glory may shine brightly to the extraordinary advantage of the Church. Through Jesus Christ, our Lord. Amen.

FROM THE SAME PSALM:

It is the task of all believers, O great and good God, to advance the progress of Christ's kingdom [*sir*] with sincere enthusiasm, joyful admiration and zealous support, for there your goodness is proclaimed and we are enabled to seek salvation. Christ has earned the right to have all peoples and nations made subject to his rule and to deal with us in the best way because we are his unique heritage and his own special possession. We beseech you, our king, who have been exalted to heaven and to the Father's right hand, that you deign to deliver us from the sins into which we have fallen and to lift from our necks by your mercy and power the disasters and misfortunes that threaten us, so that you alone may reign in our hearts and that all the kings and magnates and princes who hold power over affairs on earth may cling inseparably to you as their legitimate and true God. Through Jesus Christ, our Lord. Amen.

FROM PSALM 48:

O great and good God, your greatness and exceptional honor flourished especially in the Church since in her you hold sway most powerfully by your word and Spirit. But it is not just there that you are praised in so wondrous a way, rather all honor and solid delight [*51v*] in the whole world unquestionably derives from her. And because you are much better acknowledged there than elsewhere, the result is that there you are a safe refuge and fortified citadel for your faithful. Therefore the kings have gathered and the monarchs of this world have conspired, as they have desired, to attack her; may they be forced to stop what they have started so that, as they experience the presence of your power and might, stricken with fear and terrified with trembling they may break off their endeavors. Those whom you strike with terror are overtaken by pain like that of women giving birth. Therefore, O God, may our sins not conquer your goodness; we have indeed sinned seriously and we do not deny it, but together with our own sins we acknowledge your kindness and beg for it so that we may be finally reconciled to you, not because of our merits but because of the goodness, favor, and grace of your Son. Please grant that the enemies of your Church may be dispersed, as ships in the middle of the sea are often pounded by a tremendous crash from winds that are whipped up unexpectedly. Then just as we have heard with our ears from the Holy Scriptures that your abundant promises are proclaimed, so may we see them happen with our eyes. We have already begun to hope [*52r*] and believe in the things which your words propose to us; we beg you to make these events take place so that thanksgiving with great acclaim for the benefits received may be joined to the preaching of your name and your goodness and that everywhere men may acknowledge that anything which comes from you is pure justice. May you be our God, I say, our God as long as we live here and for eternity. Through Jesus Christ, our Lord. Amen.

FROM THE SAME PSALM:

All creatures bear shining witness to your goodness, O great and good God, but the Church is the special work in which you are uniquely praised and glorified. For this the whole world rejoices because true doctrine is found there, where you are acknowledged and we are summoned to Heaven. Everything found on earth which is joyful, happy, and blessed flourishes in her. So it is no wonder when hostile powers move against her with threatening, wrathful, angry attacks. If you assist, protect, support, and defend her, whether they like it or not, the rulers of this world and the princes of darkness are forced to fall into confusion, flee headlong, [*52v*] and be thrown into complete panic. Your power smashes their impotent rage, but your faithful are then delivered from their sad cares. Sometimes we do not realize these benefits because we live evil and troubled lives, driven into many and diverse sins, partly through weakness, partly through ignorance. We beg you, then, because of the great honor of your house, that you blot out anything we have committed against you so that you yourself may rule and govern us in that same Church for the praise of your name. Through Jesus Christ, our Lord. Amen.

FROM PSALM 49:

We pray to you, O almighty God, that by a faith joined to the teaching of the Holy Spirit we may inwardly reflect, when afflicted by troubles due to the wickedness of our enemies, how much they rely on the wealth and good fortune which they are enjoying. They fail to recognize that there are no riches on earth which men can use to redeem themselves from death and eternal damnation. Hold in check, good Father, our affections lest they cling to things that are so transitory. May we be warned about our common weakness and the misery which engulfs our whole human race by death itself, which [*53r*] stalks us all at random. Regardless of how wise or foolish men are, it is not granted to them to escape death and enjoy forever the goods they have produced. We also openly confess that we have fallen frequently here, because relying on worldly powers we have dreamed up marvelous victories and triumphant ceremonies as if our names should be extolled beyond all measure. We have not kept squarely before our eyes how passing is good luck and the favorable successes of the flesh and how all who trust in them perish at last like cattle and are herded into hell and oppressed by eternal night. Forgive us, O God, this crime, and after we have put aside groundless hope in worldly resources, receive us whom you have rescued from hell and death. Grant that we may have nothing to fear from those who greatly multiply riches and honor for themselves and their houses. All these things can provide them with comfort only in this life so that they can better devote their talent to what pertains to the flesh. Lastly we ask you, O God, that you free your Church from those enemies who do not acknowledge the honor and authority conferred on them by God and not only die like cattle but who, after dying and being stripped of their present goods, [*53v*] undergo eternal punishments. Through our Lord, Jesus Christ. Amen.

FROM THE SAME PSALM:
The renowned oracles of sacred doctrine, O almighty God, which you have deigned to utter in sacred Scripture, should be listened to with eager ears. There is nobody, either obscure or famous, who should not devote his total attention to what you say. Above all you warn us against placing any trust, which we should put in you alone, in the goods of this world, which are empty and transitory. There is nothing in human riches, strength, splendor, or honor that can redeem us from death. Indeed, it is the lot of mankind that these things change quickly and pass away in a moment, nor can someone who relies on them long retain his eminence. When they wilt and die, his tarnished glory also withers away. We therefore ask you, good Father, to forgive us for clinging till now with such lasting and tenacious attachment to these goods. Pull our hearts away from them and join them as closely as possible to you and your words so that we find nothing more attractive than following you and [*54r*] eagerly carrying out what you command. Let us not become like oxen and perish like speechless animals. Through Jesus Christ, our Lord. Amen.

FROM PSALM 50:
O strong and good God, in your mercy you have deigned to gather us to yourself from all the ends of the earth, beginning with the Apostles whom your gifted with the mighty Spirit of your Son on Mount Zion. The only reason you wanted to gather your good and chosen people in such a wonderful way was so that the true way of divine worship (in which the solid perfection of believers is undoubtedly rooted) might gain public acceptance among all nations and that we might learn that piety does not consist only in outward rite and deaf ceremonies. These ceremonies would please you if they were testimonies to faith, but they are so devoid of faith that they are hateful to you and totally detestable. This you seek above all: that the glory and praises of your name come forth not only from our words and thoughts but also from all the actions of our lives. You wish us rather [*54v*] to carry out in good faith

whatever things we promise you, provided that we are convinced that they both conform to your word and promote piety. Moreover you require us to call upon you when we are crushed by troubles and thank you, as is fitting, when we are delivered from them. You demand these actions as major principles of our religion. But we, O God, have sinned very sadly and unhappily because we have brought very little faith to our rites and ceremonies and have usually treated the Holy Scriptures with hostile hearts estranged from them. We were resistant to discipline and have ignored your commandments right and left in favor of our wicked desires. But now because of your inexhaustible kindness and goodness forgive us for these evil ways. Also deliver from their evil deeds those who are wrapped up in robbery and unchastity, who blaspheme your name, and who speak evilly of your Church and Gospel. They think that you forget the outrages that they commit since you seem to put up with them patiently rather than avenge them. Train your eyes for once on them and do not permit them to plunder us as if there was nobody to deliver us. Through Jesus Christ, our Lord. Amen.

[55r] FROM THE SAME PSALM:

You have shown us, O good and great God, by your harsh sentence how the cases of mortals are decided before your supreme tribunal, so that you do not want debates over victims and outward sacrifices, for you hold always under your power the calves, goats, wild beasts and finally all the animals of the whole world, nor have you ever wanted these animals to be offered to you except in so far as they bear clear witness to faith, religion and inward piety. Above all you have demanded from the human race that they give thanks for benefits received, that they attribute to you the gift of all the goods they enjoy, that they strive earnestly to undertake for the glory of your name everything they attempt and plan, as they promised they would do, and that they call upon you alone in their troubles and disasters. As you know, O God, in this we fall far short. So we beg you that out of your goodness you pass over and forgive all the punishments and guilt we have incurred so far. May we not make use of your words for our condemnation. May we not be condemned by your sentence as insolent, covetous, and accursed, but may we earnestly offer you a sacrifice of praise, [55v] and may our lives be conformed to the measure of your commandments. Through Jesus Christ, our Lord. Amen.

FROM PSALM 51:

We join in prayer to beg your mercy, O great and good God, that we may be cleansed, washed, and scrubbed from our iniquity, crimes, and disgraceful acts. We acknowledge and confess how until now we have done evil before you, but our sins will never succeed in making you unjust and less faithful. We know very well that we do not deserve that you fulfill the splendid and abundant promises you have made to us, but here there is need that your trustworthiness and constancy come to our rescue. You see how corrupt and vicious from our birth we have emerged into the light, for earlier we were conceived in iniquities. Cleanse our hearts and deign to adorn them with a splendor acceptable to you. Give us a pure heart and an upright spirit, holy and willing so that you will not cast us out as wicked but that we may receive true joys and solid happiness. If you were to free us from the sins that accuse us as guilty of eternal death, [*56r*] our lips would suddenly be loosened to praise you. Grant, we pray, that we may approach you with the one sacrifice in which you delight, that of a contrite spirit and a humble and broken heart. Then our present troubles will be alleviated and the praises with which we glorify you will not be unwelcome to you. May you proclaim your goodwill toward Zion, that is, toward your Church. You see how many dangers beset her, how she is tried without and within. We beseech you to deliver her not only from her outward enemies but also that you reform and restore her so that you possess her as a spouse who is seen as unworthy of you. Through Jesus Christ, our Lord. Amen.

FROM THE SAME PSALM:
We acknowledge, O almighty God, how deadly is our falling into the sins by which we have contaminated our souls. It is a great burden to us and pains us bitterly, but we cannot wash away the stains we have contracted by own powers or by any sort of good works. There is only one shelter left: that we come to you as the fountain of mercy so that you may take pity on us and [*56v*] wash away the faults, cleanse the iniquities, blot out the sins, and purify the vices which have infected us from our conception and birth. For if you were generously to forgive the evil deeds and crimes that burden us, then indeed you would be revealed as faithful and wholly consistent in your promises. May you deign to sprinkle us with the blood of your only begotten Son, for only by that can soul and body be remade for eternal happiness. We desire to have a new heart created within us and to be endowed with a new spirit so that without coercion but freely and very willing we may offer you that sacrifice of a broken and downcast spirit which you are wont never to spurn. Finally having thereby made atonement and been purified by your favor and mercy, may we always offer you a sacrifice of praise. Through the same Jesus Christ, our Lord. Amen.

FROM PSALM 52:

Those who have enjoyed success in their evil endeavors and acquired some power by their crimes are inclined to boast about it arrogantly. They always amuse themselves with curses, and they take supreme and refined pleasure in backbiting, lying, and deceitful talk. [57r] Meanwhile these wretches do not realize how unexpectedly and suddenly they are going to be overturned in their fortunes and how they will be deprived of these kinds of transitory goods and of eternal salvation, so that they will find no place in the land of the living. O great and good God, we rely above all on your mercy and goodness, and now that you have wiped away the sins which we have so often fallen into because of our human weakness, we pray that we may live in a humble spirit. May we not treat any of your gifts arrogantly but gain wisdom from the fall and overturning of proud men, who made not God but riches and worldly success their strength and foundation. Grant, we beseech you, in your kindness and paternal love, that we may cling firmly to you alone and live fruitful lives like green olive trees that flourish in your Church, and that we may give you fitting praise because you lavish riches on your people. Through Jesus Christ, our Lord. Amen.

FROM PSALM 53:

The furious impiety of the wicked has spilled forth into such madness that, persuading themselves that God does not exist, they indulge in a life of total corruption [57v] and befoul themselves everywhere with damnable practices and filthy behavior. Just as they do good to none, so they everywhere seek their own advantage at the cost of others. But God, whom they ignore, is not unmindful of their actions. He fills the heavens with his majesty and also observes the deeds of humankind; alas, he finds not even one person who is devoted to pursuing uprightness, faithfulness, and justice. All have gone astray from the straight path; they oppress the weak, do not worship God rightly, and do not call upon him. But the time will come when those who are now so secure will be shaken by a mighty fear. Those who seem to be achieving happiness through their wickedness will finally be deprived of all their goods when they go to encounter an angry God. Hence we pray to you, O heavenly Father, that you desire to favor us who take refuge in you and that you loose the chains of sins which bind us fast, that we may rejoice in lasting happiness before you and enjoy eternal blessedness with you. Through Jesus Christ, our Lord. Amen.

[*58r*] FROM PSALM 54:

When misfortunes toss your people about, O great and good God, and their souls are immersed in grave concerns, they put aside human resources, in which you have taught them not to hope, for they are indeed worthless. They come to you as their solid strength and call upon your invincible name; this comes from the bottom of their hearts so that you can rescue them from men who are fierce, harsh, and cruel-hearted and rise up to attack the saints, whom you yourself have chosen to inherit your kingdom. They devise atrocities against your people made even more cruel because they never turn their eyes toward you in reverence. But because of the sins we have committed, we already feel the threat of just retribution and heavy punishments; we beseech you that you spare from punishments the suppliants who have repented for having offended you. In your mercy stand by them when their enraged enemies attack them. Although our merits hardly demand it, still your faithfulness, truth, and promises give assurance of protection. When you have answered our prayers, we shall earnestly gather together in songs of praise to you and shall manifest our grateful heart in the joyous throng of the devout[*58v*]. Through Jesus Christ, our Lord. Amen.

FROM THE SAME PSALM:

We call upon your name unceasingly, O almighty God, since we experience your ready assistance in the extreme anguish of your suffering Church. Now there is need for you to protect us from the hands of the godless with the strength and invincible might with which you are endowed. Although our corrupt behavior and the evil life we have lived so far do not deserve it, still we know that your mercy is such that you do not spurn those who seek refuge in you, however wretched and unworthy they be. Therefore because of your mercy and not because of our good deeds (since we have none, we cannot boast about them), O God, listen to our prayers and kindly give ear to the words that we pour out before you in our prayers together. You see how those who are alienated from you conspire and rise up against us; since they do not keep their eyes on you and your word, they strive to overturn your Church with their whole effort. We pray that you be our helper, that you strengthen the souls of your servants, that you turn back on the wicked the evils they deserved [*59r*] so that we may fervently confess your name and extol everywhere your goodness because we have been freed from all oppression and because we shall see your enemies experience everything which all the faithful should wish to happen to them. Through Jesus Christ, our Lord. Amen.

FROM PSALM 55:

We are forced by the extremely urgent needs of the Church to cry out daily to you, O great and good God. Our soul cannot be at peace when we observe and experience those who wish evil upon the Gospel and work so zealously for the destruction of the people who believe in you. We fear, worry, and shudder; we all but desire to have wings like a dove so that flying away from these evils we might at last find rest and peace in you. But such affliction is what our sins deserve; by them we have long and seriously offended you. Undoubtedly those sins have brought these evils upon us. But we beg you, good Father, not to be more influenced by our sins and crimes than we can bear. In your mercy deliver us from deceitful and misleading statements and suggestions. Watch out lest the Church catch the plague from those [*59v*] who sometimes seem to be her children and who along with us partake in her from the sweet nourishment of your sacraments. We now cry out to you, we urge with insistent petitions that as you have often wonderfully helped your people in other ways, so be willing at the present time to save us from destruction. Do not allow the covenant your peace-loving people have with you to be violated. We have indeed cast upon you all our burdens and weighty cares. May you deign in your might to take them up, along with us. Otherwise we faint and groan under their weight, so please foster and increase our weak hopes with your prompt help. Through Jesus Christ, our Lord. Amen.

FROM THE SAME PSALM:

We are suffering serious misfortunes, O almighty God, which force us continually to beg your aid. We are constantly afflicted by the world, the flesh, the devil, the enemies of truth, and misfortunes. This is why we repeatedly and strongly hope that the feathers and wings of doves be given to us so that we may use them to fly away from here as fast as possible to you. Here we have nobody except you to rescue us from these great evils. Indeed, so unreliable is the hope [*60r*] which is placed in men that you discover your worst enemies are those you thought were most indebted to your kindness. Everywhere poisoned tongues scourge the devout; violence, quarrels, injustice, oppression, trickery, and deceit lurk all about. Hence we cry out to you with our whole heart to cleanse our souls, wipe out the sins which stain us so sadly, and condescend to take unto yourself us who trust in you alone. We cast on you our burdens and troubles, and since we have all but collapsed under them we pray that you support us with your goodness and power, lest the hope that we have put in you weaken and collapse. Rather may it daily emerge more and more strong and steady. Through Jesus Christ, our Lord. Amen.

FROM PSALM 56:

Wicked men, O great and good God, are trying to swallow us. They attack and assault us with all their strength. But because your power is above that of all the princes and kings of the earth and because our trust is in you alone, may you now take pity on us. We confess that we have incurred your grave displeasure [*60v*] because of our sins when we so wretchedly spurned the teaching of the Law and Gospel, which you proposed to us, that we have been a continuous disgrace to that teaching till now. Now this pains our souls, and relying on the death and blood of Jesus Christ, your Son and our savior, we implore from you forgiveness for all our sins with earnest and burning prayers. Since you have taken us into your grace, we shall fear not the slightest what the flesh does against us. You will stand by your cause, and you will see how all day long the wicked vilify your religion and your worship and how they continuously plot evil against your people. When they treat those you have redeemed so wickedly, how can they escape your anger? You cast down your opponents when you are aroused against them. It is not your practice to ignore the sighs and tears of your poor; all our prayers are already written down in the book of your providence. Listen to them, O God, heavenly Father, and since we call out under the prodding and prompting of your Spirit, drive your enemies into flight. Stand up for your army, defend, strengthen and confirm it. If you are for us, we shall not fear what [*61r*] men do against us. After you have delivered us, we shall glorify forever your promises and words. Bring it about, O God, that after recovering peace and tranquillity we may dwell continually in your sight and be ever directed by the light of your countenance. Through Jesus Christ, our Lord. Amen.

FROM THE SAME PSALM:

While we live here, O almighty God, we can attain no peace because of the pressure of our sins; we are attacked on all sides by the deadly incursions of hostile powers. Indeed, unless you are with us, it seems that we will be immediately swallowed up. For our defence, every time a mighty fear arises in our timid souls, we pour out our prayers to your mercy, which shines and glows most widely, so that we really take to heart and hold in esteem your words and promises. When we have been strengthened by them, we shall overcome with a stout heart all the sad, terrifying, disagreeable and hard things that crop up. O good Father, just as you have gathered and written down our tears, so may you free your people from the chains and shackles of hardship when we call upon you. [*61v*] Because you are good, purge away our guilt and grant enough strength and firm faith that no power of evil men may terrify us. Because if you rescue us above all from eternal death, we can fulfill our vows to praise your name forever. Through Jesus Christ, our Lord. Amen.

FROM THE SAME PSALM:

Daily we continue to pray for your mercy, O almighty God, when those who try to swallow up the Church never stop attacking her in various ways. They are many in number and are growing immeasurably in strength. There is nothing that strikes more terror into us than our own sins; by them we have grievously offended you and make ourselves completely unworthy of your favor. But because you are kindest of all, we have not given up hope; we keep before our eyes your promises, whose words and statements we praise, agree with, and embrace with faith as much as we can. Therefore, good Father, make us fear no more than is right what our flesh can do against us. We know that the wicked are now [62r] spreading false tales about us everywhere and aiming all their machinations against sacred doctrine. They watch for and seize upon every chance to demolish the Church. Do not despise, O God, the prayers and sighs of your faithful people; strengthen us and confirm us so that we are in no way held back by what men are going to do to us. Deliver our souls from sin and destruction so that now and after this life we may be granted to enjoy your joyous and blessed light. Through Jesus Christ, our Lord. Amen.

FROM PSALM 57:

Except for you alone, O great and good God, there is no other refuge. We entrust to your defense our whole salvation so that we may be protected by you until the anger abates in those who are causing your Church to suffer violence. Hence we call upon your name forever since it is by your license and power that all things come to pass for all the devout. We pray that you do not allow our sins to restrain your goodness. We confess that they are infinite and most grave, so that we do not doubt that they must be forgiven us [62v] through our one mediator, Jesus Christ, by whose favor your people, not only in heaven, are saved. But because of your faithfulness and goodness all those who strive to oppress your faithful people will finally be put to shame. You yourself, good Father, see how his Church is forced continually to carry on amidst lions and flames, amid powerful armaments and extremely poisonous tongues. Therefore show and proclaim your power for her salvation so that the nets and snares set for your saints may bring harm only to their makers. May you grant us a stout heart and a soul steadfast in confessing and praising you. May we know and acknowledge that your goodness is so great that it should be glorified not just by the voice but also by lyre, by harp, and by every kind and manner of praise. Your goodness reaches beyond the clouds even up to heaven, and as it day by day becomes magnified and better known, so by it you exalt yourself even in our own age and you manifest your power in defending us. Through Jesus Christ, our Lord. Amen.

[*63r*] FROM THE SAME PSALM:

In troubles and extreme disasters, O great and good God, nothing lifts and consoles the soul more than clinging to your goodness as tightly as possible by the anchor of trust. So we rightly come to you when we seethe and are inflamed with our vices; daily we call upon you when overburdened by our baggage of sin. We beseech you to send us help from heaven; otherwise we shall not survive safe from the lions, spears, javelins, and treacherous tongue which Satan uses to attack your Church in wondrous ways. Show yourself and manifest your infinite powers by rescuing us. Thus your goodness and faithfulness, which far surpass the clouds and heavens, will become manifest in their enormous greatness. We will joyfully give you the thanks which we owe for your having saved us, and we will redouble your name and praises forever. Through Jesus Christ, our Lord. Amen.

FROM THE SAME PSALM:

O almighty God, while the Church is being so constrained by the enemies of your name and teaching [*63v*], we trust in you alone and take refuge under the protection of your wings. We acknowledge that we must cry out to you unceasingly since you alone can advance our cause. We do not deny how evil our merits are, so that we are rightfully all but destroyed by our present disasters. We can put forward in good faith nothing of what we have professed in name and outward show. Because you are goodness and mercy themselves, it belongs to you not to reject those who seek refuge in you. We beg you, send down protection from heaven to deliver your believers from the insults of the wicked. The Antichrists roar like lions against your Church, and each day they become more inflamed with hatred for your word. So show yourself, good Father, and make your glory manifest since you are glorious beyond all others. Tear up the traps, fill in the ditches, render ineffective the ruses which they set for your gospel so that day by day, more and more, our soul may grow strong in confessing, glorifying, and extolling you above all things. Through Jesus Christ, our Lord. Amen.

[*64r*] FROM PSALM 58:

The princes of this world are assaulting the Church wickedly, O almighty God, because they do not judge aright about divine and heavenly matters. Ceaselessly they ponder iniquity in their soul and plot only acts of violence against your elect. But what else are they going to do? At birth they went forth into the light as evil and had a deadly poison inserted in them by nature just like serpents. This poison could never be extracted from them by all of God's exhortations and words, for they throw these aside, not unlike asps avoiding the magicians' charms. Our sins have fully merited that we should be afflicted by such ferocious enemies of your faith and teaching. We now confess our sins and pray that they be forgiven us because of your mercy. We then ask this of you: that you yourself smash and destroy the teeth of the lions. May they flow away like water, and like a broken arrow and like a snail which is covered over by its shell may they no longer harm your faithful ones. May they grow weak like a premature infant, and lastly may their assaults flash into fire just as [*64v*] a flame which stirred up among thorns is easily extinguished. But may you, O God, make joyful your just ones so that observing the massive retaliations which you yourself extract from the enemies of your religion, they may see the reward laid up for your faithful. May their virtue be strengthened because they realize that you lay down harsh judgments upon the earth. Through Jesus Christ, our Lord. Amen.

FROM THE SAME PSALM:

The Antichrist and all his minions, O great and good God, now desire nothing else in their hearts against your Church but iniquities and unjust plans since they put on a show for themselves of wanting a council[5] to be held about piety and religion, but in fact they are engaged in nothing but lies. They have been far from you from their early manhood and have always up to now taken delight in their errors. Now at last they want to vomit out the poison which they have kept ready like an asp; they cannot be so charmed by the words of your Holy Scripture that they want to hold back from their evil efforts. Heavenly Father, it is not us who deserve to be destroyed by them because of our evil deeds, [*65r*] for we have possessed and known well the path

---

[5]Representatives of Charles V and Paul III worked out plans for the Council of Trent in May and June 1545 as they prepared for the First Schmalkaldic War. Trent opened on 18 December 1545. On 12 June 1546 the Catholic Estates at the Diet of Regensburg accepted the Council; the next day the Protestant Estates rejected it. On 16 June 1546 Charles V declared the Protestants rebels and the First Schmalkaldic War began. He won a decisive victory over the Protestant forces at the Battle of Mühlberg on 24 April 1547.

of truth and life, which is your mercy, although we have always turned aside from it toward wicked desires. Deal with us according to your glory and the dignity of your name. Do not repay us according to what we ourselves have deserved but what was proclaimed to us by your promises. Smash to pieces the efforts, power, and might of the enemies of your name and of your teaching; destroy them and make them completely ineffective so that the just may take solid delight when they see that you have taken up their cause, and while you are executing this righteous judgment, may they experience that justice has its reward. Through Jesus Christ, our Lord. Amen.

FROM THE SAME PSALM:

The behavior of the wicked is so corrupt and profligate, O almighty God, that very little or nothing wholesome is left that can be discerned in their judgments. They weave plots, they employ violence, and already from their tender years onward they have deserted you and have lived enmeshed in their inveterate evil deeds. Their savage acts [65ᵛ] bear comparison with snakes, lions and any sort of fierce animal in their hardness of heart, rabid anger, and untamed cruelty. Therefore we ask you not to let us fall, as our sins deserve, into such madness that we trust and rely on them and forsake you, who are the fount and source of all good. What would be equally destructive would be our following their judgments and attitudes. Make us think, we beg, the exact opposite of them, and meanwhile may their ability to do harm grow weak so that their power and plan be reduced to passion and impotence, like that of men who are disarmed even though they do not lose their desire to do harm. May their efforts perish in a flash, and may the Church of the devout rejoice when it realizes that you reward the just with the fruits of justice and extract punishment from the wicked as they deserve by their evil. Through Jesus Christ, our Lord. Amen.

FROM PSALM 59:

We ask you to deliver us, O almighty God, since we are hard pressed by the enemies of your teaching and religion. It is now your task to defend us from evil men who eagerly long for slaughter and [66ʳ] increase their strength and power by great conspiracies so they can exterminate your saints from the earth. They do not in the least assault us because of the sins and crimes which we confess that we have committed; rather they run to the attack purely out of their hatred for piety and religion. But may you, O God, who commands all creatures, first forgive anything we have done against you, then bestir yourself and finally give thought to the cause of the devout. Our cruel enemies wander about, howl like dogs, and run around all over the place. In dealing with our causes, they talk exclusively of arms and swords. But may you, O God, laugh at them and hang them up by the nose. We look to you alone for help since you are a citadel and mighty fortress for us. Make the Church so share in your wondrous goodness that she may see her hopes fulfilled against the enemies of religion. Do not destroy them by some ordinary way but by a kind of punishment that people will not easily forget. May you make them wander forever as beggars because of the abominations, lies, and perjuries they were involved in. Finally break them utterly, break them, I repeat, [*66v*] so that they become a laughingstock to ordinary folk and everybody will know that you are indeed the God of your Church, in which you are marvelously extolled as the firm strength and safe fortress to all who call upon your name with sincere faith. Through Jesus Christ, our Lord. Amen.

FROM THE SAME PSALM:
Because we are hedged about by human weakness, O almighty God, and restricted in soul by the chains of grave sins, we daily beg for your mercy so that kindly and forgiving you may turn to hear us. We are tried, assaulted and attacked in wondrous ways by hostile powers, and since our natural powers here are wholly languishing and have proved completely useless, do you, O God, rise up and deign to cast down with your might everything that hinders our salvation. May you in the end mock and deride the man who chooses to pit himself against your will rather than accommodate himself to it, as is proper. We have put the strength of our safety in you alone, for we have not the least doubt that you are our good. Thus, even though the enemies of your name surround us and somehow besiege us by spreading around a blinding darkness, [*67r*] we rely on your goodness, and trust that their malice will fall upon themselves rather than upon us. May it then come about as we hope: your goodness will serve as citadel, refuge and fortress for us, who eagerly want to celebrate and extol your surpassing honor and outstanding kindness. Through Jesus Christ, our Lord.

FROM PSALM 60:
O great and good God, you sometimes have castigated your children with fatherly severity so that when they are brought low by hard times and broken by troubles they may finally realize they have sinned. Then yearning for you they may desire to escape the vices which have earlier engulfed them. Then at last, since you are good and infinitely to be loved, you show yourself completely placated and gracious. Therefore we ask you, heavenly Father, to

keep up this same long-standing practice and deign to deliver your suppliants from the sorrows and lamentable trouble which our sins daily bring down upon us. We have no doubt that will happen since what you have promised to believers has hardly escaped our attention. That picks up our spirits. We rejoice in it [*67v*] and finally use it to convince ourselves that we have been truly and firmly received into your favor, even though we could once see ourselves as rejected by you. Keep bringing us help so that relying on your protection we may bravely conduct our affairs to the honor of your name. Through Jesus Christ, our Lord. Amen.

FROM THE SAME PSALM:

Often enough, O great and good God, you seem to have cast your faithful people from you and scattered them to distant places, as if you were extremely angry with them. But again you win them over, and in your goodness you turn your favor and kindness toward them. This stirs up our confidence that you, who now seem to be striking the earth and destroying its inhabitants with new and unusual fear, will come to heal its wounds. Although you sometimes may want to try your people with harsh and bitter misfortunes, as if you were to give them a poisoned cup to drink, still to those that honor you, you unexpectedly hold up the banner of salvation so that, in fulfillment of your promises, they may live in happiness before you. Now turn your eyes away from the sins we have committed, for we can hardly deny that we have acted wickedly and perversely. [*68r*] But since you forgive those who call upon you, stand by your church at last, and, as is your practice, save her with your right hand. O God, for a time you seemed to have rejected us. But now come forward. Arouse yourself and bring us help. We are not wrong in begging your aid, for our experience has taught us that human powers are useless. Assist those who have put their hope in you. Help them to act bravely so that through you they may win victory over their enemies. Through Jesus Christ, our Lord. Amen.

FROM PSALM 61:

We pour out prayers to you, O great and good God, because extreme anxiety afflicts us over the grave temptations which we are suffering. We want you to hear us since you are exceptionally fatherly and outstanding for your marvelous paternal care. Don't let your family die in misery, even though the devil is busy trying to snuff out your grace in them and burying your gifts. Provide them with fortress and safe refuge at your side, to which you may draw us with your support when we cannot climb up by our own strength.

Then we will be taken up to the tabernacle of your presence under the protection of your wings [*68v*] and thereby be delivered from the threshold and jaws of death. We have indeed trespassed against your law and have befouled the holy body of your Church with our sins, but while we confess this and beseech you for mercy, we experience great relief. Now, relying on your goodness, we need not fear any bitter misfortunes; on the contrary, our soul glows with a burning desire both to glorify you and to make an overflowing return for all that we owe you because of what we profess. Through Jesus Christ, our Lord. Amen.

FROM PSALM 62:

O great and good God, since we are convinced that you are our bastion, citadel, fortress, and salvation, we keep our soul in peace and quiet, even amid afflictions. We are certain that you will strip the devil and his minions of success regardless of all the snares they set for us. All who set themselves against you are unable to survive, and their hope deceives them in the end. We therefore beg you that, having blotted out our sins, you continue to work for our defense, as you have been doing so far. We do not deny that we have sinned very often because we are weak. [*69r*] But since you are our helper, we shake off all our fear of worldly men—we recognize them as empty show, so empty that if they were weighed in a balance, they would turn out as being more empty than emptiness itself. Just as we do not fear them, so we also ask that all our confidence may be drawn away from ill-gotten wealth and passing riches. May we always keep before our eyes you, who are just, kind, and of invincible might. Through Jesus Christ, our Lord. Amen.

FROM PSALM 63:

O great and good God, in this life where we undergo practically every harsh, terrifying, and painful experience, we seek, desire, and eagerly thirst for you alone. We want to look directly at your singular power and marvelous beauty, for mortal men can encounter nothing more blessed, nothing more pleasurable, nothing more sweet than that knowledge. Please allow us, O heavenly Father, while we are thanking you for the benefits you have conferred, to untiringly proclaim your name and beg you continually in ardent prayers and petitions [*69v*] for what contributes to both your glory and our salvation. These are indeed the joys of the faithful. There is our soul fed with true and lasting happiness since even when it is in bed at midnight it does not forget your goodness. Our sins, into which weakness and ignorance drove us, stand in the way of this our good. Blot them out in your mercy, we beg you.

Be our helper, just as you began. Protect us under the wings of your favor. Join our hearts to you forever. May those who persistently and obstinately resist your glory fall headlong into death's bottomless whirlpool, but may we rejoice and glory forever in your consolation and help. Through Jesus Christ, our Lord. Amen.

FROM PSALM 64:
Heavenly Father, except for the fact that we are of listless spirit and totally stupid, we would be aroused daily to call upon you in our prayers. Satan and his evil satellites are advancing our destruction day and night, and our impure flesh constantly tries to drive us headlong into transgressions against your commandments. Since our soul is being completely torn apart by lying tongues, deceitful words, sharp stakes, [70r] and deadly darts, and since our strength is completely exhausted and drooping, we fly to you, our true port of safety. We pray that, as you understand that we have been crushed by wicked and toilsome burdens on account of sins and faults that we have committed, in your mercy forgive and forget whatever stain and guilt clings to us. So protect and defend us that we may turn over to you all the burdens which have weighed so heavy upon us. Thus we will rightly rejoice, and with no regrets we will glory in the fact that we have entrusted our whole selves to your fidelity. Through Jesus Christ, our Lord. Amen.

FROM PSALM 65:
So many and so great are your kindnesses to all mortals, O great and good God, that glory, praise, and honor is owed to your name everywhere and by everyone. What can be more delightful for men than the ready hearing you give them when they call upon you in their troubles? Is there any other good that should give us greater joy than how you render yourself satisfied and generous despite our iniquities? Why should we not [70v] be happy when you join us to yourself in the sacred assembly and feed us with spiritual goods and heavenly delights? You deal kindly with all creatures for the sake of your elect; you sustain the mountains, you smooth the seas, you settle down the uproar of the nations, and you refresh the cultivators of the earth with the brightness of the heavenly fires and illuminate them with great joy. Give timely and abundant rains that make the soil fertile and cover the fields with every kind of fruit so that both animals and men may have enough food to eat. You are the author of such great benefits, and you give us this also: that we may give due thanks and that we may use the things you give us for our salvation. Through Jesus Christ, our Lord. Amen.

FROM PSALM 66:

O great and good God, your power and invincible strength is such that in the end you usually bring under your control the enemies of your name and glory, regardless of how hard they try to oppose you with their mad fury. The godly reflect on this in their hearts and adore you, voice their praises, and faithfully worship your excellence. As [71r] you once opened the sea for the sons of Israel, turned aside the waters of the Jordan from their usual course, and drove their enemies from their ancestral seats even though they appeared unconquerable, so we pray that you now desire to act on behalf of your dear ones. May they luxuriate in heavenly gifts and not faint when tried by temptations, but after being tried, refined, and cleansed by misfortunes may they shine with the brightness of virtues. May you give them refreshment after the afflictions and agitations of soul which you, their Father and Creator, have prepared, so that they may at last render you prayers of praise and songs of celebration. Let us rouse ourselves, I pray, to worship and honor him, calling to mind as carefully as possible the benefits which he has conferred on us in his goodness so that moved by our gratitude he may henceforward hear our prayers with greater kindness and willingness. Through Jesus Christ, our Lord. Amen.

FROM PSALM 67:

Mortals ardently desire two things, O almighty God, namely, that they enjoy the favor of your divinity and that the light of your countenance enlighten them. We feel our lack of them, which results from the sins we have committed [71v], and we therefore pray that the medicine of your mercy may heal our wounds, that your kindness may forgive the sins we have perpetrated, and that your joyous light may scatter the dark clouds which we ourselves have brought upon us. If we achieve this goal, even though we are wrapped in the darkness of this mortal life, we can easily recognize the counsels, arrangements, and plans by which you rule, protect, defend and marvelously watch all things with infinite goodness and fidelity. When we have noted and reflected carefully on these things, we will glorify you with all nations. May we be flooded with a sweet happiness because you govern all nations, provinces, and kingdoms with right judgment and exquisite justice. If all people gave universal recognition to what is a simple fact, all people would give you universal praise. Grant, good Father, that we may seek and obtain these two things. Be not slow in adding to them a happy yield from the earth. The more generous you are to your dear people, the more you will be feared and the more earnestly honored throughout the whole world. Through Jesus Christ, our Lord. Amen.

[*72r*] FROM PSALM 68:

O good and great God, you are the fount and source of all good things, and both our salvation and everything pleasant in life flows from you. Unceasingly you confer and heap upon your people so many benefits that it is impossible to reckon their number. But first we must not be silent about how happily and favorably you yourself have waged our wars against sin, death, the devil, and all evils so that the main opponents of our salvation felt your presence when you conquered and smashed them and extracted punishment from them. Therefore we should give you earnest thanks in psalms, praises, godly hymns, and every kind of song. That we do not do this is a spiteful spirit but with souls clear and cleansed from carnal cares, we pray that you forgive what we have done either through the darkness of ignorance or the weakness of soul. Just as you have continuously defended your people so far, keep on protecting us from the tricks and deceits of the hostile powers so that you may also be universally acknowledged for so favoring believers that you sufficiently supply them with invincible strength and courage. Through Jesus Christ, our Lord. Amen.

[*72v*] FROM THE SAME PSALM:

Since your might is such, O great and good God, that none of your enemies, however powerful, can stand up against you, we beseech you in your mercy that you rise up with all your might to help us. The sons of Israel experienced your saving presence that was always with them when they had to clash with their enemies, even though kings and skilled armies were aroused against them. When you lift up your power and strength on high, do not disdain, we pray, to turn your face toward us who are struggling with Satan and the flesh and its passions. We indeed acknowledge that our salvation must be credited to you alone. Likewise we take refuge in you, who are the fount and root of all good, and we pray that we may recount the praises which your name has earned after we have been delivered from the evils surrounding us. Through Jesus Christ, our Lord. Amen.

FROM THE SAME PSALM:

So great is your power and might, O great and good God, that when you arouse and engage yourself [*73r*] all who attack your name and your kingdom with hatred are instantly scattered and thrown into flight. At this time we therefore do not doubt that the powers of both Satan and his minions, who keep on attacking us from every quarter, will be dissolved just as smoke disappears and mist evaporates. Therefore great pleasure and supreme happiness await believers. We earnestly pray that we may be able to attain them so that you may release us, we beg, from the baggage of sins that greatly burdens us. Reconcile us to yourself and enrich us abundantly with the Holy Spirit. Since you are the Father of orphans and the Avenger of those who are harshly afflicted, may you deign to deliver us too from the chains of our sins. Defend us no less than you protected the children of Israel in the desert. As you see, we are very much disfigured by sin, therefore may the splendor of your favor and grace attend us so that our soul may be reformed and made resplendent for supreme happiness. Through Jesus Christ, our Lord. Amen.

FROM THE SAME PSALM:
Such is your wisdom, O great and good God, that you have countless ways and infinite methods for saving your people and [*73v*] for destroying the wicked. Accordingly, when you restore your people who are oppressed by both sin and Satan, you also score sweeping and glorious victories. Those victories beyond any question merit that all who belong naturally and rightly to Israel should celebrate your praises and triumphs with enormous joy. We ask that, using your special and outstanding power, you increase more and more each day with a joyous success those gifts of salvation that you have begun to confer on us. By those gifts we will offer to you, who are carried in noble triumph above the heavens, not brute animals as victims but ourselves as a stainless and welcome holocaust. Thereby testimony will be given to us and even everyone that to you alone belong the supreme strength and infinite majesty by which you lead the elect to the happiness they hope for. Through Jesus Christ, our Lord. Amen.

FROM PSALM 69:
O almighty God, our weak human nature is daily tossed and turned about by infinite troubles. That would not be so [*74r*] lamentable if those who faithfully worship you were not seen as being more harassed and afflicted than the other people amid our universal misfortune. But that is the way it is. Stormy seas, sticky mud, and huge hurricane waves of temptations all but suffocate those who believe and trust in you. The way they bear these things with patient and steadfast souls, as regards their own advantage, certainly helps but little the salvation of the weakhearted who see what is happening, unless you come quickly to help because of the goodness and kindness with which you are endowed. That which seems to have cast down weak souls will marvelously refresh them. If you hear our prayers, as we trust, and snatch us from these great dangers as we beseech you, then these tribulations will bear no

mean fruit. We ask you, good Father, to grant that those who are now almost consumed with zeal for your glory may obtain from you what they are praying for: both the expansion of your kingdom and the salvation of those who are fighting against that kingdom. Through Jesus Christ, our Lord. Amen.

[*74v*] FROM THE SAME PSALM:

Your kindness and goodness toward men was such, O great and good God, that you allowed your Son and our Lord Jesus Christ to be subjected to extreme insults and supreme derision so that even when he had a tremendous thirst in his last hour they would not reach him a drink except one made sour by vinegar. If we forget about these things, either we show ourselves as having lost our faith or we make ourselves guilty of the most hateful ingratitude. May we keep before our eyes the severe punishment which you finally visited upon those wicked men who raged so violently against your beloved Son. May that example move us to restrain ourselves from sinful acts and evil living. To us he is now even more renowned and exalted than he was then because it is on our account that he is even more afflicted by injuries and insults. Therefore we beg and beseech you that you deign to nurture a sounder mind and a zeal for better things in us, who profess your name and worship. Through the same Jesus Christ, our Lord. Amen.

[*75r*] FROM PSALM 70:

O great and good God, we fly to your steadfastness and mercy in our daily prayers because we see that nothing in this life is without dangers or is safe from the enemies of our salvation. Because of their hostility, deceit, and cruelty we experience everything as dangerous, hostile, and burdensome. Since we are conscious that our own faults are not light and since we are not ignorant that we undergo punishment from your justice for our sins, we pray that, because you are good, you will forgive us for what we have done shamefully and that you will simply wipe away or mitigate in your gentleness and kindness the punishment that is rightly and deservedly owed to us. That way all who opposed your worship, which we profess, will blush and be put to shame when you help us. Conversely those who are zealous for your name will rejoice and be glad. So don't delay any longer in bringing help lest the wicked again and again throw against us the charges they have prepared to make. Through Jesus Christ, our Lord. Amen.

[75v] FROM PSALM 71:

Since it is clear to us, O almighty God, that prompt and ready assistance is always provided to those who take refuge in your protection, therefore we put our entire confidence in you alone so that our trust and hope may be eagerly directed toward the same one from whom help is ever to be sought. From their first years you help, foster, and benefit those who worship you so that if sometimes you seem to have forsaken them, it is usually counted as something extraordinary. Therefore we trust that, since you have always been near us from our conception in the womb, you will not be distant in our decrepit old age and our last days. Hence we daily give and will give the praise and thanks we owe you, as we hope to do forever, since your bounties toward us are countless. Moreover the more your goodness and greatness are glorified, the more they are recognized as surpassing all the power of praise. Still we beseech you to add to your other benefits this too: that just as you sometimes expose your people to bitterness and adversity, so may you also deign to console and revive them. Through Jesus Christ, our Lord. Amen.

[76r] FROM PSALM 72:

Because we will have our Lord Jesus Christ as our most just judge, it is right that we always fear and honor him. Since he now has supreme power from the Father, he watches very carefully that the just gain in strength and restore and spread his worship as far as possible. Therefore we ask you, heavenly Father, that before we are brought forward for judgment at his tribunal, we may be redeemed from the sins of which we are guilty. May we be reborn in his Spirit and abound in good works so that we are not condemned for our evildoing. If we recognize that we have achieved this by a strong and firm faith, we shall count ourselves thereby truly blessed and lastingly happy, and we shall extol and exalt your name and glory with the highest praises so that, if is possible, the whole earth may be filled with the knowledge of you. Through Jesus Christ, our Lord. Amen.

[76v] FROM PSALM 73:

O great and good God, your goodness toward those men who revere you with upright and sincere devotion is enormous, but human weakness being as it is, the happiness of the wicked more often strikes the eyes of your elect. When they see how successful in their every effort and desire are those who hold in contempt all law, both human and divine, and who have fallen far from piety, they think and shamelessly assert that you no longer have any care for us. We beg you, keep the feet of our faith from faltering. Support us with your hand when we slip. Clamp down on our mouth and thoughts lest we begin to think that our efforts to worship you have been vain and wasted. Strengthen us so that we may await with patience and Christian toleration the outcome and final success of our affairs. Then when your supreme tribunal opens, there it will be shown how justly you govern all things. Meanwhile grant that we may be gripped by no greater desire than that of having our souls tied and linked to you by an indissoluble bond. Through Jesus Christ, our Lord. Amen.

[77r] FROM PSALM 74:

If it were to happen, O almighty God, which we do not doubt often occurs, that we provoke your wrath against us because of the sins that we have just committed and we bring down the heavy whips which chastise us: remember, I entreat, your goodness and promises which you know we have laid hold of by faith. Do not hand our souls over to the power of those who oppose your glory and our salvation. They strive for nothing but destroying your works or making them useless and bringing to naught the salvation of the human race which you purchased by your mercy. All their efforts are finally aimed at making your name blasphemed and vilified. We ask you to remember how you previously conferred benefits on us. Do not put an end to the work of redemption you have already begun in us. Arise, O God, and assist those who call on you lest the plans of the wicked enjoy success either against your glory or against our salvation. Through Jesus Christ, our Lord. Amen.

[77v] FROM PSALM 75:

We desire, O almighty God, to glorify your name and your marvelous deeds. So that may happen, we ask you with our whole strength that you defend your people from these terrible dangers, lest they perish. Let not your sight fall on our sins. Above all, do not count against us the fact that, when you called us to you and proposed a program of true piety and granted each of us freedom to live by your word and our Christian profession, we ourselves not only acted with cold hearts but also cast aside like ingrates the discipline and a life worthy of that faith which you have given us. So do not pay attention to how much we have sinned, or what we have deserved, or how much your justice can rightly demand from us. Be gracious to us through the favor of your beloved Son, our sweet Lord Jesus Christ. Put yourself between us and our enraged and potent enemies. When it seems a good time, lay down your fair and righteous judgment against them. You support the earth and the whole universe; all creatures strive after you, so if you stand for us, nothing will be able [*78r*] to set itself against our achieving salvation. Not only have the foolish and wicked Antichrists lifted up their horns, but they have fallen into a terrible rage and frenzy against us. They utter unspeakable blasphemies against you, and after having their necks broken they cast off from themselves every yoke of your word. We can see no firm help, O God, either from east or west or from any quarter. As you are our judge, it belongs to you alone to decide to lift us up or cast us down, whenever you wish. Since you have the cup in your hand, let them drink it dry and drain its dregs; from it may they fall into a stupor so that they do not accomplish their design against your Church. Then we will proclaim you forever and sing psalms to your name, for the horns of the wicked will lie broken, and the just will be allowed to rest quietly in you. Through our Lord, Jesus Christ. Amen.

FROM THE SAME PSALM:

Almighty God, we have decided to praise and glorify you because you are always present to those who call upon you out of sincere faith and because you manifest your presence by giving them singular gifts. We thank you especially because you have deigned to gather unto yourself from our group [*78v*] a Church. Since it is right that you reign in her and declare your might, we urgently ask you to there strike down impiety and likewise uphold innocence and religion. May all that is earthly from the world or the flesh quickly melt away; may all that you have given in our rebirth by your heavenly Spirit be strengthened. Make the just and the elect strong like mighty columns, but may those who are earthly and fight against your name and teaching buckle and collapse. We beg you, good Father, to see to it that the foolish stop their folly in time and the unjust cease at last to misuse the forces which they seem to have drawn up against religion and your holy Church. Let their harsh sermons, raging insults, and rebellious blasphemies cease. Do not pay attention here, O God, to what our sins deserve. They are serious—that does not escape us, and we don't deny it. In your mercy wipe them away lest they make us drink dry the bitter cup of your wrath. Let all who search after injustice drink and even squeeze dry all its dregs so that the Church may continuously keep in mind your judgments and offer earnest praise when she sees how [*79r*] the horns of the wicked are broken and how they stand upright and safe who have dedicated themselves completely to justice and religion. Through Jesus Christ, our Lord. Amen.

FROM PSALM 76:

It has pleased your goodness, O almighty God, and was not required because of our merits that your word became known to us and that the Holy Gospel of your Son was preached in our midst. We recognize this as a singular and wonderful gift, even as we recognize how hard pressed we are by our wickedness. Beyond question we have behaved toward you with shameful ingratitude, for we have not at all lived up to our knowledge of your word and your teaching. Because we repent of our iniquities and want to correct our mistakes, we still ask you to help the fallen, reach out your hand to those who call on you, and forgive us who bitterly regret having offended you. In accord with your promises, we are your tabernacle and dwelling against which the wicked have set up camp so that they may destroy us completely and utterly. Break their spears and bows; cast away their shields, swords, and arms. [*79v*] You can do this effortlessly, for your power is more splendid and magnificent than any mortal rulership. May your power despoil and pillage them. Let your rebuke cast both their infantry and their cavalry into a stupor. And when those who took so much pride in their strength have slept out their sleep, let them find in their hands nothing to help them or give them pleasure. We, however, know how terrifying you are and how nobody can stand before you when your wrath has been enkindled. We therefore ask that you arise and save your gentle people. May your enemies' wrath, which has rebelled against you, give way to your praise. Since you can curb the spirit and ferocity of princes, do not allow us to fall before them. Stand by us in such a way that when we have secured victory we may fulfill with eager heart and ready will the pledges we owe to you. Through Jesus Christ, our Lord. Amen.

FROM THE SAME PSALM:

In your Church, O almighty God, you have chosen a house and a dwelling place for yourself where you can be acknowledged and where your name may be magnificently glorified. You have driven out of her shameful spears, bows, swords, [*80r*] shields, and all warlike catapults and military machines, which have been built by the opponents of your teaching and the enemies of the religion you have established. Because of this, I say, you deserve glory and admiration before all the robbers and tyrants of this world. Accordingly we call upon you not to depart because of our sins from the praiseworthy and glorious custom of your majesty. As we have indeed deserved, your church has been afflicted and badly treated for a short time, but for the glory of your name may you render weak as sleepers those strong men who oppose both her and you. May their strength fail them if they should want to misuse it. Let their infantry and cavalry become useless at your rebuke. As we know, O God, you alone are to be feared so that nobody can bear up under your wrath. Arise then to judge the cause of your Church so that your help may keep safe her kindly citizens and that everything her disdainful enemies have contrived against her may be turned to your praise. We understand how all the kings of the earth stand in fear before you and how you have taken the spirit out of the princes of this world. Grant then, O God, that we may perform with supreme eagerness and heartfelt joy the acts of thanksgiving which we promised you for such a great blessing. [*80v*] Through our Lord Jesus Christ. Amen.

FROM PSALM 77:

We call out to you with heart and voice, O almighty God, fully confident that since you are our God you will hear us amidst our current needs. With repentance and prayer we call upon you while we are being oppressed by hardships and afflictions all around. We have no other firm and solid consolation. While we have a troubled soul and a restless heart, what else is left to us except to call on you amidst the sadness and grief weighing upon us? Above all our sins oppress us. We know that we have offended you by them; we experience and feel a troubled, wounded conscience. So our soul endures sadness and affliction; we are sunken in fear and sorrow; our whole strength ebbs away. Our eyes keep watch for you, and we beg for your mercy with a stricken mind and a downcast heart. Alas, O God and good Father, will you withdraw from us forever because of our sins? Will you stop showing how gentle and kind you are in dealing with us? But you are patient and long suffering by nature, [*81r*] so your mercy and goodness, which are infinite, will not depart from us. You, O God, are the Father of mercy: Do not forget to be merciful. We have deserved your wrath because of our wasted lives, but with your lofty right hand you can easily change our lives and ignore our sins. When we recall your works, we are confident that you will do so. You have grown accustomed to working marvels in delivering your people, so now use your fortitude against a wicked people who have attacked us, your flock, with deceitful tricks and warlike savagery. Deal with them as you did in ages past. We know the power you used to redeem Israel from the Egyptians. The waters, the deep, clouds, thunder, lightning and all creatures contributed at your command to the [Israelites'] salvation so that you led your people like sheep through Moses and Aaron to where you wanted.[6] Even so, O God and good Father, assist your armies so that saved from our enemies we may be drawn by faith and a pure

6Ex. 12:51; Is. 63:11-14.

life to you, our happiness and our hope. Through Jesus Christ, our Lord. Amen.

[*81v*] FROM THE SAME PSALM:

In these difficult times, O almighty God, we keep looking to you; we weary you every day with our burning prayers and promises, and we fly unto you as our only salvation while the Church is faced with so much danger. Our sadness increases and our sorrow grows no little bit when memories of past times come back. In those days secure in mind and safe in soul we could devote ourselves in peace and serenity both to your teaching and to praising your name. But because we have grossly misused the gift of so much security and deep tranquillity, it was right and just that we experience the hand of your severity and justice. But we now pray, good Father, that you forgive any sins we have committed against you, for it is impossible for you to forget how to take pity on your people lest you cast us away forever. Since your promises have to take place sometime, do not deprive us of your mercy. We remember well the past deeds that you performed in delivering the Israelites from Egypt. As soon as the waters of the sea saw your power, they rose up [*82r*] and were stirred in wondrous wise. You fought against the wicked with dark clouds, thunder, lightning, winds, and a black storm. Therefore just as you then snatched away your people Israel, so now deliver the Church from the fury of Satan and the assault of his minions. Through Jesus Christ, our Lord. Amen.

FROM THE SAME PSALM:

O great and good God, to the same degree that we are hard pressed by troubles we have become accustomed to come to you with our burning prayers. So now when we feel and daily experience more and more how the Church is tortured and troubled in cruel ways, we come to beg your kindness in deigning to be her help, just as you did repeatedly in her first days. Doubtless neither your upright nature nor the supreme steadfastness with which you are endowed allow you to desire now to gather up and withdraw your goodness for those you hold dear since you have always been kind to them. Hence we beseech you to preserve toward us your old ways, just as then when you manifested your invincible power in freeing the Israelites from the [*82v*] bondage of Egypt. Now use the same power to lift up, foster, and restore the Church. That way the greater your care for her is, the more clearly it will appear that she has been powerfully rescued from the devil, sin, and death. Through Jesus Christ, our Lord. Amen.

From Psalm 78:

O almighty God, it has been carefully handed down to us in sacred scripture how mighty were the deeds you performed in setting at liberty your children in Egypt. We have also known that everything set down in those divine utterances contributes greatly toward our consolation. We now urgently beseech you that amidst our present misfortunes you earnestly recall to our memory by your Spirit those deeds so that encouraged by them we may place our trust in you alone. You led the sons of Israel from Egypt by working terrifying wonders against Pharaoh. The sea rolled back, the clouds protected them, fire served as a guide for their journey, the rock gave forth water, and the heavens gave manna and meat. Mount Sinai displayed you for them to see when you deigned to give them a law through Moses. Since you wrought so many great deeds for them, do not desert us so that [*83r*] the devil and the Antichrist can scatter the sheep of your flock. We have indeed sinned against you, frequently and seriously, but the Israelites rebelled against you in the desert more than once, and they contradicted you when they believed your words less than was right. There you punished them bitterly, but you still did not allow your inheritance to be destroyed, for you were fully aware that they were flesh and worthless in spirit. That is why you were so touched by mercy that you rescued them from their troubles. O God, we beg you to deal now in the same way with your Church; deliver and defend her not less than those men in the past, after several lashes. Through Jesus Christ, our Lord. Amen.

From the Same Psalm:

O great and good God, we acknowledge the supreme ingratitude of the human race, which is clear from our actions. But since individuals can easily not know themselves, this is made much more clear in the history of the ancient fathers which the sacred scriptures faithfully commemorate for us. We hear that you set free the Israelites with wondrous deeds when you led them out of Egypt, guiding them in the desert, defending them, [*83v*] and teaching them with such zeal and care that anything greater cannot be imagined or thought of. But it is recounted of the same people that they were so ungrateful and forgetful of those benefits that they kept complaining about God, who was their maker, deliverer, and guide. Certainly they were never guiltless of that sin. We therefore ask you, best of fathers, that as you in your mercy have chosen us and have conferred upon us the highest ornaments of your grace, never let us forget them. Rather constantly stir us with your Spirit to thank you for them. That thanks will glorify you and strongly encourage us to live a good life. Through Jesus Christ, our Lord. Amen.

FROM THE SAME PSALM:

O great and good God, you frequently deigned to protect and defend the fathers in the old law by marvelous wonders. You commanded that these same wonders be both narrated to posterity for its use and set down in writing for their eternal remembrance so that those who learn about them with faith may both admire your goodness to the ancients and conceive the firm hope that you will also be no less gentle, [*84r*] trustworthy, and kind toward them. Thus when they shall have studied how the fathers were punished by the severity of your justice they will also warn themselves that they will not be spared when they have kept on provoking you with their iniquities. We therefore pray, heavenly Father, that those events may be fruitfully recounted to us. Just as they were delivered from Egypt, we too have been delivered from eternal destruction through your favor. Moreover, we hope again and again that you grant to us that, unlike those who complained in the desert about your goodness, we will not be stirred up by our desires so that we excite your wrath unto our destruction. Through Jesus Christ, our Lord. Amen.

FROM THE SAME PSALM:

We can fully understand, O great and good God, how harmful is the desire for evil pleasures, both because they incite us to hurl complaints against you, who are supremely good, and because by indulging them to our heart's desire we incur the harsh punishments of your justice. The Holy Spirit now opportunely reminds us how all this happened to the sons of Israel in the desert. Thereby we are taught by another's danger [*84v*] and made more careful not to get ourselves caught up by a like fate in similar misfortunes. Accordingly we ask you to hear the prayers in which we beg that we may be constantly mindful of you. May the idea never arise, either in our hearts or words, that you who are the highest truth should mislead us. But if sometime we lapse out of weakness, take pity on us, for you know that we are both frail flesh and utterly weak spirits; may you thus be led by your mercy partly to lift us up after we have fallen and partly to give us strength lest we be thrust down into eternal destruction. Through Jesus Christ, our Lord.

FROM PSALM 79:

O almighty God, you have chosen us to be your inheritance and you will undoubtedly not fail to do anything that might contribute to helping us, enhancing us, and making us happy. You have given us knowledge of the Holy Scriptures, the preaching of the Gospel, the administration of the sacraments, and countless other things which add to the development of this inheritance of yours. But alas, we have been ungrateful for all these splendid and singular gifts and [*85r*] have performed none of the things demanded. Hence wicked nations quite rightly have been stirred up through your anger to attack the Church and to pour out like water the blood of your people and your inheritance. They account us a joke and laughingstock, and what is even more pitiful, it is not our sins they persecute in us, but you yourself, your Holy Gospel, and pure worship and religion. Accordingly we pray you, God and good Father, not to be forever angry with the sheep of your pasture. Pour out this wrath of yours, which our sins have made blaze out against us, on the nations who have not known you. Do not allow the wicked to devour your Church. We beseech you by your mercy and by the intercession of your beloved Son, our Lord, to remember no longer our old sins. Because our salvation rests on you alone, help and set free those who are calling on you, at least on behalf of the glory of your name. Be merciful to our sins, otherwise the wicked will say that you have turned against your own cause. Do not reject from your sight the groans and tears of the afflicted. Forgive us for our sins against you and deign to show on our behalf the power of your help so that [*85v*] we, your inheritance, your people, the sheep of your pasture, may confess you forever and celebrate your praises down all generations. Through Jesus Christ, our Lord. Amen.

FROM THE SAME PSALM:
Almighty God, we pray that we may take a salutary warning from the striking examples of your severity: how you overturned the kingdom of the Israelites and plunged the people who were rebelling against you into massacres, pillaging, plundering, fires, captivity, and all sorts of sorrows. Thereby may we undergo repentance with an eager heart and through that repentance may we be delivered from the heavy punishments which we have fully merited by our countless sins. It is right for you to take into account your most holy name: for if you empty your wrath upon us, the wicked will think that you did not want to bring help to those who worship you and call upon you. They have grown accustomed to hurl insolent jibes at your Church whenever any adversity or calamity befalls her, and they say, "Now where is their God?" "What good does their religion do them?" This kind of insult redounds against you, against your teaching, and against the Holy Gospel. [*86r*] So we pray that mindful of the sheep of your pasture you defend and protect us so that we may everywhere declare and proclaim your praises unceasingly. Through Jesus Christ, our Lord. Amen.

FROM PSALM 80:

It has always been your practice up to now, O almighty God, to stand by your people like a shepherd and to lead them like sheep under your protection. We now beg, let your power be aroused amidst such great dangers. Let your face shine upon us. Arise and come to save us. We acknowledge that, because of the iniquities and grave sins we have committed against you, your anger against us has not been without cause. We confess that your justice was being carried out when these massive evils, which now press upon your Church, overwhelmed her. But now when we deeply regret all the sins we have committed against you and we implore your kindness and mercy, why are you still angry with us? How long will you put up with the quarrels, insults, and outrages which evil and perverse men use to attack you through us? Turn toward [*86v*] us in these hard times, good Father, the gentle and serene countenance of your goodness. Be mindful of the singular benefits you have conferred on your Church. You have constantly fostered, endowed, and ennobled her with the abundant gifts of your Spirit. Do not now hand her over to be despoiled by wicked savages and cruel Antichrists. Do not allow that such a delicate and prized vineyard which you have planted and developed with your own lofty and mighty right hand should be shamefully and sadly hacked down, burned over, and pulled up by the roots. Look down from heaven and see us crying out to you. May the wicked perish from the rebuke of your frown, for they constantly blaspheme your name, your Gospel, and the holy worship which we offer to you. We, who are the work of your right hand, feel the salvation and help coming from you. When we call upon your name, you so revive and strengthen us that we can never desert you but are always guided in all our actions by the light and brightness of your countenance. Through our Lord, Jesus Christ. Amen.

[*87r*] FROM THE SAME PSALM:

In your mercy, O almighty God, you have been pleased both to be and to be called the shepherd of your faithful. From your lofty throne, on which you sit above the cherubim and all the heavenly powers, stir up, we pray, your might and saving power to save us. You sometimes seem to be angry with your faithful and to expose them in some ways to the mockery and jokes of the wicked, but now finally turn your face of grace and favor toward them. Do not allow the Church, the vineyard which you have planted and cultivated with wonderful foresight, to be ground underfoot and torn up by savage impiety. We beg you to set her up again and restore her so that you may lift up what has been brought low by hypocritical theft, replace what has been destroyed by tyrannical arson, and make whole at last what is crippled and mutilated. Let your hand be prompt and ready to defend us so that we whom you have restored to life may call upon your name and that we whom you have enlightened with the sight of your mercy may live safe and sound for you alone. Through Jesus Christ, our Lord. Amen.

[*87v*] FROM PSALM 81:

We have no small reason, O great and good God, for celebrating your praises with glad and joyous hearts since in your goodness you set us free from the slavery of sin and the tyranny of the devil. Since we confess you as our God, we pray that you be pleased to grant us this, that we may listen to you alone, worship you alone, and account nothing better than or equal to you. When we sometimes dared to do that, we had to undergo no light or ordinary punishment, because left to ourselves and without you, who are the true God, we have sunk to our lewd desires and followed our base passions. We now think that no greater disaster can befall men than that plague. That led us to ask again and again that we hear you and thereafter walk in your paths; with that achieved, we know for certain that you will carry through your promises so that you will hold in check the enemies of our salvation and you will in the end make us dine forever on sweet and indescribable delights. Through Jesus Christ, our Lord. Amen.

[*88r*] FROM THE SAME PSALM:

O almighty God, because of your supreme benefits we ought strenuously to give you both thanks and praise so that we glorify your name not only with our voices but also with musical instruments. It so happens that due to our misdeeds we see the Church beset by extreme danger. This drives us to confess and bewail our sins before you. In your goodness you have long wanted us to be free from the tyrannical slavery of the Antichrist, but we wretches have shamefully abused the gift of liberty and peacefulness. More than once you have summoned us to judgment like the Israelites through both the sacred scriptures and the ministers of your word. "Hear me, my people, and acknowledge me as your God," not, I say, only in words but in the heart, in deeds, and in sincere worship. But we, alas, have turned our heart away from your words, so that our sins have continually increased beyond measure. The enemies of the Church, who would have been undoubtedly overthrown had we trusted in you, are now terrifying to us. We, who could have enjoyed your sweet gifts in peace [*88v*] and quiet, are now smitten every day by greater afflictions. But we request that out of your singular kindness you do not

desert the Church which is beset with so many troubles. Be willing in the end
to stand by her so that she may be able to preserve forever and hold onto the
worship and teaching that you have handed down to her. Through Jesus
Christ, our Lord. Amen.

FROM PSALM 82:

O great and good God, you govern all kingdoms and earthly powers;
unless your Spirit guides and establishes them, they cannot dispense either
justice or fairness to the people. Accordingly we ask that you be pleased to
bring help to our mortal affairs, which have been troubled more than enough.
Preserve and enhance good princes but rebuke the evil and violent ones so that
they do not fail to lay down justice for the poor, that the oppressed may be set
free, and especially that godliness may flourish and grow. Just as you have
been pleased to enlighten our magistrates, princes, and king with your divine
name, so we also pray that in your goodness you bring it about that by their
efforts and ministry the faithful may honor you while living here [*89r*] and lead
holy lives so that they along with their rulers may be led to you, who are king
of kings and lord of lords. There may they together enjoy eternal blessings and
supreme happiness. Through Jesus Christ, our Lord. Amen.

FROM THE SAME PSALM:

We confess, almighty God, that your people, who have failed to obey
you, are often forced to submit to evil powers and unbelieving princes. This is
not something we can complain about, as if an injury had been done us: for
we have sinned so seriously and stubbornly against you that we have fully
deserved not just these punishments but much harder ones. Still, relying on
your words and promises, we earnestly beg you again and again to want to
assist your Church in these difficult times. As you have deigned to honor
higher powers and magistrates with the name and title of gods, be willing to
direct their meetings with your justice and act as judge among them lest left to
their lust and sensuality, which otherwise beset our corrupted human nature,
they sinfully oppress the Church and yield to impiety what is not proper.
Good Father, just as we pray [*89v*] that you become involved with them in
governance, so we do not doubt that with your assistance there will be freedom to deliver the poor, the orphans, the afflicted, and the oppressed from
their grave and acute dangers. We ask that you do not hand your Church over
to the power of those who dwell in darkness and try to overturn everything
that is right, just, and devout because they do not understand their duty. Since
it by your doing that they, who without realizing it have been lifted up to

being called gods and exalted sons, deserve to be cast away and destroyed like the worst of men. The Church is your inheritance, O God, so assist her, take her cause under your own care for judgment. Through Jesus Christ, our Lord. Amen.

FROM PSALM 83:

Almighty God, every day the hatred, armies, ambushes, and lethal plans of the enemies of our salvation increase so much that we are forced to call out constantly. Their every endeavor has no purpose but this: that we may be torn from you and nobody can be found who either trusts in you or invokes your name purely and rightly as he should. Our own flesh, our senses, and wicked men have conspired together with these rulers of darkness [*90v*] against your Church, and finally all our earthly and worldly feelings and faculties have risen up against her. So we pray that you be not silent nor keep quiet nor hold your peace. Just as of old you saved the Israelites by overthrowing the Egyptians, Midianites, Canaanites, and Philistines, so today rescue those who have entrusted their whole selves to your trust and protection and whose strength, power, and safety is hidden in you alone. Put a limit to the arrogance of those who are hostile both to us and to you so that all may understand that you alone are the God whom they should devoutly worship and chastely invoke, while casting aside all superstitions. Through Jesus Christ, our Lord. Amen.

FROM PSALM 84:

The ancients were gripped by a desire, O almighty God, to approach the place which you had appointed for your tabernacle for that time. We too come forward with the same desire that we may see the Church restored and that you grant that congregations of the devout may legitimately gather to celebrate your praises, [*90v*] to listen to sacred doctrine, and to receive the sacraments rightly. This is why we pray to you, our King and our God, that we may finally someday rejoice there, for we have no doubt that whatever happiness there can be here in this life is found in the holy gatherings of the devout. Hear then our prayers, good Father, and grant that we may make your house just as you wanted it to be. It will be happier for us to live even one day in it than for a long time in the tents of the wicked or that we should tarry in one not legitimately convened, even though it be fully stocked with all the pleasures of this world. So because you are our light and our fortress, make us gather on earth to glorify you so that our hope may grow of finally reaching you in the eternal tabernacles of heaven. Through Jesus Christ, our Lord. Amen.

FROM PSALM 85:
Almighty God, because of your glorious and magnificent mercy you show yourself favorable toward your Church so that we may be freed from the horrible slavery of sin. Till now we were [*91r*] slaves of the flesh and wretched captives of the devil, but you have deigned to forgive us all our iniquities and cover up all our sins. So now, although we are ungrateful and unworthy of your benefits, we ask that you hold back your wrath and anger. You are rightly aroused against us, but for the sake of your name allow this anger which has been stirred against our sins to be held in check. Lead us back onto the path of salvation for it is incompatible with your kindness for you to be angry at us forever or that you stretch out your indignation and wrath though many generations. Deal with us in your usual way and not according to our merits. Scatter and put to flight our enemies from whom you wanted us to experience your anger over our sins. When angered you kill, but when pacified you give life and show your mercy and salvation, for you have set before us destruction to terrify and punish us. Henceforward make us, who have insolently rebelled against you, to listen obediently to what you are telling and ordering us. May your mercy and truth be joined together in us, may your peace and justice be locked onto our hearts with an unbreakable latch so that when you rescue us from the savage Antichrist and his cruel minions, [*91v*] we may yield you a rich harvest of justice and holiness. Through Jesus Christ, our Lord. Amen.

FROM THE SAME PSALM:
O great and good God, because we are your sheep, your people, your inheritance, we fully believe that you will be gracious to us, and so gracious that you forgive our transgressions and sins and remit the punishments they deserve. We ask that you hold back by your fatherly care the anger which we have kindled, and that you dissolve the wrath which we have provoked against ourselves. It is not your nature, even though our sinfulness deserves it, to remain angry forever nor to stretch out your anger over a long time. Quite the contrary. Everywhere you manifest your goodness, and you are wont to offer salvation to all who seek refuge in you. Grant, good Father, that we may listen when you speak, for you always speak for our peace and good. If that happens, we shall not only have been saved and adorned with glory, but also everything we have will be filled with goodness, truth, justice, and peace. Our faith will abound, and through it you shall generously justify us. [*92r*] We therefore pray that we be not lazy or unfruitful servants but instead advance continually in holiness and innocence before you. Through Jesus Christ, our Lord.

FROM PSALM 86:

Great indeed are our misery and poverty, almighty God, therefore what we need most is your salvation. When we fly to you for safety and protection, we encounter our serious sins, our corrupt life, and evil habits. We don't want to conceal them from you, nor could we if we wanted to. You see all our evil deeds, and we confess to you that we have committed those sins. We did wrong, and were disobedient, arrogant, and rebellious toward you. We deserve far greater troubles than the ones we are suffering. But you are our God and loving Father; incline your ear and hear us. Take pity now on us who cry out to you every day and lift up our eyes and hearts to you in this very hope: that because you are inclined to forgive, rich in kindness to those who call upon you, and mightier in your works than all [*92v*] the gods, do not spurn us in our great trouble and tribulation. You are great, you work wonders, you alone. So teach us your paths, make us walk in your truth. Call back our wandering heart to you so that it may greatly fear your name. You have given us a splendid share in your mercy, but because we were ungrateful the armed camps of the wicked rose up against us and the battle lines of the damned attacked us. They pay you no heed and take no account of your teaching and name; they seek by their infamous skills only one thing: to destroy your worship and our souls by one and the same action. O God, since you are merciful, long suffering, loving, and truthful, look down and take pity on the children of your promises; strengthen and save them; march out with the banner of salvation so that our enemies may be confounded and all may see and understand that you are truly our God. Through Jesus Christ, our Lord. Amen.

[*93r*] FROM THE SAME PSALM:

When we notice our poverty in strength and planning, O almighty God, and still do not doubt that we are holy and are dedicated to you, we are driven to pour out before you continually our prayers and our entreaties and to place all our hope in you alone. Since you are meek and kind, endowed with plenteous mercy and goodness, stand by those who call on you. Teach us your plans without delay so that we may put aside all sham and hypocrisy and obey your commandments openly and fully. Just as nothing can equal your name, so we desire that it be both acknowledged and worshipped by all mortals. This will be done if, just as you often rescued your people from grave dangers, so in the present you look upon them, give them strength, and grant them true salvation when the enemies of human salvation rise up mightily against them.

We beseech you to unfurl this splendid banner so that the opponents of your glory, after taking notice of it, may earnestly be converted unto you. Through Jesus Christ, our Lord. Amen.

[*93v*] FROM PSALM 88:[7]

Because our salvation is yours, O almighty God, and we call out to you daily, incline your ear to our prayers, we pray. Do not turn away from them but admit them into your presence, especially at this time when we are so glutted with troubles. These hard and tumultuous times do not afflict us unjustly or undeservedly, for we by our vices have acted ungratefully, lived wickedly, and worshipped you carelessly so that we have brought all these evils on ourselves. We are terribly sorry and beg your mercy in all our prayers lest you deal with us according to our iniquities. May you not wish to account us among those who have already reached the grave nor reckon us with those who are going down into the pit. See how worthless are human strength, the defense of the flesh, and outward power. So make haste to help. Do not let your anger settle in upon us. Do not drown us in the stormy tempests of the Antichrist. The opponents of your name and your Gospel hold us in abomination, and our friends and acquaintances slink away from us. [*94r*] Therefore we call upon you and stretch our hands toward you. Do not hide your face from us, we pray, otherwise we will die in misery. We will not be able to endure the terrors of your justice. If our friends, relatives and acquaintances distance themselves from us, may you manifest yourself next to us and stand out by helping us. Then rescued from so many dangers, we shall confess you, not in the grave nor in death but among the living. Through Jesus Christ, our Lord. Amen.

FROM THE SAME PSALM:

While we are living here as mortals, O almighty God, we often fall away from you, and darkness clouds our minds. We, who should have made progress on your path, either fall often or lie flat like cowards. In your goodness you have been accustomed to lift from their sicknesses or troubles those whom you have embraced with your favor so that you scatter their darkness

---

[7]There is no prayer based on Psalm 87 in any of the five Latin editions of the *Preces*. This is the only psalm which Vermigli neglects, even though there is nothing in its content that might have discouraged Vermigli from basing prayer on it. Josiah Simler in his prefatory letter describes finding tiny sheets of paper written in Vermigli's autograph; among them were the scattered sheets ("chartas quasdam abiectas et dissipatas") which contained the prayers drawn from the Psalms. Given that description of the manuscript, it would hardly be surprising if a page was misplaced or lost. There is, however, a prayer based on Psalm 87 in the 1569 English translation of Vermigli's *Preces;* almost certainly the translator, Charles Glemhan, simply made up a prayer to fill the gap.

and sluggishness. We feel that you are doing that to us now. We find ourselves so depressed and bent over with the burden of disasters that we are on the edge of completely wasting away. We therefore ask you, good Father, not to rebuke us in your indignation. [*94v*] Do not consume us in your burst of wrath. We would want what has happened so far to contribute to our restoration. Look how we are now pouring out our petitions and groans before you. You see how our friends and relations are scattering all over the place and how the enemies of our salvation do not stop plotting and weaving snares and constantly thinking up deceits and tricks against us. Answer our petitions and prayers, O God, and do not suffer the enemies of your name to rejoice over us. Do not desert us or keep yourself far from us. Hurry to our help since we have entrusted our salvation to you alone. Through Jesus Christ, our Lord. Amen.

FROM THE SAME PSALM:

While we live here, O almighty God, we are encircled on all sides by evils, and we are so filled with disasters and surfeited with hardship that while still alive we walk in the midst of death. We therefore cry out with urgent and ceaseless prayer to you whom we have taken as our only salvation. We beg you to see how we have been consumed by our sins and by now almost swallowed down by total destruction. Your anger and wrath, which they have inflamed, worries us immensely and leaves us terribly torn up inside. [*95r*] Our friends, relations and well wishers cannot bring any help to rescue us from such grave troubles. Hurry then, good Father, to our support and out of your mercy forgive us what we have committed against you. If you don't do that as long as we live here, we will not find a place after the last judgment and condemnation, from which we beg you to keep us. Show us again the favor of your face, which you rightly seem to have turned away for so long because of our evil deserts; otherwise we cannot bear any longer the pangs of conscience and the harshness of your hand. Through Jesus Christ, our Lord. Amen.

FROM PSALM 89:

Your mercy, O almighty God, is widely known both because all the saints have glorified it and because it has continually revealed itself through all generations. It has led you to enter into a covenant with your elect because you want the kingdom of Christ and his seed, that is, the Church, to endure forever. No mortal has to fear that you will lack the power to carry through [*95v*] all that you have firmly and solemnly promised. The way you punished Egypt stands as monument to your power. Since yours are the heavens, the earth, the world, the winds, the seas, and everything you have created, we do not doubt that you can save the people whom you have adopted and who walk in the light of your countenance. We have need that you especially grant us this: that you be pleased to forgive us our sins. We confess that by them we have gravely offended you and that they truly afflict us and pull us greatly down by their weight. Grant then pardon to your suppliants, and be our protector against the enemies of your name. Lift up your arm with courage. Strengthen your hand to save us, and for our sake amidst these dangers grasp a weapon in your right hand lest the violence of the wicked prevail against us. Do not allow the sons of iniquity to harass us in their hatred. Strike them yourself and see to it that their efforts cannot succeed against our Holy Gospel. We call upon you as our salvation, our God and Father. Therefore preserve and protect your mercy toward us and do not weaken the covenant you have entered into with us. We have forsaken your law; [*96r*] we have not walked in your commandments; we have profaned your sacred rites; and we have not obeyed your will. We do not object to being struck by your rod or to being kept in line by the lashes of your punishment. We ask only this: that you do not take from us your mercy, goodness, and truth. Through Jesus Christ, our Lord. Amen.

FROM THE SAME PSALM:

We confess that it is the practice of the godly, O almighty God, to praise your mercy and goodness when things go according to their wishes. We indeed have effective evidence of your Spirit and grace if we keep up the same practice in hard times and pressing troubles and proclaim you as kind and gentle continually and unto all generations. We therefore ask you never to permit our minds to forget the promises and pledges which you were pleased to enter with your faithful servant David, that you would grant that the Christ, the mighty and everlasting king of all the faithful, would come from his posterity [*96v*] and that under his protection the universal Church would be defended from all hostile powers and would flourish and be endowed with every sort of good. We have experienced more than once your constant fidelity to those promises; you have often freed your people from grave and terrifying dangers for no other reason than this. This gives us courage to demand that now too when there is the greatest need you look out, as you usually do, for your faithful people in their difficulties. Through Jesus Christ, our Lord. Amen.

FROM THE SAME PSALM:

O almighty God, you have promised us in our Lord Christ Jesus not only an abundance of grace by which we shall be your dear friends, sons, and heirs, but you have also undertaken the task of bestowing so much kindness that, if our weakness is such that we fall into some sins, you will chastise our iniquities with your fatherly rod and merciful whip. But you will never turn away from the Church your kindly favor and generous heart. Remember then, heavenly Father, this covenant which you once declared to be more solid that heaven, sun, and moon. When [97r] your wrath flares up not a little because of our grave sins and you seem to cast down the cause of your faithful people and seem to show unusual favor to the enemies of your name, we beseech you to show forth then at last your ancient mercies. Do not permit us, who are the members of Christ, however unworthy, to be forever the joke and laughing-stock of unbelievers. Through the same Jesus Christ, our Lord. Amen.

FROM PSALM 90:

O almighty God, you have wished us to know that your tabernacle was not really so large that it could hold your infinite power and immense nature. So we already take for certain that you alone are the only tent, dwelling, and refuge for our weakness. We are not to regard you as a recent and new dwelling place for believers but rather an eternal one since you chose them before the foundations of the world. Our hardships and disasters on all sides drive us to you as our dwelling and safe fortress. We surely lead a hard and fleeting life, which flows like water [97v], as a person suddenly wakes from sleep and a flourishing plant instantly withers, when we are consumed by your wrath and indignation and thrown into lasting terror. We admit we have committed sins which have rightly angered you, and had you been pleased to fix your eyes on punishing them, we would indeed be destroyed by your burning anger. We therefore ask, O God, that you be willing to forgive the sins and outrages by which we have offended you so that you do not give us over to eternal damnation. Rather may we draw from our present troubles this fruit: that recognizing the power and effectiveness of your wrath and the futility and brevity of our life, we may with greater zeal come to fear you. Be yourself again, good Father, and may you now be gracious to your afflicted and persecuted children; then we shall fully rejoice and be glad, when your work is manifest to us. May the Holy Spirit, we beg, so direct us that your honor, glory, and splendor may shine forth both in us and in all of our actions. Through Jesus Christ, our Lord. Amen.

FROM THE SAME PSALM:

If we rejoice in your exceedingly abundant favor, O almighty God, [*98r*] it is because you chose to pursue us with your supreme love before the foundations of the world were laid; you predestined us to attain your eternal gifts before the mountains came to be or the earth was formed. Our joy is doubled if we recognize that aside from that we are nothing because of the weakness of our nature and the corruption of sin. We rush headlong into destruction, we flow away like water, we vanish like dreams, and we wither in a moment like grass. I ask that our difficulties, when we ponder them in our heart, may provide us with an opportunity for learning and wisdom so that we may understand how unworthy we are by ourselves of your favor and likewise how great is your kindness toward us. We beseech you through that kindness that you turn a favorable countenance toward us and designate us as your work, as indeed we are. May your brightness so shine right into our minds that our deeds may never stray from seeking your glory. Through Jesus Christ, our Lord. Amen.

FROM PSALM 91:

All who truly commit themselves to God so that they have him for their firm fortress and citadel [*98v*] find they have nothing to fear from disaster, snares, or any sort of destruction. For God protects his own people no less than birds defend their young with their wings or soldiers in war protect themselves with shield or buckler. What disease, plague, calamity, or devastation shall be able to terrify one who sincerely trusts in God? Truly, he will not have any cause for fear. Even if he has Satan and all the wicked setting great and deadly snares against him, from afar God has entrusted his safety to many angels, whose help defends him, whose hands and shoulders carry him along lest he run into troubles. The most savage souls have no power that he cannot crush and grind under foot. So if we now fear the unrighteous so much, that can be a sign that we have too little trust in you. That weak and tiny faith makes us so prone to countless sins that we are continually provoking you to wrath over our failures. We therefore pray that because you are good, you be pleased to forgive what we have committed against you, and to make us henceforward deeply in love with you so that we may in faith reverence your name and majesty and so that our prayer may become fruitful before you. We beg that you respond to our prayers [*99r*] and that lastly you be pleased to assist your Church in her hardships. Through Jesus Christ, our Lord. Amen.

FROM THE SAME PSALM:

Those who place their hope in you, O almighty God, have chosen for themselves the shade of your fidelity and the solid bulwark of your protection where they can be safe from the snares of their enemies and secure from any sort of deadly destruction. When evil men, who are really the devil's members and minions, are going to plan some evil against them, they will not be in the least deprived of God's trusty help, for he will quickly protect them like a stout shield. Serious temptations rage all round in our daily experience, and because of them an infinite number of mortals are hurled into eternal damnation, but evil will not catch up with those who are steadfast of heart and have said, "You are my God, and I have placed my only hope in you." They will stand firm and fearless while others fall. Not only will the care of the angels free them from misfortunes, but there will be no beasts poisonous or monstrous enough [*99v*] to do them any harm. We therefore ask you, good Father, not to keep us from such great benefits; grant that we may love you so much and entrust ourselves to you so entirely that we may choose for ourselves no refuge except you. Through Jesus Christ, our Lord. Amen.

FROM PSALM 92:

We are lax in extolling your name, O almighty God, when we do not focus our hearts on your wondrous works, for the moment we begin to go over them carefully in our memory and give them close attention, they first thrill us deeply, and then they drive us very forcefully and effectively to proclaiming your praises. They are truly stupid who either do not advert to them or remain unmoved by them and are just like those who perhaps are blinded by gloom when they watch the wicked go about successfully and avoid punishment for a long time. But they should learn that you want this to happen in order that they may have more to bewail when their affairs take a sudden and unexpected downturn and after the shadow of happiness they run into pure and simple disaster, eternal disaster, while the just, like cedars and palm trees, enjoy eternal and unmixed benefits in the blessed house of heaven. [*100r*] Foster this hope in us and console us with it, we beseech you, good Father, so that we may understand that you are just and fair and we may proclaim to all the people that there is absolutely no injustice in your judgment. Through Jesus Christ, our Lord. Amen.

FROM PSALM 93:

O almighty God, when we see how you have founded the earth, how it continues firm and unshakable, and how consistently and orderly it functions, we recognize in it your strength, power, and loftiness. From it we take heart and completely convince ourselves that your promises are good, true, and trustworthy the same way that the nature of things teaches us that your kingdom is strong and unshakable. Even if the enemies of our salvation seethe, prance about, keep heaping on us the waves of anger and temptations, and rise up against us like mountains of water and stormy seas, we have complete trust that we will be defended by your power and authority. Grant then both that this faith [*100v*] be continually increased in our souls and that your good and glorious promises about your Church may come true; may those promises also that you made to her in ages past be preserved in her, and thereby may your goodness and inexhaustible kindness be proclaimed more and more to all peoples. Through Jesus Christ, our Lord. Amen.

FROM PSALM 94:
The insolence of sinners, O almighty God, is staggering. Not only do they grind down the weak and hurt the feeble, but they reach such a peak of madness that they think their wickedness and outrageous deeds are hidden from you. We therefore ask that you keep far from our minds this sort of folly and that you be willing to convince us that when you created men's ears, formed their eyes, and gave them the power and faculty of understanding you were not ignorant of anything which we use them for on earth. Meanwhile so rule and direct us that we not only escape from the everlasting evils which are prepared for the wicked but that we also attain to the supreme peace and happiness which you have decided to grant to your people. Indeed, unless you stand by us [*101r*] and have protection prepared and ready to defend us, we easily fall into those evils which threaten us. We beseech you to be for us a citadel, wall, and stout shield lest it appear that our putting all our hope in you was in vain. Through Jesus Christ, our Lord. Amen.

FROM PSALM 95:
O almighty God, since you are our salvation and strength, it is fitting that we glorify you with all our power. If we want to do that the right way, we start by coming to you with a confession of our sins. Because of your goodness and not because of any merits of ours you have chosen us to be the sheep of your pasture and your people. You have done this without any contribution from us, for you are the great king above all the gods in whose hand lies not only the earth and the mountain tops but also the heavens and all creatures. We have offended you in infinite ways, we have hardened our heart against your warnings, we have given in immediately to temptation, we have

wandered astray in our hearts, we have been a burden and sorrow to you because of our sins and evil deeds. That is why you have stirred up against us such proud and [*101v*] cruel enemies, thanks to whom we have been brought to a great crisis. Nevertheless we acknowledge how wickedly we have acted and have discovered that no defense remains for us except your goodness and mercy. So we lay before your face these prayers and supplications before we perish and beg that you do not grind us up in your wrath. We beg you to wipe away the sins with which we together with our fathers have tried and provoked you. Remember that you are our God, king, and shepherd. Save, guard, and defend us from those who hate you no less than they hate us, lest you allow the work of your hands which you have begun in us be destroyed at their cruel caprice. Through Jesus Christ, our Lord. Amen.

FROM THE SAME PSALM:
So great are your majesty and invincible might, O great and good God, that they tower over everything and dominate everywhere. That is rightly so since everything from lowest to highest was created by you. There is nothing, even what is buried in the earth or found atop the mountain peaks, [*102r*] of which you are not the creator. Hence we rightly desire to extol you. Add to that the fact that you are our only protection and that we belong to you alone as your possession like flocks and sheep. We therefore worship you as a Godhead most close to us; we honor, adore, and call upon you, seeking this above all, that you do not allow our heart, which is vicious by nature, to become hardened to your warnings. We beg that you soften it by the breath of grace and the Holy Spirit and do not allow us to abuse and contradict your commandments as did the stiffnecked Jews who so often wanted to run the risk of your power. Be pleased in your goodness that what did not happen to them, to the promised land, may be granted to us, that we be not prevented from entering at last into the gate of eternal happiness after our long and lasting wanderings. Through Jesus Christ, our Lord. Amen.

FROM PSALM 96:
O almighty God, many reasons urge us to glorify you and bless your holy name, but we would not be able to do so properly unless we first drive away from us the sins [*102v*] which weigh so heavily upon us. We have received from you the noble gift of salvation through the Gospel, but until now we have been so cool toward living it out, so opposed to our calling, so negligent and contemptuous toward your commandments that we finally needed these disasters to make us face our evils. These grave dangers induced you and our

sins provoked you to showing us your wrath. Please pay no attention to what we deserve but look, O God, at how your glory is recounted among the Gentiles and your wonders are recognized by everybody. Your enemies, who are also ours, put their trust in human strength and idolatry; they would like to impose on us the same worship which they give the Antichrist. In contrast we know that you alone are the great Lord and terrible above all the gods. So we call upon you and in this hour of ours we take refuge in you, asking that you pardon our sins and show how vain are the gods of our enemies. Judge, O God, the opponents of your worship and the enemies of the Holy Gospel so that you may reign and lord it over the Gentiles, as is only right. Stretch forth, O God, your power, glory, and greatness in delivering us [*103r*] so that rescued from such terrible evils, we may render the praise and offerings that we owe you. Let the honor of your name be everywhere extolled, and may all peoples adore and reverence your majesty with pure worship. Through Jesus Christ, our Lord. Amen.

FROM THE SAME PSALM:

Your benefits to us, O almighty God, are not only constantly being conferred but they spring forth as continually new and unusual. They therefore deserve that we celebrate them with ever new praises and songs, unless we want to be ungrateful. Such is your greatness and power, such is your beauty and majesty, that you surpass to an infinite degree whatever men have ever been able even think up or imagine about your divinity and godhead. Grant us then that when we are about to venerate and adore you we may eagerly offer to your abundant glory all that we are and all that we have and that we may proclaim your kingdom to all the Gentiles, not just by words but especially by our upright and holy behavior so that it may be everywhere understood that just as we were created by you with the whole world so too we will be restored along with all things. [*103v*] Through Jesus Christ, our Lord. Amen.

FROM PSALM 97:

O almighty God, you yourself are the author of complete happiness and true joy; you are endowed with supreme severity and terrifying might, and you use these endowments in dealing with men according to your infinite fairness and justice. We therefore pray that you not seek to enkindle the fire of your wrath against us, who are otherwise deserving of harsh punishment because of our sins. Because of your mercy and because of the merits of your only Son, Jesus Christ, our Lord and Savior, forgive us the evil we have done.

Turn rather the indignation of your anger against your enemies. May they catch fire, tremble, and melt like wax before your face. May we be truly restored and reformed by your Spirit in a new kind of life and experience within us your justice and proclaim it to all nations so that they may understand it. Even though we have often wandered far from your will, which was revealed to us in the Holy Scriptures, still we regret our vices and [*104r*] we ardently desire to manifest your glory. Let us not fall short in this our hope and desire. Confound them who have no hope in you but possess and trust countless idols, which they adore, honor, and venerate. Grant at last to each of us whom you have been pleased to regenerate and revivify with your Spirit the gift of attacking with total hatred sin and whatever conflicts with your will. Then snatch the souls of your servants from the hands of the unjust so that not only we may rejoice after our escape but also that a saving light may arise on all your people by which they may be converted to you and glorify forever your memory with praises. Through the same Jesus Christ, our Lord. Amen.

FROM THE SAME PSALM:

Since it is you, O almighty God, who reign far and wide and govern all things, there should be nothing in the world that does not rejoice exceedingly over that fact. The thing which should be desired most is that, just as your kingdom is resplendent with justice and fairness, so may it also possess so much power and might that no designs and no efforts [*104v*] can stand against it. Rather everything that has been determined by your just design and outstanding justice produces good results. We therefore ask that just as the earth, the heavens, and the whole universe are shining examples of your justice and wisdom, so may the truth and purity of your worship in the Church shine forth. There may all share a common happiness because superstitions and corrupt religion have departed. May this be the reason why they rejoice who really and earnestly love God. Lastly we ask him that the light of the mind may grow within us and that in the gathering of the saints we may take joy with enormous eagerness over God's benefits. Through Jesus Christ, our Lord. Amen.

FROM THE SAME PSALM:

O great and good God, since all your judgments shine with utter fairness and justice, we have an urgent need for rejoicing and exaltation. Granted that those who are your people are afflicted for a passing moment while they live here, but the time will come when you will judge the earth by fire and by the glorious and manifest presence of your majesty and render to each according to his deeds. Then even the heavens [*105r*] will proclaim your justice, and all will be forced to confess, whether they like it or not, that you are most just. Then your Church will be bathed in true and lasting happiness. Since that is the way things are, while we are here on pilgrimage far from you, make your light and spiritual joy with great integrity of heart arise within us so that we may rightly and justly rejoice in you alone and keep constantly reminding one another to remember your holiness. Through Jesus Christ, our Lord. Amen.

FROM PSALM 98:
O almighty God, you have many times declared that it belongs to you alone to save us and that in doing so you do not need the aid and help of any creature. In the age of our fathers you performed wondrous deeds and frequently saved them by your right hand and holy arm alone. You manifested your help toward them in such wise that your mercy and goodness were made plain to all the nations. Since until now you have never forgotten your pledge and promises, you always stood by your people in marvelous ways when they had need of a savior. Hence they judged that they had every reason for extolling and glorifying your name [*105v*] with heart, voice, horns, lyres, trumpets, and polyphonic songs. Now we, who are your own people, have equal reason to ask that you do not depart from us in our days. You surely are not ignorant of the number and nature of the dangers which press upon us, and when we view the situation in the light of what we deserve, the dangers appear to us greater and harder than we can endure. We have sinned so much against you, we have broken your laws with such insolence, and we have frequently been so rebellious against you that we would seem to have lost out on our salvation if you want to deal with us according to our life and behavior. But we are striving to obtain from you this: that you deal with us in your usual way, that you forgive those who repent, that you wipe away the offense of those who call upon you, that you bring help to those who trust in you, that out of your fairness and mercy you defend, rescue, and protect us from the savage enemies of your name. Through Jesus Christ, our Lord. Amen.

FROM THE SAME PSALM:
Immense praise is owed to your name, O almighty God, by the whole of the human race [*106r*] because of the supreme and infinite benefits conferred on it, especially because you have freed us from death, not by the help of any other creature, but by the great sacrifice of your beloved and only Son. Thus we can rightly say that we have been saved by your holy arm and strong right hand alone. Most truly have you declared how observant and mindful you are

of your fidelity and goodness; all the ends of the earth and all mortals can see that from our redemption. But we are so dull, ignorant, and stupid that we have all but lost any sense of your great generosity. We have to credit this to our iniquities and sins. We therefore urgently implore your mercy that you be pleased to take away from us the grave sins that we have committed against you and free your Church from the occasions for so much sorrow. While we know that piety and religion are involved in such a crisis, we cannot sing to you in heart and voice as much as is right or in our joy urge all creatures to rejoicing. We beg that you now come and judge for yourself the case of your faithful. Lift up and sustain the sorrowful with your judgments. Refresh the downtrodden so that the fairness and justice, in which you especially excel, may shine forth as widely as possible to all people. [*106v*] Through Jesus Christ, our Lord. Amen.

FROM PSALM 99:
O almighty God, it is indeed the mighty force of your kingdom that you are wont to use in defending your faithful and laying low enemies and rebels. Our fathers experienced this quite often. Hence we rightly believe and confess that when you are the fortress of your people, those who oppose them find their earth, hearts and strength wavering, while your people are in turn protected and encouraged. Since you are so great and powerful in the Church, we beg you to throw into confusion by your power all the nations who want to destroy your kingdom. And as you are great in strength and power above all gods and kings, show yourself now on behalf of your Church as awesome and terrifying. We indeed know that you love judgment and judge human affairs with justice; we therefore want to put this request to you: that when the iniquities which we have committed bring down on us your severity, you turn your eyes away from them toward Jesus Christ, our savior, who is for us the true high priest, in place of Aaron, Moses, and Samuel. Be mindful of the prayer, sacrifice, blood, [*107r*] and tears which he shed for us on the altar[8] of the cross. Granted that our merits are worthless and we have committed infinite sins, remember that through him your name is invoked over us. So forgive, pass over, and remit our transgressions. Delay not in delivering us from such great dangers so that in our soul we may live for you and extol to the heavens your name with praise, as it deserves. Through Jesus Christ, our Lord. Amen.

---

[8]Here the translation follows the 1604 reading of *ara* (altar) instead of the 1566 reading of *arca* (money chest).

FROM THE SAME PSALM:

O almighty God, even though it sometimes seems that the wicked are raging so much that they are spinning almost everything around in circles, there is still nothing to make the faithful really fearful, for you yourself have taken command over earthly affairs, and you control with your wisdom the rudder of the whole universe. All those who hold to this conviction let other people fear but are themselves happy; filled with solid and unmixed joy, they glorify you with as much praise as they can and send up praises to you in every way. We join our efforts to them with eager heart and humbly beg you with ardent voices [*107v*] that just as you who showed yourself gracious and attentive to Moses, Aaron, Samuel and your other faithful priests when they called upon your name, so too may you be pleased to hear us at this time so that you be no less willing to defend with your presence, guidance, spirit, and grace the Church which now as much as ever desperately needs your protection. In just that way you once helped our fathers with a column of fire and clouds in the sea and in the desert. Through Jesus Christ, our Lord. Amen.

FROM PSALM 100:

O almighty God, your dignity and the enormous gifts which you have conferred upon us demand that we should come into your presence giving you thanks and, as is proper, glorifying you with supreme happiness and singular joy. But two things especially seem to hinder us, so that we do this too little. First we are burdened by countless vices, and we are so hard pressed by sins that we have hardly dared to lift up our eyes to you. Moreover by reason of our crimes we are so surrounded with fear and worry over the Antichrist that they come close [*108r*] to swallowing us up. Our experience teaches us that because of our depravity he has been so stirred up against us by your justice that, unless you support us in your mercy, human strength and help will do no good from here on. Hence we especially beg you that you free your servants from the burden of their vices and that you be pleased to give us a pure and unsullied life in place of our wicked and corrupt one. Secondly, may you be pleased to snatch your people from the jaws of their cruel enemies, who are striving to destroy forever not only the lives and possessions but also the souls of your faithful people. We beg you, who are our God, to keep this from happening. We are the work of your hands; you yourself made us, we did not make ourselves. Since we are your people and the flock of your pastures, then be pleased to be present and bring help to both the inner and the outer man so that we may at last enter the halls of your presence proclaiming your goodness with praises, hymns and songs so that due to us all the nations and all ages may have faith in your goodness. Through Jesus Christ, our Lord. Amen.

[*108v*] FROM THE SAME PSALM:

By the testimony of the sacred scriptures, O great and good God, and by the inward prompting of your Spirit we are assured that we possess your grace and favor for ourselves and our affairs, that we are bathed in gladness, and that we are enjoying a righteous pleasure. Since we have perceived by the gift of faith that you are our maker, by whom we were created and chosen out for your flock and your peculiar people, we can never get too much of giving you the thanks you deserve and of remembering such great benefits. We therefore come to you with praise and prayer and demand with all our petitions that you manifest your name to all the nations and that in your mercy you restore the Church to her proper happiness so that your mercy toward her many be obvious to all, both because of the truth of her teaching and because of the life and behavior which fully conform to the things which are truly being taught. Through Jesus Christ, our Lord. Amen.

[*109r*] FROM PSALM 101:

O great and good God, this above all you require in the life of those who profess your name and religion: that they build their life on complete fairness and justice and that they practice charity and mercy toward their neighbors. Although the Holy Scriptures everywhere inculcate these virtues, we confess that we have scarcely put them into practice, and we acknowledge before you our injustices[9] and iniquities and the cold zeal which we have shown toward the Church and your saints. We pray that you be pleased to pardon us for the treacherous and rash acts which we have done until now against your commandments and that you grant we may embark on an innocent life guided by the wisdom of your Spirit. May evil counsels have no place in our hearts, may we hold in horror anything that might turn us from justice and uprightness, and may nothing that is opposed to your law and wishes come near to our hearts or deeds. In addition, we ask you, heavenly Father, not to desert your Church in this extremely difficult time of ours. You see how the cruel, malicious, and wicked Antichrists have attacked her. They are so puffed up with pride and on fire with rage that [*109v*] they regard all human and divine rights as a joke with the same supercilious contempt. They act without a trace of

[9]Here the translation follows the 1604 reading of *iniustitias* rather than *iustitias* found in the 1566 edition.

humanity and truthfulness, they stride forth to attack everything with lies, deceit, and violence. Hence we beg you, O God, to hurry to help your people and to destroy with your power and might these wicked men who oppose your name no less than our peace and tranquillity. Through Jesus Christ, our Lord. Amen.

FROM THE SAME PSALM:

O almighty God, every ornament of holiness and virtue befits the Church, which is your house. We now see her sadly impoverished. Because you are good and desire every good (of that we have no doubts) and greatly favor her as is stated in your promises, we pray that you grant her to be so restored that all things in her may be carried out with spiritual wisdom and that you remove from her those offenses which rightly deserve eternal condemnation. May they depart who in their treachery fall away from you and who with stubborn obduracy are in rebellion against your law. May detractors be totally driven from her together with the proud; [*110r*] there is nothing they do not claim for themselves in their arrogance. In contrast may she provide there the greatest opportunity for those who search for the truth; these men not only meditate on you before you, but feed your people in the highest innocence and faith, and zealously carry out their ministry in all that leads to salvation. Keep away from her, keep away, good Father, all human deceit and painful idolatry. May every sort of wickedness at last be pulled out by the roots in the congregation of believers. Through Jesus Christ, our Lord. Amen.

FROM PSALM 102:

O almighty God, in ourselves we are unworthy of having our prayers gain access to you, for we have transgressed your commandments and law right and left, and we have lived lives totally unworthy of the Gospel and our calling. But because of your kindness hide not your face from our prayers and petitions. We are bitterly assailed and oppressed by extreme dangers, so incline your ear to us and give those who call upon you a prompt and favorable hearing. We beg you first to deliver us from our sins and vices, then strengthen our weak heart in your path, and by your Holy Spirit [*110v*] refresh our exhausted strength of soul so that we may live for you. After having been restored and renewed may we cause your name and Gospel to be spoken of favorably. Secondly, turn your power and might against those who heap countless insults and slanders upon the name of your son and his teaching. We beseech you, take pity now on Zion, that is, on your Church, for it seems time for you to favor her. We ask you to look down from your heavenly dwelling place, look into our troubles, and listen to the groans of those who are locked up, tortured, and slaughtered in horrible ways because of your name. Rescue from these great dangers your sheep whom the Antichrist has condemned not only to death but to vile curses; then your children may be able eventually to live a peaceful and tranquil life before you. Through Jesus Christ, our Lord. Amen.

FROM THE SAME PSALM:

The throng of believers implores your help, O great and good God, for it is being savagely oppressed by the tyranny of sin. The holy sap of piety in it is almost dried up; its mouth is blocked lest it sing your praises; and there is scarcely [*111r*] a member left in its body which can fulfill its duty of helping another member. Therefore bestir yourself to help us, for your strength is never diminished, and we think it is already the opportune time for you to help your Church which is so much afflicted. But if we do get your help, we have no doubt that fear of your name and sincere piety will be spread to the farthest reaches. For if you were to deliver your people from such terrible evils, you will be teaching that your fidelity endures solid and unshakable forever. Your fidelity still remains the same for your elect, even if the heaven and earth are thrown into startling changes and shaken so much that they perish. We beg again and again that your fidelity both save and restore us, not because of our own power or merits but because of the merciful and kindly efficacy of your fidelity. Through Jesus Christ, our Lord. Amen.

FROM PSALM 103:

Because of your supreme kindness toward us, O almighty God, we are bound to proclaim you constantly with our soul, heart, and all our powers and to give you worthy thanks, unless we wanted to be ungrateful and shamefully to forget [*111v*] all the things which you have given us up till now. First you freely offered us the remission of our sins in Christ and regeneration through his blood; then come your teaching, sacraments, the life of the body, and all that contributes to the conservation of the inner and the outer man. We acknowledge, however, that we have abused shamefully all these benefits of yours, we have done nothing in good faith which fully fits in with our calling. Hence we now humbly request that you be pleased to forgive our faults and amend our corrupt behavior and the foolish life which we have led until now. Do not deal with us, O God, according to our sins nor repay us according to our iniquities. Given that the highest goodness and kindness hold sway with you, are you going to be everlastingly vengeful? Or are you going to chastise and punish us in your anger? Remember that you are our Father. We therefore ask that you be moved with fatherly affection for those who worship you. You know that we are dust and empty dreams unless your goodness comes into play; we are weaker than grass and flowers. So do not pay attention to our evil deserts but look to the covenant between you and us into which you have entered. Rescue your people [*112r*] from the criminal and impious hands of your enemies so that we may glorify your deeds with the angels and the saints forever. Through Jesus Christ, our Lord. Amen.

FROM THE SAME PSALM:
O almighty God, our human weakness can never glorify you as you deserve, for not only is there question of your benefits to us by which we have both attained life and maintain and carry it on day by day, but most important of all, through Christ you have pardoned the faithful for their grave and infinite iniquities. For this ultimate and highest benefit we give you thanks — even if our thanks are not what we owe but what we are able to give. For that reason we are made more eager to make requests. We do ask, good Father, that you be pleased to introduce and conserve continually in the mouth of your Church the word of pure doctrine so that her first youth may return to her like that of eagles while the old leaven is changed. You skipped over the sins of the Israelites and not only led them to their promised abodes through Moses, whom you yourself taught, but also you showed by bestowing on them the continuous benefits of your mercy that your goodness toward them towers over and surpasses all their sins by a distance not less than that [*112v*] which separates heaven and earth from each other. In just the same way may your mercy move you, who are our Father as we are your children, for we are even now being buried by darkness and vice, unless you come to our help. Let us experience the renewal of your covenant between you and us, and after its reestablishment let us hasten by a supreme effort to give expression to your commandments and law by our holiness of life so that worthy thanks to your goodness may be given for our salvation not only by the Church on earth but also by the angels, who carry out your will with the greatest eagerness. Through Jesus Christ, our Lord. Amen.

FROM PSALM 104:
All creatures abundantly manifest to us your power, beauty, and glory, O almighty God, for we see that everything honors you as much as it can and obeys not only your words but your inclinations. We too should not lack the same zeal, especially since you have created the universe for our use and con-

venience. We realize how plants continuously sprout forth from the earth for us, how fountains, rivers, herds, rains, [*113r*] grasses, grain crops, wine, oil and all sorts of food help us, but our nature is so blind, debased, and corrupt that the more we abound in magnificent benefits from you, the more arrogantly we stray from your words and wishes. We therefore pray that in your mercy you be pleased to wipe away all the sins that we have thus far committed against you. And as we depend on your mercy for our bodily food, whether we like it or not, so may we also direct all our feelings, forces, plans, and deeds toward you alone. We pray moreover that you may not in the least turn your face away from us in this our day, otherwise we will be thrown into confusion, die, and be reduced to nothing. You, O God, do not lack resources and means to destroy your foes. As your messengers you have the violent winds, lightning, and flames of fire, and if you look down to the earth, it immediately quakes; and if you touch the mountains, they immediately send forth smoke. May the wicked Antichrists therefore[10] be destroyed so that they exist no more, and may the Church be granted peace and tranquillity to celebrate and sing your praises. Through Jesus Christ, our Lord. Amen.

[*113v*] FROM THE SAME PSALM:

It has not escaped your faithful, O almighty God, that from the beginning you created all things for the salvation of your elect. Just as we see how the whole world that you created is resplendent with wonderful and beauteous ornaments, so we pray that you may be pleased to brighten and beautify your Church, which is the gathering of your servants, so that your dignity may be resplendent in her no less than in the universe. Above all may there shine in her the pure light of your words; may the power and might of the Spirit make them effective in our hearts; may the constancy in faith of believers be so great that they may be more solid than the mass of the earth and the foundations and pillars of the world. At the rebuke of your power may dangerous temptations and the punishments of hell and the prince of darkness be driven from her. On the contrary, instead of them may the inspirations of your sweet Spirit arise like living fountains of water, and may there not be lacking a source to provide food continuously for our weakness. May our confidence in your name be a fortress into which we may withdraw. Just as there is nothing in your creatures that does not shine brightly, whether in the stars or in the variety of animals, [*114r*] plants, and rocks, so may the Church, we pray, be

[10]The translation follows the 1604 reading of *ergo* rather than the 1566 reading of *ego*, an obvious typographical mistake.

enhanced by the lamps of all the virtues. Through Jesus Christ, our Lord. Amen.

FROM THE SAME PSALM:

Everything you have created, O great and good God, bears witness by its greatness and exquisite decorations to how you flourish in your wondrous wisdom and immense might. There is nothing that does not depend on you. Every living thing is nourished by the food you supply, and anything from which you hide the sight of your face cannot last another moment, for when you withdraw your Spirit, they are immediately destroyed. So, good Father, because you are so good and mighty even regarding things which you have put at a level far below man, we pray that you extend no less your kindness toward your Church. She is indeed your work since you rejoice and take delight in her and care for her with your keenest providence so that in her your majesty may stand forth most clearly. That way we can continually hold delightful discussions among ourselves about your will and with unceasing praises rejoice that you have removed from her all wickedness. Through Jesus Christ, our Lord. Amen.

[*114v*] FROM PSALM 105:

O heavenly Father, your wonders urge us and your commandments earnestly teach us to seek your face, that is by reminding ourselves through pure worship and steadfast prayer in sacred gatherings that you are our God, who has made us through Christ into the true Israel and through faith into children of your illustrious servant Abraham. As is fitting, we therefore ask and approach your presence beseeching you to take away from us sins and all impurity of life. We confess that we have previously sinned seriously in heart and voice. Unless you hasten to help us, our sins will pull us down into the deep. For as we have observed, the enemies of your name have risen up and prevailed against us and are daily strengthening themselves against Christ, your Son and our Lord and Savior. We acknowledge that we have brought all these evils down upon your Church because until now we have lived a life unworthy of your name and of our calling. But we call on you to be mindful of your covenant by which you promised that we would be a connecting link for your inheritance. [*115r*] This pact of yours is not something ephemeral but everlasting. In other times you were wont to chastise kings to keep them from harming your elect; you succeeded on earth, as often as you wanted to, in defending and protecting your saints. In Egypt the heavens, the elements, and all creatures fought for you to save your people. Therefore, as then you did not forget your covenant, show how you remember it at the present time. Wicked men, the devil and Antichrist are striving by every device to swallow us up. Renew on our behalf your marvels, O God; we have no help, but protect us under your wings, stretch them out over us to defend us so that we may be allowed to live for you in safety and quiet. Through Jesus Christ, our Lord. Amen.

FROM THE SAME PSALM:

O almighty God, there can be no more illustrious or noble desire for holy men than to recount in their souls your marvelous and singular deeds and to glorify them in word and song as splendidly as possible since they are now followers in the faith of Abraham and are not unworthy sons of the holy fathers of old, members of Christ. [*115v*] Taught by the instruction of his apostles, we summon up in our memory how devotedly you observed the covenant which you entered into at the beginning with your Church. You were always a secure protection and solid defense for your elect when they placed their trust in you, and while you were defending them, there was nobody who could hurt them. Moreover when you did strike the earth with some disaster in the severity of your justice or harassed it with severe hunger and lack of food, all that was for their salvation and ultimately contributed to the glory of the Israelites. Warned by these events we take heart and approach you on our knees that today you be pleased to be mindful of your covenant as regards your Church no less than you were of old. As you see, she is hard pressed on all sides by many troubles; we beg you, good Father, who alone can do it, either to command all these troubles to depart or grant them power to purge away our vices. Through Jesus Christ, our Lord. Amen.

FROM THE SAME PSALM:

We hope, O great and good God, that you may be pleased to increase the congregation of your children both in number and also in faith and in all the adornments of your grace. Just as you gave Aaron as a faithful pastor to the children of Israel when they had already grown into a numerous people, [*116r*] so now may you prepare for your Church holy, learned, and wise ministers by whose work may our Egypt fade away and may their teaching, by which they instruct us, daily set us aflame so that each of us grows enormously rich in fine spiritual fruits. Never deprive us, good Father, of the light of your scriptures and the guidance of the Holy Spirit, otherwise we will both wander in misery through the desert of this life and perish wretchedly. When the infinite dangers of temptations threaten your faithful people, may they not lack the strength of your grace and favor so that while they live here they may be strong in spreading your kingdom to many people and attain in the end the dwelling place of eternal happiness which you have promised. Through Jesus Christ, our Lord. Amen.

FROM THE SAME PSALM:
Since the scriptures rightly reproach the ingratitude and rebellion of the children of Israel against God (for they annoyed him constantly with their complaints), we pray to you, heavenly Father, that you so rule and govern us with your ineffable mercy and fatherly kindness [*116v*] that we may not be found like them. They easily forgot about your works by which you set them at liberty, they clung to alien gods, they defiled themselves with carnal pleasures, and finally they both spurned the attractive land that you had promised them and befouled it with their grave and shameful iniquities. Because of these enormous sins you frequently punished them with fatherly discipline, but you never forgot the covenant which you entered with their fathers, for such is your goodness. We pray, O God, that you correct your Church that same way with your usual leniency when she sometimes has a serious lapse, thereby keeping intact your eternal pact which you have renewed with us through the death of your only begotten Son, our Lord Jesus Christ, who lives and reigns with you forever and ever. Amen.

FROM THE SAME PSALM:
Your goodness toward the congregation of your faithful people, O almighty God, is such that they can hope for and promise themselves the same thing now that you wrought previously in setting your people at liberty, if they remain in the covenant which they have entered with you. Just as [*117r*] the persecutors of your Israelite people were harassed and then crushed by your power, so too, when it will seem opportune to you, all who set themselves against your Church and truth will perish by the power of your Spirit. We therefore now ask from you for this especially, that while we are pilgrims in this life away from you and are walled in on all sides with infinite dangers, you illuminate the night of our darkness with the light and fire of your Spirit. May you be pleased to moderate by the sweet cloud of your grace the agitations of many-sided temptations so that we may accomplish the journey through the desert of this life safe and whole and that we may rejoice in having come at last to you in the eternal tabernacles after having cleansed our souls. Through Jesus Christ, our Lord. Amen.

FROM THE SAME PSALM:

O great and good God, our faith is more feeble and weak than it ought to be. That is why we sin like our fathers while our mind does not cling faithfully to your promises. But you are good, for just as you did not deal with the children of Israel according to their infidelities but delivered them from the slavery of the Egyptians with a strong arm and mighty power, [*117v*] so stand by us, we beg, and overcome and lay low the sins which have led us into captivity, just as you drown the Egyptians in the bottom of the sea. That way, after we have been deeply touched by the realization of your goodness, let us have a more solid faith and constancy, and in the desert of life do not let us indulge our passions lest, like the Israelites who provoked you to wrath by their various desires, we too should enkindle your anger against us. We pray that we may constantly keep before our eyes their sufferings and punishments so that warned by another's danger and evil, we may conduct ourselves with greater caution and prudence in your house, which is the Church. Through Jesus Christ, our Lord. Amen.

FROM PSALM 106:

Good Father, because of your supreme goodness and eternal mercy all of us are bound to glorify your name with all our might, for you have very often revealed the immense might of your powers in saving the devout. We now ask you to deign to visit and console your Church with that same power. That way she will not be so much persecuted by the fury of the Antichrist and the machinations of the wicked. [*118r*] Since the Church is your inheritance, we want very much to see her peace, joy, and happiness. We know very well and we confess frankly that we, like our fathers, have acted wickedly, have sinned gravely, and have deserted you, our God, in our utter wretchedness. But despite that we do not lose heart when we see how in dealing with your people of old you always showed yourself as one who heaped them with unbelievable benefits. When they repeatedly forgot those benefits and turned aside to idols and wickedness, you not only did not destroy them utterly, but after chastising them in a measured and fatherly way you restored them to their original tranquillity after their return to your path. O God thrice blessed, be pleased to save us, in no way because of any merits of our own but only because of your name, that as we have been gathered from different nations, so may we confess your praises for having snatched us from such great dangers and proclaim your honor. Through Jesus Christ, our Lord. Amen.

FROM THE SAME PSALM:

O great and good God, your kindness and wondrous goodness is such that the more we [*118v*] recognize it in your works, the much more difficult it seems to honor them with just and worthy praises. But what is continually brought home about your goodness to the mind of onlookers is that those are blessed who do just and upright deeds and contrariwise those are unhappy who stray far from your laws in their life and behavior. Accordingly we ask you that by the grace and favor of our Lord Jesus Christ you preserve us in the task of obeying your holy will and that you call us back from our innumerable serious sins. Lastly may you be pleased to save the Church, not because of her merits but because of the dignity of your name, lest forgetfulness of your benefits ever creep up upon her. If we do not keep your blessings before our eyes constantly, we easily yield to worldly and carnal desires. Keep far from her factions and envy which by the devil's craftiness are wont sometimes to oppress your faithful ministers. And just as long ago the prayers of Moses brought you to spare your people, whom you had determined to wipe out, so may you grant us pardon for all our faults and offenses. Through Jesus Christ, our Lord. Amen.

[*119r*] FROM THE SAME PSALM:

O almighty God, the fathers in the desert serve as an example to us; they dealt with you so negligently and so irreverently that they annoyed you almost continually or at least with no long breaks in time. They did it by tempting you, complaining about you, and turning away from you through evil omens. Therefore you were rightly and deservedly aroused against them, and sometimes your wrath even went to the point of handing them over to their enemies for very severe chastisement. These events ought to have been a lesson to us, above all so that we would avoid the sins which we know were responsible for alienating them from you. But as we are weak and inclined to evil, just like them we have terribly defiled ourselves with those same sins; we have therefore not just once felt how you, since you are just, have handed us over to be tortured by our own desires. But now seeing that we have already suffered enough punishment, we beg you that, just as you brought aid to the Israelites when they returned to you amidst a storm of troubles and did not forget the covenant you had entered into with them, so too be pleased to stand by us and to deliver us from the errors and slavery of sin into the grace of Jesus [*119v*] Christ our Lord and your own Son, who lives and reigns with you forever and ever. Amen.

FROM PSALM 107:

Those sailors owe a great deal to your kindness, O almighty God, who when they are horribly tossed about by stormy tempests and wind-driven waves are saved by your prompt help because they have called upon you with faith. Show no less power in supplying a life-giving abundance of water to dry and sandy terrain. Change and convert sterile soil and make it fruit bearing. When the sins of men deserve it, by a striking change you make pleasant and fertile land into the opposite, sterile and unfruitful desert. So that you may be acknowledged at last and mortals may appreciate your supreme power, you expose great kings and princes to contempt and shameful mockery, and you lift up the poor and the weak to powerful kingdoms. We therefore ask you, do not allow us to be drowsy when thinking about these things; indeed, grant this one thing: that taught by these events we may entrust our whole selves both to your goodness for help and to your law for guidance. That way, with you as our leader, we will swim out of the waves of the world; [*120r*] our souls, which so far have been sterile in good works, may then be most prolific in them; and we, whose labor has resulted in an extreme dearth of good, may be led by you to riches of the kingdom of heaven, which you have made. Through Jesus Christ, our Lord. Amen.

FROM THE SAME PSALM:

O great and good God, it is right for all those whom you have snatched from terrible dangers to sing your praises and give you the thanks you deserve. They experience your mercy every day whose journey goes astray along blind paths, through remote and deserted places, and runs into danger from beasts and bandits. You do not in any way deny them help when they pour out earnest prayer to you. You are also at the side of those who are oppressed by captivity, iron chains, and dark dungeons. Neither do you desert those whom deadly diseases have already almost destroyed, for you once determined that a person who begs for your help from the heart would never do so in vain. Therefore we, who long ago wandered far away from the paths of devout and holy living, now seek refuge in you. We, who are so terribly oppressed by the tyrannical slavery of sin, call upon you and finally urgently ask in all our prayers that you deign to heal our sickness of soul [*120v*] so that we may live forever for you and that you thereby gain eternal praise. Through Jesus Christ, our Lord. Amen.

FROM PSALM 108:

Strengthen and teach our hearts and souls by your Spirit, O almighty God, so that whatever misfortunes they encounter or however they are shaken with fear and dread of the enemies of religion and piety, they may still not thereby be deterred from singing your praises. Stir up within us, good Father, the talent, thought, and intelligence to rightly understand your goodness and to recognize the unwavering trustworthiness of your promises. These two things are so outstanding about you that they surpass in their greatness not only the highest clouds of the sky but they also reach beyond the heavens themselves by a vast distance. Accordingly we dare to ask and request from you that, after pardoning our countless serious sins, you be pleased to reassert your honor and show your glory to the world by rescuing the Church from the jaws of the Antichrist. Recall that she is your inheritance and your chosen possession, even though you sometimes seem to have rejected her because of our iniquities [*121r*] or to have excluded her from your protection. But given your goodness and fidelity, you can hardly have really forgotten about her. Hence we trust in you alone, for we have already found out very well how useless is human help. Stand by us then, and grant that we may act with steadiness and courage for your name and for your Holy Gospel. Through Jesus Christ, our Lord. Amen.

FROM THE SAME PSALM

When we mull over in our memory and heart the treasures of your promises, O almighty God, we are wonderfully stirred to glorify your name. That zeal then grows stronger when we find by experience that you perform most faithfully what you have promised you would grant. So far your have given us many things even things we did not deserve, but there remain some things for which we pray again and again so that they may happen more quickly. You have begun to rescue us from our enemies: may those good beginnings go forward to their conclusion. So far we have been freed from our sins so that as long as we really believe in you, they will not be imputed to us unto death. But they still weigh upon us; [*121v*] therefore day by day may we more and more throw off their yoke with your support. You are the founder of the kingdom of your Son, who is the true David; we pray that you may take care to spread it and make it illustrious to the point that both among the Gentiles everywhere and among us especially it may be honored and called upon in a chaste and holy way so that your Church may carry out splendid deeds for your glory and not be dragged back from the path of right religion by the enemies of godliness. Through Jesus Christ, our Lord. Amen.

FROM PSALM 109:

It is you alone, O almighty God, whom we acknowledge and confess as the source of all we have. We consider it supreme happiness to live under your care and religion. We account nothing more dear or important than to devote ourselves to the praise and celebration of your name. Do not at this time hold back and remain silent against the wicked and deceitful enemies of your Church; it is not only with lies and blasphemies that they rebel against you, for they wage war against us with raging hatred and savage cruelty and forget all about humanity and godliness. You know, O God, how peace-loving we have been until now toward them; [*122r*] we loved them in our hearts and we earnestly prayed for them both in public and in private. Now they repay us for these supreme benefits with terrible afflictions and injuries. So rise up against them, O heavenly Father. May the curses and blasphemies that they have been constantly mouthing overtake, fall upon, and crush them. May they get the rightful reward for the hatred and injuries with which they have treated you especially and us, your people. Kindly Father, do not treat us as our sins deserve. We have sinned so much and been so evil in your sight that there are no punishments, however heavy, that we do not deserve. But do not pay attention to us—look to the glory of your name. Help and save us out of your goodness since we are poor and afflicted. May the Antichrists be disgraced and clothed with shame; let mockery be their daily cloak. Be close to us with your help and save the souls of your faithful people. Through Jesus Christ, our Lord. Amen.

FROM THE SAME PSALM:

Since you are the God, heavenly Father, whom we glorify as our God, do not be silent or acquiesce when your Church is so oppressed. Meanwhile nothing is heard anywhere except pure blasphemies against you, against your teaching, and against [*122v*] your people—and mainly from those people for whose salvation the Church has been continually praying to you! You know how we have always desired peace and every blessing for our enemies; but now they are all puffed up with passion because they think they have seized the right time for overturning your heritage. They therefore deserve that you give them for their evil deeds just and fitting punishment and everything which we have just heard your Spirit threatening against stubborn and incurable sinners. But we too have guilty consciences because our lives have been completely unworthy of you and your teaching. First we confess that our sins are grave, then we pray that out of your mercy you deign to forgive us for them. Lastly, be pleased to bring help to your afflicted people so that we can confess and glorify you in large and devout congregations, because you have taken upon yourself to be a defender who stands ready at the right hand of the poor and of those who are almost destroyed, and because you preserve their lives and religion from the power and rage of the Antichrist, who now seems to be claiming unjustly and taking over for himself everything to their detriment. Through Jesus Christ, our Lord. Amen.

[*123r*] FROM THE SAME PSALM:
O great and good God, you are both the worthy and the rich subject of all the praises which the Church pours forth. It does not escape you how liars and deceitful men are scheming every day against her. Because she is kindly, she loves them with motherly charity and begs from you their salvation with prayers that are both ardent and frequent. But since these men do not change for the better but become stubborn and stuck in their evil ways, we beseech you to curb at last their rage and to put some limit and end to the affliction of your servants. You see how everything has already been almost reduced to extreme weakness so that there is nothing in your worship that is not close to defilement and shameful corruption. Hurry and help us, so that it may be understood that you do not lack the power and wisdom to rescue your people. That will help wonderfully to broadcast your name and praises. Because your Church already has a profound lack of spiritual goods and powers, make good the shortage from the overflowing treasures of your light and doctrine, of your graces and gifts. Through Jesus Christ, our Lord. Amen.

[*123v*] FROM PSALM 110:
You have granted to your beloved Son, our Lord and Savior, Jesus Christ, O almighty God, that he sit at your right hand endowed with full and universal power so that he presides over and commands all things. There shall never be any of his future opponents whom you will not in the end make into a stool for his feet; we therefore beseech you to examine how in these days the wicked and cruel Antichrists have been stirred up so that they dare openly to say about Christ, "We don't want this person to rule over us." They cannot get enough of proclaiming their deadly hatred both against him and against us, his people. Send down from heaven then, O God, the scepter of your power and the rod of your anger upon them so that through the Holy Spirit and the Gospel your Son may hold sway in the midst of his enemies. Grant that freely and spontaneously they may be his people and may they join together in the great multitude to defend his holy kingdom with their prayers and resources. We are indeed unworthy of such a great blessing because of our sins, for so far

we have lived with such little faith in you. But do you, O heavenly Father, place before your eyes not us but your oath [*124r*] in which you established your Son as both prince and priest in your Church for her salvation. Therefore grant in this hour that the princes, kings, and powers of this world, which have risen up so much against her, may be struck down by your furious wrath. Pass judgment upon those blasphemous and polluted enemies so that this holy kingdom of the Gospel may be spread through all the parts of the earth and so that Jesus Christ, your Son, who seems to be somehow persecuted in us, may be acknowledge as lifting up his head in splendor and glory. It is through him that we ask all these things, who lives and reigns with you forever and ever. Amen.

FROM THE SAME PSALM:
O great and good God, you have conferred on Jesus Christ, Your Son and our Savior, the exercise of supreme power over all created things. Thus he sits at your right hand so that in the end all hostile powers will be subjected to him as a stool for his feet. We pray that now when the Church is in such need that he be pleased to stretch forth and exercise his power. May he stir up ready and willing coworkers for such a wonderful, distinguished, and useful task, who fired by zeal for his dignity and esteem [*124v*] may shore up true doctrine, restore right behavior, and reestablish probity of life among his faithful people. Since we acknowledge and confess that we have been polluted and defiled by countless sorts of serious crimes, we pray that we may be exonerated by the expiation of Christ, the mediator and priest. Unless he, who has been set up as our priest in the line of Melchizedek, does so, there is no other way we can obtain expiation. After our sins have been wiped away through him, may you turn your wrath away from us and unleash it against the stubborn and rebellious enemies of religion. Pass judgment on the ungodly nations so that when your severity is seen, realized, and made clear, you may be extolled by the common praises of all, as you have fully deserved. Through the same Jesus Christ, our Lord. Amen.

FROM THE SAME PSALM:
We have known, O almighty God, that the dissolution of the world has been postponed so long and that Jesus Christ, our Lord and your beloved Son, has been taken up beyond our sight to your right hand for no reason other than this: that in the meantime all the enemies of Gospel may be laid prostrate beneath his feet and that his [*125r*] teaching, which driven by the Holy Spirit has been spread from Mount Zion out through the whole world,

may both propagate and bear fruit far and wide so that you may now have voluntary worshipers rather than people who have been constrained and coerced. True worshippers will count it a blessing not only to risk all they have but even their very lives for its truth. Since it is recognized that you, good Father, will really perform these things and have added an oath to do so, we now call upon your fidelity to carry them out with all possible speed. Pronounce sentence, I beg, on behalf of your Church, which has been so long and so bitterly attacked by the prince of darkness. Crush the instruments of the devil and the raging power with which the powers of hell have kept her under siege so that Christ may at some point lift up among us his resplendent head, who lives and reigns with you in the unity of the Spirit, forever and ever. Amen.

FROM PSALM III:
Great and marvelous, O almighty God, are all your works. Were we to examine them with devotion and faith, we would find in them nothing which would not provide our souls [*125v*] with supreme satisfaction. But alas, when we are weighed down by our corrupt life and very many sins, we are unable to devote sincere and devout meditation to the greatness and justice revealed in your works. Still we cannot fail to say that you are generous and merciful when we go over in our memory the gracious deeds you have performed for us and for our fathers. Since you never deserted your people, providing them food and giving them the inheritance of the Gentiles which you promised lest the covenant you had entered with them be abolished, do not forget us now in your mercy. Rather show yourself a lover of judgment and truth, manifest the fairness, justice, and uprightness of your will. You know full well the reason why we are so harassed by our enemies, namely how they have embraced hostility and hatred against piety, religion, and the pure invocation of your name. They cannot bear that the Gospel flourishes in our churches. That is why they are getting ready so eagerly to devour us. Send redemption to your people. May the covenant which you have with the Church be holy and everlasting. In its name we call upon you to rescue us so that all may recognize your goodness [*126r*] and fear and stand in awe of your majesty and that we may sing your praises forever. Through Jesus Christ, our Lord. Amen.

FROM THE SAME PSALM:
If we examine your works intensely, O almighty God, we are driven to confess with our whole heart their justice and rightness, for we find in creatures nothing except what is magnificent, exquisite, and splendid. Moreover the evidences of your goodness toward men which you put forward deserve to

be remembered forever and never to be surrendered to oblivion in the coming centuries. So far you have never allowed it to happen that you deserted your faithful, for always you were fully mindful of the covenant that you had entered with them. You supply enough of what is required for the health of the body; you endow them with a magnificent inheritance and provide them with wholesome precepts and teaching. Besides that, you add enormous promises backed up by your steadfast truthfulness, and lastly you are wont to rescue them from slavery and oppression. Relying on these arguments, we now humbly come before you and beg that you be pleased to forgive the terrible sins by which we have offended you and to deliver us from threatening evils so that we may be free of fear, delivered from the wicked, and deserve to attain to the fear of you, which is the beginning of wisdom, and to a right understanding of your law. Through Jesus Christ, our Lord. Amen.

[*126v*] FROM THE SAME PSALM:

O great and good God, we owe you the unfeigned praise which is poured forth privately and publicly from the heart, because the deeds by which you have preserved us for yourself deserve such universal admiration that devout people cannot examine them without feeling supreme pleasure. Neither do we doubt that you are still prepared to do for our salvation deeds that will deserve to be held sacred in our memories forever. We harbor no suspicion that you would ever be able to forget the covenant which more than once you have deigned to enter into with believers. The scriptures keep before our eyes and frequently remind us how you stand continually and steadfastly behind your commitments. Not only did you lead our fathers out of Egypt, but in your wondrous kindness you supplied them with food in the desert and established them in the land of Canaan, as you had promised. We therefore pray, good Father, that your mercy and truth be made no less manifest toward us. Send forth the mighty power of your word so that by it the worship of your name in the Church may be set free from error and darkness, and because the right worship of you is the beginning and pillar of all wisdom, may it at length be our happy lot to attain it. [*127r*] Through Jesus Christ, our Lord. Amen.

FROM PSALM 112:

Good Father, because we did not worship you with proper zeal and did not obey your commandments as we ought to have, these hostile and difficult times have now befallen us. Those who obey, love, and reverence you according to the ordinance of your word live truly happy lives, do not dash off into darkness, grow strong in justice, and use good judgment in arranging all their affairs. O almighty God, may your mercy sew back for us what our guilt has ripped off. Grant this first, that henceforward we may not swerve in the least from the path you have laid out. Secondly, may you strengthen our souls and hearts so that we do not fear the evils that befall us any more than we ought. Shore up the weakness of our minds and grant that we may rely on you alone. May the horn of your people be exalted and lifted up in this war which is so dangerous and fierce. You see how much our wicked and accursed enemies are whipped into rage against us. If they had the power to do so, they would destroy not only us and all we have, but they would also cause the destruction and abolition of all your worship, piety, [*127v*] and religion in the churches. They have bared the teeth of their cruelty, and they are in a merciless rage with their savage arms. Therefore bring them to naught with your invincible power and supreme strength; destroy their efforts so that they may fade away empty-handed and all their execrable desires perish, for the praise and glory of your name. Through Jesus Christ, our Lord. Amen.

FROM THE SAME PSALM:
O almighty God, the fear of you, namely inborn godliness, makes those men truly happy who are touched by no concern except the immediate execution of your will. Thereby we are led to request your mercy so that you may be pleased to restore your dilapidated Church. For there is no other way that her posterity, which is your posterity, can ever emerge either illustrious or powerful. There is no other source from which to expect an abundance of spiritual gifts, nor can light burst forth any other way amidst errors and the darkness of calamities. Besides, if as we pray, godliness revives in her, our sincere duties of charity toward our neighbors will be carried out without fail. Instead of himself, each person will look after his brothers. Each will govern his actions not by chance or impulse but by a spiritual standard. [*128r*] We therefore request this as a chief priority: that you solidify our confidence in you, from which neither storms of troubles nor the pleasure of good fortune can tear us in any way. Through Jesus Christ, our Lord. Amen.

FROM THE SAME PSALM:
All those live in happiness, O almighty God, who strive with all their might for true godliness and the observance of your commandments. May we in the similar way see why it has been quite consistent with your justice that we are harassed in these difficult present times, for until now we have been cold in devoting ourselves to your worship and careless in obeying your law as

was proper. In your mercy, do not, O God, decide to punish our sins as they deserve, but in the deep darkness of these dangers cause some of your light to shine upon us by which godliness may be restored in your Church and holy religion may flourish. Grant besides that our heart may be so strengthened by your word and promises that, even if we were to hear about serious evils hanging over us, still we would not be moved or stagger. Support us yourself and bring it about that in this fear [*128v*] we may rest solidly on you alone. The Antichrist will become enraged over that and grind his teeth, and the enemies of your name will grow faint. But the praise and glorification of your mercy will shine forth and be visible to all. Through Jesus Christ, our Lord. Amen.

FROM PSALM 113:
We ought to glorify your name, O great and good God, with all our power and total effort, but we have not lived that way before now nor advanced your praises as we should have. On the contrary, through our fault and wickedness your truth and the Holy Gospel have been in bad repute, and what ought to have been highly esteemed among all peoples is generally held in contempt because of our defect. We therefore acknowledge and confess that you are afflicting and oppressing us so that we may recognize your justice and judgment. Nonetheless we pray that you finally come to our help since none can be compared to you in goodness and kindness. Thanks to your infinite greatness it has been your practice to look into not only the things which are in heaven but also to lower yourself to study the events happening on earth. See the afflictions of your Church [*129r*] and take note of the oppression of your people. Because we have hitherto lain in the filth of our sins, we are now being crushed under the weight of our enemies, as we have deserved. You are wont to lift up the poor from the dust and to raise the needy from the dunghill. Deign to stretch out your helping hand to our princes and armies and so to aid your Church lest she be completely sterile. Grant that sometime she may be able to rejoice in peace and tranquillity. Through your word and Spirit grant her to be for you the mother of many children, who will glorify your name, as is fitting, with perpetual praises. Through Jesus Christ, our Lord. Amen.

FROM THE SAME PSALM:
All those who are dedicated to your worship with faith and sincere devotion, O almighty God, owe your name undying praises, which they pay to you in all places without cessation through all the years, days and hours. In that way the greatness of your goodness is proclaimed among us so that everybody

ought to confess that you are no less kind than you are invincible. Granted that you are said [*129v*] to have established your royal court on high in the loftiest regions of the heavens, nonetheless you reach down with your providence to all the lowly things which take place in the crannies of the earth below so that nothing can take place either in heaven or on earth without its being clearly and plainly seen by you. Therefore since we know that you are not ignorant of our doings and that your perpetual practice is to raise up the needy and the weak, provided that they trust in you, from the foul and filthy dust to noble and glorious kingdoms and often to endow childless and sterile women with a large family, we humbly implore you to take pity now on the afflictions of the Church so that through you she may finally be bright and glorious, for she now goes about dirty and dust covered. May she who seems to have passed childbearing take a solid and rightful joy in the number of her children. Through Jesus Christ, our Lord. Amen.

FROM PSALM 114:

When you brought out the people of Israel from the slavery of Egypt by your invincible power, O most merciful God, and the Egyptians had undergone enough heavy retribution for their cruel and stubborn hearts, you undertook to care for the Jewish nation with fatherly diligence and singular compassion. [*130r*] You openly revealed yourself to them by marvelous displays and overflowing favor: by dividing the Red Sea, in the wondrous quaking of Mount Sinai, by the retreat of the Jordan waters, and by the marvelous flow of water from rock. We can understand clearly from these, that all things obey and turn out well for those whom you have been pleased to write down on the page of your saints. This stirs up within us a lively hope that, since we undoubtedly belong to your people through the adoption of faith, it will transpire that, just as we have already been rescued by your grace from the disaster of eternal death, so also everything created, whether it bears a favorable or hostile appearance, will happily contribute in the end to the salvation of your holy Church. As we feel that our sins are rightly and justly causing this great delay, so we pray that it may be gloriously accomplished, thanks to your mercy and promised favor, and that it may be in the name of our Lord Jesus Christ, your Son, who lives and reigns with you forever and ever. Amen.

FROM PSALM 115:

When we invoke your mercy, O almighty God, to deliver us from our pressing [*130v*] troubles, we do so not only so that you may refresh and benefit us but also that your name may emerge resplendent from our deliverance. We see that if you permit your people to lie prostrate, in the future it will be easy for the children of this world to hurl at them the reproach that the trust which they put in you alone was worthless. As far as we are concerned, we have been enlightened by your grace and know well that all the good things of this world, from which unbelievers fashion idols for themselves, have no power or ability to make men happy, even though they worship and reverence them. Hence we understand that we have this left to do: that all those who are endowed with fear of you and who belong to the spiritual Israel and have been grafted into the kingdom and priesthood of Christ should make you alone their defender and help. But when they shall have done what they are bound to do, each day they will achieve a greater increase of true blessings. Accordingly we earnestly beg you that you, who dwell in heaven and have determined that we are to inhabit the earth while we are engaged in this life, may grant us to live in such wise that you permit us to conduct ourselves the opposite of the dead who keep silent at your festivities. Rather we desire to proclaim forever your praises in word and sacred ceremonies. [*131r*] Through Jesus Christ, our Lord. Amen.

FROM PSALM 116:

You manifest your love for the devout most, O almighty God, when you assist those who call for your help in the midst of their misfortunes. The more serious the troubles from which you rescue them, the greater is the evidence of your good will toward them and the more are all hearts set afire so that they seek refuge in you when hard times come upon them. We, who have been completely dejected and weighed down beyond what we can bear by the burden of sin, humbly call upon you. We have experienced how men are liars and how every hope is hollow which has been put in things created. We ask you with all the urgency we can muster that you forgive us for the outrageous and shameful deeds we have committed and that you turn aside from your Church the punishments which our sins have fully earned so that, helped and filled with rejoicing before you, we may drain the cup of thanksgiving and give witness to everybody about your superb paternal care over us. Just as right from the beginning you have always had a care not only for the death of your saints but also for their sufferings and sighs, [*131v*] so we pray that you may now take pity on the Church, which is fainting and almost destroyed. Through Jesus Christ, our Lord. Amen.

FROM PSALM 117:
You founded the human race, O almighty God, so that all nations might come together in joint praise of your name. To accomplish this, in ages past you predestined patriarchs, prophets, and apostles for this task, and now when everything has been defaced with darkness, abuse, and defilement you have gathered us into the Church for that same work. So that we can carry it out as smoothly and skillfully as possible, we pray that our iniquities and sins do not block our path. Just as we confess that they are countless and serious, so we urge humbly that you forgive them and blot them out. As you see, we are already so encircled by dangers and so close to being crushed that we have taken you alone as our only refuge. We beg you to look after how our faith is propped up by your Spirit lest it collapse amidst these troubles. Place before our eyes, we pray, the goodness which you have always bestowed upon the godly so that [*132r*] fully and clearly recognizing it, we may not harbor doubts about whether now too you will be the trusty protector of your Church. Through Jesus Christ, our Lord. Amen.

FROM THE SAME PSALM:
When the human race was suffering from total blindness, O great and good God, and was overwhelmed by infinite misfortunes, your indescribable kindness stood by it. Because of that kindness you deigned to hand over your only begotten Son, our Lord Jesus Christ, for the salvation of the world. We therefore owe you undying thanks, for we see that we have been saved not in the least by our merits but by your pure and solid goodness. Since we have experienced you to be so steadfast and trustworthy in your promises, it is right that we do not doubt that the few things that still remain to be fulfilled will come to pass, at a time which you have predestined, through your supreme mercy and inexhaustible goodness. Accordingly we ask you to so strengthen our hearts with the spirit of faith that we may believe without the slightest doubt and not only lay hold of the good things you offer us but also that together with all nations and peoples we may give you in the Church the thanks you deserve for all your generosity. [*132v*] Through Jesus Christ, our Lord. Amen.

FROM PSALM 118:
All those who fear God are grafted into Christ, are filled with religious zeal, and daily encouraged and invited by new reasons and infinite blessing to glorify his name. When they recognize how great is the power of the divine goodness and how prompt he is to help those who call upon his goodness and

rescue them from all danger and anxiety, then they are led to a level of security and trust where they have nothing to fear from the might of men, however powerful they be. Because that is exactly how we now feel, we entrust our salvation to you alone, O almighty God, and we beg you to be pleased to protect the Church, which is already walled in on all sides and besieged by terrible dangers. Our iniquities deserved far worse things. We confess, O God, our sad and serious offenses against you, but there is need here for your singular kindness so that your mercy may overcome our evil deeds. Grant that, chastised by you like disobedient and rebellious sons, we may not be handed over to destruction and death, [*133r*] for that would keep us from celebrating, praising, and magnifying your deeds in the gathering of the just within the gates of your kingdom. Grant that we, who are now reproached, rejected, and almost made a laughingstock for everybody, may be lifted to such pitch of justice, holiness, and upright living that all people may realize that whatever we are striving for or have striven for in religion is not the work of men but is your very own work. Through Jesus Christ, our Lord. Amen.

From the Same Psalm:
We are constantly battered by such heavy storms of troubles, O almighty God, that we need to have sole recourse to your mercy so that we be cast down beneath them. But now we have really found out that human powers can do nothing to oppress those whom you have destined for salvation. Hence when we see how those who trust in men are being fed on false hopes, we conclude that the highest wisdom of the godly is never again to put their trust in any mortals but to place their hope in you alone. We therefore pray, good Father, that even if you sometimes become angry over our sins, and quite rightly, you may chastise or hammer [*133v*] back our stubbornness but still without our falling away from you. This will indeed happen if you deign to build us upon that firm cornerstone, who as he was rejected and reproached by men so has been lifted by you to the topmost pinnacle of glory. Through our Lord Jesus Christ, your Son, who lives and reigns with you forever and ever. Amen.

FROM PSALM 119:[11]

O great, good and everlasting God, by your indescribable kindness and supreme and abundant benefits you have constantly labored on our behalf, but in contrast we, who should have carried out your commands with complete dedication, have sadly transgressed them and have heaped upon ourselves the very evils which are oppressing us. We cannot rightly complain that we have received worse treatment from the Antichrist and his adherents than we fully deserved. We have experienced that you have chastised us not by your anger but by your paternal mercy. Hence we fly to you who are striking us and ask these things: that you open the eyes of our mind with your healing light so that we may not be blind to your marvelous works; that while we are on pilgrimage in this world, [*134r*] your commandments may not be hidden from us. Make our heart continually burn with ardent desire for what you have commanded. Grant that henceforward we may not deserve to be objects of scorn along with the debauched, nor condemned with curses because we have strayed far from your precepts. You see the reproaches and insults that our enemies heap upon us at random and how the princes and rulers of this world, after they had conspired against us, have striven not just in speech but with a total effort to turn us aside from your undiluted word, from sacred worship, and from your pure ceremonies. So confirm and revivify us with your power that we may experience that your promises are true and certain. Through Jesus Christ, our Lord. Amen.

ALEPH א בBETH

Among mortals those should be accounted as truly happy, O great and good God, who have placed your law constantly before the eyes of the mind. They adhere to its form in initiating their actions and employ its rule to what they have already begun so that, if they have perchance gone astray in some respect, they may correct their course and redirect it toward justice. They live their lives in innocence and will not be put to shame when their actions are examined by a fair assessment. This works best [*134v*] when it has been put to diligent use from a tender age. But we realize, good Father, that all human effort is quite useless and worthless unless you assist with your Spirit and teach our hearts, for otherwise what profit shall we gain from meditating on

[11]This is by far the longest of the Psalms, with 176 lines. It also provides the basis for the longest of Vermigli's *Preces*. In the Hebrew, Psalm 119 is something of a tour de force, for it is an acrostic, that is, divided into a section for each letter of the Hebrew alphabet, in order; each verse in a given section starts with that letter. Vermigli divides his prayers based on this Psalm by a pair of letters which follow the order of the Hebrew alphabet.

your law except cold and damnable erudition? We therefore beseech you to supply by your grace not just strength for carrying out the measures that you command in the law but also that you bring it about that your precepts may please us more than all of our own endeavors and that we may take more delight in fulfilling them than in any carnal or worldly pleasures. Through Jesus Christ, our Lord. Amen.

GIMEL ג ד DALETH

Since our strength depends on you, O great and good God, and without your help we cannot accomplish anything that pleases you, we rightly take refuge in you so that by the help of your grace we may indeed conform our actions to your laws. That can in no wise happen if you do not remove from our eyes the curtain that evil desires keep putting between us and sound teaching. The result is that we pay no attention to the beneficial things it commands us to do. Also keep far away, we pray [135r], the swelling of the mind and the elation of the heart by which we are sometimes inclined to overestimate human institutions and inventions so that compared to them your institutions seem vile to us. This mainly happens when we fear to undergo the contempt and hatred of great men and of this world. Therefore when we find our hearts so torn between opposites, do you, O God, refresh us with your word and be pleased to calm the cares of our hearts and our excessive anxiety with spiritual tranquillity and to prevent us from being deceived by the lies of this world, which otherwise are so enticing. For if you shall have once enlarged our anguished heart with your Spirit, nothing shall be able to block us from running as fast as we can to carry out your commands. We beg you with all the intensity we can that we may be able to attain this in the end. Through Jesus Christ, our Lord. Amen.

HE ה ו VAU

When we consider how weak are our abilities, O almighty God, and conversely what the perfect fulfillment of your law entails, we realize clearly that to obey it we absolutely have to have your powerful [135v] help. Be pleased then first to teach us yourself the real reasons for your commandments and secondly to illuminate our intelligence and mind that we may understand the things you have taught us. We have need then that you grant power and proficiency in carrying out what we have learned from you, for otherwise the knowledge will do us little or no good unless we are provided with at least the beginnings of obedience. The evil inclination of our heart greatly hinders that, and finally our feelings and perverse emotions oppose it. Hence we pray that you yourself help us with your grace and generous favor so that all our offenses and daily sins against your law may be forgiven and not be counted toward our eternal death. But meanwhile may your mercies manifest themselves, O God, in the salvation and defense of the Church. You see how she is being harassed by dangers, reproaches and many afflictions. Do not permit her to be snatched away from you and stripped of your word, and of rightful, holy, and sincere worship. Through Jesus Christ, our Lord. Amen.

ZAYIN ז ח CHETH

We take refuge in you, O almighty God, in this difficult time when we see your Church to be greatly afflicted, and [*136r*] that because of our evil deeds. We have sinned against you, have acted wickedly, and have transgressed your law in countless ways. There is only one thing that raises up our hope and provides us with great consolation in these troubles: because we know that you are fully mindful of your promises regarding your servants. Our sins and our past life accuse us bitterly. We therefore ask you to revive us and lift us up with your mercy, which we see is offered to us among the promises in the holy scriptures. We beseech you to keep us from turning aside from the law which you have deigned to propose to us. Regardless of how the wicked harass and mock us, we desire to cling to you inseparably. On many other occasions you have taken up the case and cause of your servants when disasters have almost engulfed them. So now do not desert those who are calling upon you. Your enemies want nothing else than to take away from your Church her sacred scriptures, her ceremonies, and all pure worship. Since you alone are our lot, we look up to your face with our whole heart. Before the crowd of reprobates and criminals swallow us up, come and help us in your goodness so that day and night we may devote ourselves to glorifying you because of your just judgments. Through Jesus Christ, our Lord. Amen.

[*136v*] ZAYIN ז ח CHETH

We have conceived no other hope of salvation, O almighty God, except from your faithful promises. From them alone do we draw solid consolation whenever the flesh, human reason, the devil, or the ungodly savagely mock us. We take courage against them all from the fact that you will follow through completely on all that you have promised, for when we mull over in our hearts your fidelity from the earliest centuries, it is clear that you have never deceived anyone. Grant then that day and night we may rest immovably upon this solid rock, impregnable bastion, and well placed anchor. Since we have no doubt that you will play your role to perfection, all that is left is for us to execute the charge given us with complete dedication so that we may increase our stride and pace to full speed in carrying out your law. We beg you, good Father, that you make us stop our delaying. Regardless of the wishes of all the ungodly, who are always setting up obstacles, let us comply with your commandments, and may we join as our allies all those who give you pure worship so that [*137r*] just as the earth is everywhere filled with your good things, so day by day may the number of those who call upon you keep increasing. Through Jesus Christ, our Lord. Amen.

TETH ט ' YODH

Almighty God, until now it has been your practice to deal graciously with your servants. Especially when through your mercy we have been led to a knowledge of the Gospel we had a singular experience of your benefits. But we honestly confess and acknowledge that we have befouled them by our sins. Not only did we pervert ourselves by those sins, but thereby your name and the teaching of your Son were blasphemed among unbelievers, and many were driven away from the path of truth by our fault. We now therefore beseech you, heavenly Father, to make us appreciate rightly and understand you so well that we may cling to your word and precepts with total constancy. The afflictions we are undergoing are effective spurs to make us return to your path. Since you are good and generous to all, do not allow those whom through Christ you have adopted as your sons to wallow in shame. The more the devil, the Antichrist, and his minions [*137v*] bend their best efforts to pull us away from you, do you act against them, we beg, so that we may keep your commandments with our whole heart. May the fact that she is afflicted by these ungodly persons turn out to the good of your Church. Soften our heart, which is otherwise sluggish and fat, unto a rich understanding of your words and law so that the Church may value them more than gold, silver, and the treasures of the world. Desert not, O God, the work of your hands which you yourself have made and embellished. May the evil people be put to shame who try to destroy your ways with perverse zeal. But may those who worship you and accept your promises in good faith finally rejoice in you. May they enjoy your goodness and forever live for you. Through Jesus Christ, our Lord. Amen.

TETH ט ' YODH

There is nothing we have hoped for longer and more eagerly, O great and good God, than to obtain from you the gift of understanding your statements in their right meaning. We desire it so much that we are also prepared to pay any amount of trouble for it. So if it seems right to you to bring your elect back to that conviction by a stroke of hard luck or misfortunes when they have fallen short, take the measures which seem best so that we may devote ourselves wholeheartedly to your law. [*138r*] Since you deigned to fashion us in our mother's womb with your hands, may you again so favor and enlighten us that we be not blind to your words of truth. While we make these requests, good Father, we are eagerly seeking not our own consolation but that of all for whom your law and truth carries weight; they will be wonderfully overjoyed if they see that all of us cling to you with sincere hearts. Hence we earnestly request that your will, which you have declared to us in the sacred scriptures, may be for us dearer than gold and more desirable than all riches so that we may embrace it with our whole heart and that nothing we embark on may bring disgrace on us or on the Church. Through Jesus Christ, our Lord. Amen.

Caph כ ל Lamedh

O almighty God, since in these times of ours we have a special respect for your promises and our heart is almost broken in waiting for your help while salvation seems to be vanishing before our eyes, we need you to assist and console us. We beg you not to pay attention to our weak faith, vices, and the evil deeds by which we have heaped shame upon your name and brought your Holy Gospel into ill repute. [*138v*] Bring it about, O God, that in the time that still remains in our lives we may atone for all of that by devout and religious actions. For if we were able to obtain that request, we would not be in doubt about your judgments being handed down against the enemies who are persecuting us so bitterly. You see how undeserved it is, for even if we have sinned so seriously that we have earned even harsher punishments than these, still it is hardly because of our sins that our enemies have dug these ditches for us; rather they persecute us for having partly reformed religion and for having restored your worship. Indeed they want us to be killed. Good Father, in your goodness encourage and strengthen us. Grant that your word may abide forever in the Church, and make us rejoice and find refreshment in it, lest we perish in this affliction. Since we belong to you and find only disappointment in human help, save us yourself and protect us from threatening dangers. Through Jesus Christ, our Lord. Amen.

Caph כ ל Lamedh

Our spirits have already grown faint from anxious longing, O great and good God, while we hope for help and salvation from you alone. [*139r*] Day and night, I say, we look up to you that at some point your servants may finally come to enjoy the promises they have hoped for. Meanwhile we hope that it may be granted to us that we may in no wise be forgetful of your law while you put off helping us amidst our troubles. Just as your law remains constant in the beautiful decoration of the heavens and because of your law an unshakable stability holds sway on earth and the helpful and marvelous change of seasons keeps going on, so likewise, we pray, may the passage of time not destroy your law in our hearts and breasts, for if we do not keep constantly reflecting on it, we will easily perish amidst our afflictions. It is your word which gives us life, for if we shall have believed in it, we attain to salvation and justice and are not greatly disturbed by injuries from our enemies. Good Father, grant us this: that it may never happen in our hearts and that may we prefer to see everything else come to an end before we see your words disappear or become blotted out in the Church. Through Jesus Christ, our Lord. Amen.

Lamedh ל מ Mem

O great and good God, those who devote themselves to your words in the end draw no little fruit from them, for [*139v*] they not only surpass their enemies by their understanding and knowledge of heavenly things but also outstrip those who gained a great reputation from both great learning and from the experience of a long life. So that we may not be cheated out of such an advantage, we pray that spurning the debauchery of sin we may find our delight above all pleasures in your word. Because this life of ours is surrounded on all sides with blinding darkness, we cannot possess any better lantern than your pronouncements to give light to our minds. They should direct our human journey like a most pure light; this is especially true when the situation itself indicates how each of us because of terrible dangers is constantly carrying his life in his hands. All around there is no lack of the minions of the hostile powers who are setting a thousand traps for our salvation. We therefore ask you as earnestly as we can that you deeply move our hearts to fulfill your precepts, which you have been pleased to endow with marvelous promises. Through Jesus Christ, our Lord. Amen.

Mem מ נ Nun

Such is the power of both your law and your words, O almighty God, that those who love them and continually reflect on them grow wiser each day and surpass in intelligence all other mortals, even if they are learned [*140r*] and advanced in age. This sort of study helps in wondrous wise to draw our steps back from the path of depravity and strengthens our otherwise unsteady strides lest they sinfully go astray from your commandments. Since we have wretchedly fallen in our past life and sinned shamefully, it is perfectly obvious how we have disregarded your just words, promises, ceremonies, and your whole law. Hence we hardly have cause to wonder or complain that you are now unjustly afflicting us: because of our clearly depraved and corrupt behavior we deserve that our wicked and cruel enemies have so risen up against us. That certainly would not have happened to us if we had made continuous use of your commandments and words as a lamp for our feet. But we now beseech you, O God, through the depths of your infinite mercy that you be pleased to look upon the terrible crisis into which our soul has been led. We pray that you grant pardon for our sins and that you render our hearts readily inclined to carrying out your commandments and that you snatch us from the snares which the enemies of your holy name have set for us. Do not permit the destruction and disastrous death of those whom you have picked out as your own unto an eternal inheritance. Through Jesus Christ, our Lord. Amen.

[*140v*] Samekh ס ע Ain

Those who are enlightened with your Spirit, O almighty God, attack with utter hatred all that partakes of iniquity or sin, and they have therefore made you their refuge and their shield. Because they see very clearly that those live in contentment and happiness whom you yourself strengthen with your power and might and whom you uphold and favor, they are delivered from the gravest perils. Conversely, all who withdraw from you and depart from your commandments suffer terrible punishments. Accordingly we pray that led by the same evidence we may both cling to you alone and become most careful about your commandments. The flesh and hostile powers are carrying on a constant vendetta against us. Do not allow us to be handed over to them for destruction, but keep us attentive to your words, and make us rejoice in them as in the highest pleasures. To attain that, we need to have you teach us the mercy that is yours. An understanding of things divine is never mastered without your Spirit. Help us yourself to judge as rightly as possible concerning your law. Through Jesus Christ, our Lord. Amen.

[141r] Ain ע פ Pe

Your words, O almighty God, are everywhere so worthy of admiration that there can never be a time when they are not of concern to the godly. We therefore ask you that as you are full of mercy and goodness you look upon us with deep contentment and so mold our thoughts and actions that we may not give the least heed to impiety, than which nothing is more worthless. Since we are human and hence surrounded by the weight of our flesh, do not let its weight crush us but rather breathe forth the spirit of repentance so that we may pour forth rivers of tears in the greatest abundance over the faults that we have committed everywhere. We have you for our just judge, who will not connive at sins nor allow them to go unpunished, and your judgments and laws are filled with so much justice that there is nothing contained in them about which any creature might rightly find fault. Silver and gold that has been carefully refined by fire does not equal the purity of your judgments, so again and again we beg you not only to make us know them but also obey them as far as possible, given our weakness. Through Jesus Christ, our Lord. Amen.

[141v] Pe פ צ Zade

Our mind has been clouded by dense darkness because of our inherited disaster, O great and good God, lest it be able to understand your commandments clearly. We are so strongly inclined by our inborn desires that we are extremely attracted to what displeases you, and when we summon our heart to serve you, we are unable to bear up under the insults which the wicked hurl at us. We therefore ask you to enlighten our mind, bridle our evil passions, and so strengthen us that should any dishonor threaten us because of your Gospel, may we embrace it with a stout heart. With steadfast hope and solid faith in your promises may we resist those who are mocking us, and may the power of your truth smash to pieces the wickedness of perverse desires. Let no earthly power deter us, good Father, from bravely defending your decrees before all men, however splendid and magnificent they be. Make your decrees, I beg, so sweet and pleasant for us that we may conclude that there is nothing in life preferable to them. Let nothing prevent us from devoting ourselves to carrying them out with hearts completely eager. Through Jesus Christ, our Lord. Amen.

[*142r*] COPH ק ר RES

With our whole heart and undivided trust we humbly beg you, O almighty God, that we may be as careful as possible about obeying your laws and commandments. The drives of the flesh and the ferocity of our fallen nature and of our deep-seated sin drive us powerfully to violate your commandments. Since we are enmeshed in so many serious and shameful sins, it is no wonder that, because you employ justice and severity toward your people, you have permitted the Antichrist and his scoundrels to harass and terrorize us. But now for the sake of your goodness and mercy pardon, we pray, all our sins against you, and turn your gentle eyes and countenance toward the state of your Church, which is virtually in rags and tatters. Redeem her, as you used to do so often at other times, from threatening dangers since it is only your guidance and governance that can save her. May salvation be far from the wicked, as is just, for they have completely ignored your word, your law, and your commandments. Quite otherwise is the case of those who hope in you: they have your promises, which all possess the highest and most complete truth, about their salvation. So that your truth may be preserved unharmed and inviolate, save us yourself, since it is for the sake of your name that [*142v*] we are in so much danger. Through Jesus Christ, our Lord. Amen.

COPH ק ר RES

O great and good God, because through carnal attraction any alternative seems more attractive than your law, we therefore fly to you for refuge in our daily prayers that you guide us by your Spirit in the observance of your law. Lest we cry out in vain, soften our heart and bend our souls that they may have no greater concern than obeying you in all things. May we meditate on this alone though the watches of the night and at the break of day so even when there is a swarm of things pulling in other directions, we may be fortified by your protection against them. Just as your decrees are certain and solid, so we cling to them steadfastly. For anyone who departs from them and heads in another direction wanders very far from salvation. If that were to happen to us, since we are weak, help us quickly. Lift up the fallen. Defend us with your protection, even though we have a poor claim to it. You know, good Father, how many people are trying to kill us, so hasten with immediate help and vastly strengthen the confidence in your promises among those who call upon you. [*143r*] Through Jesus Christ, our Lord. Amen.

SHIN שׁ ח TAV

O almighty God, quite without any reason the devil, the Antichrist, and the princes of this world are persecuting your Church and seem so puffed up and angry against religion that the faithful are quite rightly terrified. Only your word can renew and restore their happiness, so stir us with your Spirit so that we may always be utterly devoted to it. We know that peace arises, increases, and continues for those who love your law so that nothing can ever really hurt them. If we are now lacking in this true peace and consolation in our hearts, this undoubtedly has to come from the fact that we have ignored your word and followed your law too little. Forgive, we pray you to forgive, every wicked and criminal act that we have committed against you so that henceforward we may no longer distance ourselves from the justice of your commandments. We therefore request for ourselves true and lasting delights in which our hearts may live and so live that they may strive to the utmost to voice your praises. Up till now we have wandered about [*143v*] like brute beasts, good Father. Since you are our only salvation, call us back from our wanderings and sins so that you may keep all of us wholly dedicated to your will. Through Jesus Christ, our Lord. Amen.

SHIN שׁ ח TAV

Even if the hatred and deceit of those who in this world constantly oppose your will, O almighty God, are strong and powerful against our weak spirit, still on the other hand the pleasure which your words give to us is so great that they are more valuable to the godly than the best spoils and the richest plunder. They encourage us each and every day to give you thanks as often as possible. Only one thing remains: that you do not allow us to be tricked out of the salvation which we are expectantly awaiting. For this reason we pray that you be pleased to lend a ready ear to our prayers so that (as the justice of your law is everywhere so true and solid) you provide us so abundantly with your Spirit that we may carry out as far as the weakness of our powers allow what we have already chosen to do under the Spirit's inspiration. May the power and extraordinary strength of your Spirit make up the difference when the weakness of the flesh fails us. [*144r*] So far we have strayed in many ways, O Lord, like foolish and misled little sheep, and unless you go looking for us because of your providence as a fatherly shepherd, we shall easily perish in our evils. So do not let us any longer wander about in the dark endangering ourselves among wolves. Through Jesus Christ, our Lord. Amen.

FROM PSALM 120:

Every single day we fly to you, O almighty God, worn out and harassed by harsh and deadly misfortunes, as you can see. We humbly beseech you to hear us at last in order that your Church may be rescued from the tricks, lies and deceits of the Antichrist and his minions. The blasphemies, insults, and reproaches with which they attack and tear apart your Holy Gospel can be compared to deadly arrows and hotly burning coals. They cause the hearts of the devout to be stricken with enormous suffering and inflame souls with zeal and a righteous anger for the glory of your name. We acknowledge that we have deserved full well that we be afflicted by this sort of unclean pestilence and raging plague, for we have grievously sinned against you and your law. But by the innate and inborn [*144v*] kindness with which you are endowed we pray that just as we greatly desire true peace to worship, glorify, and honor you, so may we be able to attain it some day by your favor, even in the teeth of those who harbor the deepest hatred against the peace and tranquility of believers. Through Jesus Christ, our Lord. Amen.

FROM THE SAME PSALM:

We know by experience, O almighty God, how the sins and lies of corrupt doctrines have brought affliction and hardship upon the Church. Accordingly we ask you to rescue her from this sort of disaster. Now at last we are beginning to understand how deceitful and crafty have been up to now the seductions of the Antichrist. Now may the power and sharp spears of your word be ready at hand to confound every intrigue of Satan. Better yet, may you yourself transfix this plague with the mighty throwing spears that you sometimes use against impiety so that all their malicious traps may be burned up, as by blazing coals. Otherwise if you do not save us with your strong and mighty hand, our pilgrimage amid evils and miseries will be endlessly protracted. [*145r*] For there is no hope of peace where your truth is held in bitter hatred—indeed peace each day seems the more remote for your Church the more she loves and pursues it. So when there is perpetual war to be waged against spiritual wickedness, do not deny your help, good Father, to those who call upon you. Through Jesus Christ, our Lord. Amen.

FROM PSALM 121:

We are extremely worried, O almighty God, as we wait for help in this difficult situation of ours; we lift up our eyes to you alone. We know that your power created heaven and earth, and so we also believe it can rescue us from current dangers. We confess that our sins have been such that we deserve to be punished by these afflictions. When you called us to the Gospel, we did not respond with the right sort of worship and honor but concentrating exclusively on our own endeavors, we sadly put your honor and glory in second place. Please do not on that account, O God, examine anew this ingratitude and the sins we have admitted, rather because of your mercy prevent our steps from slipping, [*145v*] keeping them firm in your law and commandments so that they do not turn aside from them. Moreover, do not seem sleepy or drowsy in protecting and guarding your Church which is so gravely afflicted. If you have been accustomed to defend your people from the sun in daytime and from the coldness of the moon at night, do not despise us, who are suffering from the bitter and repeated fury and rage of the Antichrist. Do not merely save our souls and lives from his schemes, but above all protect your religion, which he is attacking most powerfully. Direct the beginnings and the ends of our actions in the narrow ways of your words so that they may remain forever steady within their straight path. Through Jesus Christ, our Lord. Amen.

FROM THE SAME PSALM:

O almighty God, as long as we are suffering during these sad and disastrous times, we lift up our hearts and eyes to you alone as one who we do not doubt possess supreme power over all things; accordingly we urgently and ardently implore help from you. Since you used this outstanding power in creating heaven and earth, the very situation now demands that you help your Church with the same power, for [*146r*] she is close to being swallowed up by the jaws of cruel enemies. Do not allow, we beg, the feet of our faith to slip and waver, for that faith by itself (it is by such infirmity that we are clothed all round) is rather weak and inconstant. We first deserted you and wretchedly turned aside from the law and decrees of your will, but may you be pleased, we beg, to treat us not because of what we are but because you are limitless goodness and supreme kindness. Protect the Church by carefully hedging her in and walling her about with your defense, for if you desert her, who are otherwise the guardian of Israel, there is no way she can stand. If she is stripped and bereft of your protection, who else can save her by his care and help? Grant that we may regroup our spirits and redirect them to you so that we may have you as the guardian of both ourselves and all our affairs. Through Jesus Christ, our Lord. Amen.

FROM THE SAME PSALM:

Since we are constantly subject to evils while we live here, O almighty God, we are therefore searching round with our eyes for a source which might provide solid and firm assistance. It is you above all that our faith encounters, [*146v*] for we see that you founded all things right from the beginning and that you foster by your perpetual goodness everything that exists, both in the heavens and on earth. We pray that just as your supreme providence regarding other things is not accustomed to break down, so too may you deign to act toward us as a most watchful shepherd. May we be everywhere protected, we beg, by your goodwill so that we may not burn with overheated, evil desires nor may either our charity to our neighbors or our devotion to you be extinguished by the coldness of infidelity in our hearts. May our daily prayers and petitions obtain from you that we be kept pure from the disease of sin, and may our life be such that whether going or coming we may be cleansed of faults and endowed with virtues. Through Jesus Christ, our Lord. Amen.

FROM PSALM 122:

O almighty God, holy people continually encourage one another with wonderful speeches to sacred worship where your name is extolled with praises, the faithful are instructed in your word, and the sacraments are rightly received. But now we see that we are close to having this blocked by [*147r*] the Antichrist, very much to our sorrow. Because he is damned and debauched, he busies himself with nothing else but repeating the pattern of the holy city of Jerusalem: whenever it started to be rebuilt and reestablished, it fell apart in the end and indeed totally collapsed so that there no longer remained a place for pure worship and devout prayer. Good Father, you see full well how much trouble that scoundrel is causing and stirring up. We ask with burning hearts and strong feelings that you put aside for a short time our sinful merits and be pleased to obtain what contributes to the peace of Jerusalem, that is, of your holy Church. Since we have shamefully transgressed and wickedly violated your laws, we do not rightfully deserve that anything good be promised to us. But when we look to the honor of your name, our confidence returns, and we boldly pray that you be pleased to stand by those who are united in the name of Jesus Christ and are calling upon you through that same name so that some day we may be allowed to find rest in the true Jerusalem after you have rescued us from the enraged and violent attack of the Antichrist. May all who belong to the Church and believe her holy teaching become through your kindness mutual friends and loyal brothers. Through Jesus Christ, our Lord. Amen.

[*147v*] FROM THE SAME PSALM:

Although your Holy Scriptures everywhere teach us, O great and good God, that heaven is your dwelling place, the same Scriptures nonetheless indicate that your goodness is such that the Church too both is and is called your chosen home. Accordingly when we are about to come together in the gathering of the saints we pray that we do so with joyous and eager hearts. With utmost generosity you have showered your Church with splendid and outstanding gifts, and nothing more is needed toward beautifying her, whether something that might contribute to her spiritual elegance or to the rich abundance of heavenly benefits. Since you have made her completely perfect, this alone remains: that by our prayers you grant that she have her members united with one another in perpetual concord. May her meetings contribute to your pure worship, may they therein reach pure and sincere decisions about the Scriptures, and may your kingdom day by day expand her boundaries, and may all these things be consolidated in your peace and in the tranquillity of the Spirit. May we obtain lasting and solid goods for your house and for our neighbors when requesting peace and happiness for her. Through Jesus Christ, our Lord. Amen.

[*148r*] FROM PSALM 123:

No help is left for your people, O almighty God, except from heaven, for the forces of the Antichrist and his hostile designs have grown so powerful that the situation is little short of the abolition and total destruction of true piety and right worship. We therefore lift our eyes heavenward to you so that your help may revivify us and that we may escape such great dangers. Like servants and handmaidens we look to you with eager eyes as the only refuge of salvation. Just as they depend exclusively upon their lord or mistress, so we daily cry out to you until you take pity on us. Do not be so hostile and angry over our misdeeds, which have all but overwhelmed us, so that you assign avenging them priority over considerations involving your name and glory. We pray you to forgive your humble servants so that nothing may subtract from your mercy and supreme goodness. Take pity on us at this time, O God, take pity on us like one who is not ignorant of how many insults and reproaches are everywhere being directed against your Church. Do not allow the arrogance and contempt of the wicked to go any further. They are already so immensely puffed up by successes that it seems that they cannot be kept down by human forces. May you who [*148v*] are invincible and almighty put an end and limit to their rage. Through Jesus Christ, our Lord. Amen.

FROM THE SAME PSALM:

Although you have made your dwelling place in the highest heavens, O great and good God, still you never cease from stirring us by the Spirit, by whom you teach the hearts of believers so that we hasten to obtain help from you alone in our constant petitions and prayers when we are undergoing trials, tribulations, and dangers. Accordingly, the eyes of our faith now look to you alone, heavenly Father, just like servants directing their whole attention to the hand of their masters and like young handmaidens watching the hand of their mistress. Henceforward our eyes will keep track of how you take pity on us. Be favorable to us, we beg, as befits your mercy, and do not allow us to be a laughingstock and joke for hostile powers. We doubt not that you fully understand how the rich and proud of this world contemn and despise your Church with great haughtiness. We therefore ask you again and again to bring help quickly and not allow her to be corrupted by superstitions and errors [*149r*] nor be oppressed by the power of Satan and the wicked. Through Jesus Christ, our Lord. Amen.

FROM THE SAME PSALM:

Good Father, look down from heaven upon us who have lifted up our eyes to you alone and with your help protect us who are currently hard pressed by such great dangers. Since you created us and we are rightly and legally yours, act the good master and do not scorn your servants who in this crisis look to you as their only refuge. We truly acknowledge, I say we acknowledge, that we deserve the troubles into which we have fallen because we have committed sins and grave misdeeds against you. But we pray that moved by your mercy toward your servants you will blot out because of your kindness and goodness whatever offends you in them. Pay no attention to our unworthiness, O God, but look upon the reproaches and insults by which you are insulted in us. For when enemies mouth blasphemies against your faithful, they are hurled not against us but against your name; when they go on the rampage with arms and violence, they are mainly on the hunt for your worship, religion, and word. They are striving to destroy these utterly if they succeed. As long as [*149v*] they see themselves as going from strength to strength and carrying out their plan, they become extremely insolent, but your Church, after being treated by them with utter shame, has nobody except you, her Lord, in whom she can seek refuge. We beseech you to drive away these injuries and evils which they are inflicting; in this we seek only that you vindicate the honor of your teaching and your Holy Gospel, lest the wicked hold them up for mockery. Bring it to pass, O God, that when they experience the power of your truth they may come to acknowledge you as God, whether they want to or not. Through Jesus Christ, our Lord. Amen.

FROM PSALM 124:

Unless you, O almighty God, are pleased to support us with your help and power, the Antichrists are so bent on rising up against your people that they seem to want more than anything to swallow us all down alive. Their rage is so inflamed that if you do not stand by us, they are going to eat us up and devour us. If we examine our sins, we surely cannot deny that we have fully deserved it. Are there any punishments or penalties that we can consider as unjustly imposed on us by you, given the ingratitude we have shown toward you? So much [*150r*] have we transgressed your commandments that no punishment is so severe that we both do not really deserve it and are seen as deserving it. But be pleased to assist the holy Church, if not for our sake, still for the sake of the glory of your name, lest the surging torrents overwhelm and suffocate her by the force and flood of their waters. Turn away, we beg, their mouths and teeth from your saints lest they tear them apart like prey. They hunt for nothing else with their traps and evil skills than to ensnare and catch in the nets of their wickedness those who have devoted themselves to reformed worship and heartfelt religion. Hasten, O God, to our help and free us from the nets of such cruel hunters. We beg you, who made heaven and earth, to cause our salvation to be attributed to you alone. Through Jesus Christ, our Lord. Amen.

FROM THE SAME PSALM:

If you yourself, great and good God, do not right now suppress and smash the rage and madness of the Antichrists, so that they are unable to accomplish against your people what they have already thought up and worked out with one another, [*150v*] they will gobble down the whole Church alive. They rise up, growl, rush out, and swell up with rage so that your faithful are now about to be overwhelmed unless you quickly stop and roll back the tempest of wickedness and waves of the devil. We beg you, heavenly Father, to turn away your wrath from us and do not punish us as we deserve for the abominations we have committed against you. We do this not only so that you take us into account, but also so that you do not let down your own name, your teaching, and your promises. Bring it about that someday we may say, "Our God must indeed to be glorified and praised, for he has not allowed his Church to be scattered by the savage rage of wicked men but has rescued her by his glorious and powerful arm from the snares and jaws of criminal conspirators." Cut their nets, foil their stratagems, make their powers wither which now strike utter terror into all who love you, O God. It is to you alone, who created heaven and earth, that we look for help. Hence we beg you, because of your supreme goodness and kindness, to show yourself favorable to our prayers. Through Jesus Christ, our Lord. Amen.

[*151r*] FROM THE SAME PSALM:

O almighty God, those who belong to your inheritance and are the true Israel attest along with us that, unless they had been helped by your favor and powerful assistance, more than once they would have disappeared after being swallowed down and completely eaten up by the enemies of our salvation. For it has been our experience that whatever help could have come to protect us from elsewhere would have had no strength. The violence and impact of those who attack us is like the waters of a hurricane when it suddenly inundates the fields. Their cruelty equals the savagery of wild beasts, and they employ such cunning and hidden snares that compared to them fowlers and hunters have no skill at all but would seem like complete simpletons. Accordingly we give you thanks for all that we owe you for having rescued up till now your simple and helpless flock from such great dangers, and we request that henceforward you do not allow that same Church of yours to be persecuted by either force or trickery so that day by day we may trust in you alone more and more. Through Jesus Christ, our Lord. Amen.

[*151v*] FROM PSALM 125:

O great and good God, since human help is weak, uncertain, and deceptive, we are clearly being taught to transfer all our confidence to you alone, for the steps of those who rely on you neither go astray nor grow unsteady. Since it you who have promised to make firm Mount Zion, that is, your holy Church by your protection so that it may stand forever against all the attacks of her opponents, we beseech you that you look upon her in this hour and not allow the rod of sinners to take violent action against her. If she be forced to fall under the control of your enemies, even those who seem to be just will easily yield to wickedness. Be pleased, O God, to chastise with another kind of punishment our sins, which are grave; for now, we ask only not to be oppressed by the Antichrist. Protect the congregation of your faithful by encircling them with mountain-like defenses to keep the wicked enemies of your name from being able to wreak havoc on them as they please. At the present time deal graciously and kindly with those who possess some zeal for morality and rectitude. But as for those who [*152r*] not only contemplate

wickedness in their hearts and engage in unspeakable crimes but also devote
their every effort that your word may never flourish, that true religion may be
completely destroyed, and that any sincere invocation of your name be
uprooted—let them at last feel and experience what the workers of iniquity
deserve. May peace and tranquillity prevail and come to unite your Israel to
you more and more; may she become constantly committed to your praises.
Through Jesus Christ, our Lord. Amen.

FROM THE SAME PSALM:
All those, almighty God, in whose souls a faith in your promises has
been planted and renewed remain unshaken like the most solid mountains in
these turbulent times. Indeed, their solidity and constancy is such that they are
no less confident of being armed by your protection and defense than was the
city of Jerusalem with its protective rampart of mountains which loomed up
all around her. So now when the stain and glitter of the wicked [*152v*] are
totally concentrated on scattering and persecuting the Church, do you, good
Father, stand by her and show her how you have a special love for her. But if
our horrible sins, which we openly and sincerely confess, have merited that we
be stripped naked of your help and handed over to the ferocity and cruelty of
the Antichrists, please do not take account of what is rightly owed for our misdeeds but remember that we have been entrusted and consigned to you in
Christ. Do not deal with us in your wrath contrary to your past, long-standing
custom, by which you never granted power to the tyranny of the wicked so
that they might persecute the faithful over a long stretch. For if your judgment
did not call a halt, men who are steeped in justice might dare to desert justice
and give way to depravity, as commonly happens. Be good, kind, and generous, O God, to those who nurture zeal for piety in their hearts, and switch
your wrath rather toward those who both contemplate and do nothing that is
not vicious, foul and wicked. In your mercy preserve and increase for your
Israel her ancient peace. Through Jesus Christ, our Lord. Amen.

[*153r*] FROM THE SAME PSALM:
All those who put their faith in your truth, as is right, O almighty God,
stand firm as the mountains and strong as rocks regardless of how the devil
and the world stir up a storm of temptations against them. Just as cities are
fortified and girded round with ditches, towers, and mountains, so likewise
God protects like a shield and covers like a mighty rampart those whom he
favors and has written down on the page of the elect. Not without reason do
we therefore call upon you, good Father, not to allow the wicked to extend

their tyranny over the Church of the just lest those among the faithful who are still somewhat weak may see how the fortune of the wicked is prospering and begin to imitate their vices and sins with evil zeal. Instead defend and advance the saints; give your kind assistance, we beg, to those to whom you have already granted that they follow you with undivided heart and sincere faith. But repress with your strength and power those who offer opposition to godliness and to the glory of your name, so that your Church, which is the holy Israel, [*153v*] may not be cheated of the salvation she waits for. Through Jesus Christ, our Lord. Amen.

FROM PSALM 126:

O great and good God, hitherto it has been a captivity worse than iron which has oppressed your Church under the tyranny of the Antichrist. Nonetheless in your goodness you have deigned to redeem her, to our great joy and to the great and intense hope of those who still strive for Christian liberty. For now we beseech you that (when it seems that the devil and all the enemy powers are employing all their strength and using all their skills to hinder the good work that has begun) you be not forgetful of your Church's captivity, which you have to a degree begun to reestablish. True, she has acted very ungratefully toward you in not valuing the benefits she has received at their true worth. But for the sake of your usual mercy, do not cut short the work of restoration that remains; indeed, just like swift river beds of your grace and the overflowing streams of your Spirit are to fields baked at noonday, so deign to grant that we can harvest with joy no meager fruit from the seeds of the prayers which are now sown with tears. That way the Gentiles, whose hearts are uncommitted [*154r*] as they observe the troubles that the enemies of your name inflict upon us, may in the end come to proclaim abroad that you have treated us in a wondrous way. Thereby, after these sorrows, may we attain not only the happiness we hoped for but a saving happiness. Through Jesus Christ, our Lord. Amen.

FROM THE SAME PSALM:

Since it seems to be your practice from the earliest times, O almighty God, to help with a unique and marvelous providence those who hope in you when they have already run into a desperate crisis. Thus, when you present them with such an unexpected deliverance, they seem to be experiencing things in a dream rather than in reality. We in no wise despair over the lamentable situation of the Church because we know quite well that it is easy for you, even very easy, to fill our face with smiles and our tongue with joyous laughter so that even our enemies would be forced to say, whether they like it or not, "Their God has indeed wrought marvels for them, when quite beyond their hopes he brought them over to such glorious joy and supreme happiness." We therefore beg you, good Father, that out of your goodness and mercy [*154v*] you pardon the offenses by which we have stubbornly provoked you because of our thoughtlessness, weakness, and innate corruption. When we have been returned to our original grace with you, we may experience no less a change in our affairs than did those who were flooded with a fresh and unexpected abundance of water after being reduced to exhaustion by the parching south wind and the scorching noonday sun. We pray you to grant that what we now sow with tears we may someday reap with pleasure so that we may finally harvest the rich fruits of consolation out of the prayers which we daily pour out humbly before you. Through Jesus Christ, our Lord. Amen.

From the Same Psalm:

When it sometimes happens, O great and good God, that the Church is completely delivered by your singular kindness from the captivity and tyranny of the devil and she sees that all those who are both her members and yours are completely free of errors and darkness, she is flooded with happiness so that she is going to think she is dreaming about so much good rather than having really attained it. Then she may well call herself happy and thoroughly enjoy that solid gladness. She may not only render you undying thanks, but [*155r*] there will be nobody who does not wonder at how great and good are the deeds you have performed for her. We therefore pray that you now at last grant these things to come to pass and that you take pity on a captivity that has been so long and wretched. Deliver your people from dark dungeons and loosen with your usual kindness the chains with which the sons of Adam, whom you have redeemed, have been kept in bondage for so long. May you make joyous and fertile the hardened and thirsty soil of our souls by the life-giving waters of your grace so that the sowing in tears which the godly did in the time of their captivity may some day yield for them the joys they have longed for, and so that the sad and oppressed who till now have cast their seeds with prayers and sighs may harvest with happiness and rejoicing the solid fruits of true devotion and pure religion. Through Jesus Christ, our Lord. Amen.

From Psalm 127:

It is an uncontroverted and settled principle, which all godly men hold to, that a family cannot be set up nor any commonwealth kept going unless you, O almighty God, forward and favor its beginnings.[12] We, who are not ignorant that the Church stands above any honorable house and the largest commonwealth of this world, [*155v*] know for certain that she cannot possibly continue without your support, especially at this time when so many of the engines of both the devil and the Antichrist are attacking her. We therefore demand from you, good Father, with unflagging prayers something no human work, dedication, or effort could achieve, for it has been your practice to grant your people, as if from a dream, things that would otherwise have been most difficult and almost impossible. First, take away our sins, which seem to be the main obstacle to your bringing help in our current shortage and disaster, for they and not anything else divide and pull us away from your mercy. When you shall have forgiven them, as we earnestly petition, increase the Church with numerous progeny. If she should bear you children who are worthy of you and your Spirit, they shall go forth like arrows from your invincible arm against the enemies of godliness and evangelical teaching. Fill our sound congregations and colleges with courageous men, who neither back down nor surrender when they protect your truth by word and deed. Through Jesus Christ, our Lord. Amen.

[*156r*] FROM THE SAME PSALM:

Without your goodwill, O almighty God, all our strength and efforts are in vain. If no private house can be constructed nor any city built without your help and favor being present, how much less could the Church be restored, or be increased, or continue unless you are very much at hand with your Spirit and grace? In vain have men labored, rising early in the morning and enduring long fasts to wear themselves out in toil and trouble without purpose and profit. Accordingly, we earnestly beseech you, O God, do not deprive us of your presence and help in anything we start. Certainly nothing that has ever been collected and restored from the ruins of the Church has been successful without you. Rather you granted this achievement to your fellow workers that, as if through a dream, you had completed on hidden and miraculous principles such a great project for which, if judged aright, human forces would seem to have been completely unequal. Because we have been ungrateful and have terribly abused such great and wonderful benefits, you have now rightly begun to try us with such enormous difficulties, from which human effort and ingenuity cannot free us in the least. [*156v*] Therefore, because of your

---

[12]The U. S. Dollar bill still prints the motto "Annuit coeptis": God has favored the beginnings [of the American republic].

accustomed mercy, deliver us who seek refuge in you when we least expect it or do not know that we are vulnerable to many dangers so that set free we may acknowledge you as the sole author of true salvation. Through Jesus Christ, our Lord. Amen.

FROM THE SAME PSALM:

All who are working at anything without your help and grace labor and wear themselves out in vain, O great and good God. All those who do not have you as their helper cannot protect themselves from their enemies. Since the Church always needs building up and the city of our congregation needs protection, we call upon you to give assistance to the builders and greatly help our fighters. So that we may attain this more easily, multiply the offspring of your Church who can be sent forth like arrows to raise her up everywhere by your word. May they be so skilled and practiced in dealing with your words that when they carry out their vocation, they may in no wise be put to shame. Through Jesus Christ, our Lord. Amen.

[*157R*] FROM PSALM 128:

Nothing good or joyous can happen except to those who fear and reverence God and who walk faithfully in the ways of God's commandments by upright living. That fact now shows us the reason why we are undergoing disasters. In your supreme mercy, almighty God, you gave us your salutary teaching, but the last thing we have carried through is worshipping you in the proper way. We ranked fear and reverence for your name behind our own desires, and we discarded the discipline of your commandments. We have no reason then to complain that sufferings are sometimes laid upon us unfairly. Disregard, we pray, our iniquities and wicked deeds and because of your mercy reestablish within us fear, devotion, and holy behavior. Finally shine down from Zion, that is, from your lofty and inaccessible light, upon your suffering Church and rescue her when she is beset by such dangers. Through faith you have taken her unto yourself as a wife; grant that she be increased by the fecundity of her holy children. May she be like a vine which spreads out widely and cannot be cut down, regardless of how Antichrist strives to do so. [*157V*] We urgently ask that we obtain this especially from you, good Father: that you deign to grant good and salutary things to your Jerusalem and to send peace and tranquillity to the true Israel. Through Jesus Christ, our Lord. Amen.

FROM THE SAME PSALM:

Your prophecies teach us, O great and good God, that only godliness makes men happy, for the fear by which the godly stand in awe of you serves them as an effective bridle toward rightly going forward on the paths of your justice. Since this godliness is the distinctive ornament of your Church, we ask you that in her a continuing effort may be made by teaching and example to educate your children and that these efforts may not be ineffective and wasted. May she be daily like a fruitful woman who can be compared to lush olive trees and fertile vines. We do not doubt that these happy gifts will easily come to us at last if from the lofty dwelling place of your majesty you look down upon the gathering of your faithful with the eye of your mercy, for all true and lasting happiness flows from a sign of approbation from your immense goodness. Since we have no doubt that this contributes to the honor of your name, [*158r*] namely that the Church increase by the continuous progeny of your children, we hope to attain by our most ardent prayers that she may enjoy peace and renown both by her praises and by her purity of life. Through Jesus Christ, our Lord. Amen.

FROM PSALM 129:

You know, O almighty God, how much the enemies of your name have been constantly besieging the Church. They have always harassed her, right from her infancy. Nonetheless it is because of your favor that they have never prevailed against her; that was so that your promises might be fulfilled. Often they were seen setting the plough of afflictions very deep in her back, and with stubborn hearts they determined to gouge upon her the longest possible furrows. But you, O God, since you are just, always cut the ropes of wicked men. We now ask you not to regard what our evil deeds deserve but the glory of your name, for as far as it pertains to us, we are worthy of not only these disasters but far worse ones. But because of your mercy, do not pour out your wrath upon us but upon the wicked. [*158v*] May the wicked be put to shame and fall back, may they wither quickly like grass before they can carry to a conclusion their evil endeavors. They do not deserve that we should be praying for them to have joyous successes, for their endeavors are wicked from the start. But bring it about now that the Church of your faithful may be suffused with the blessing of peace and tranquillity. Through Jesus Christ, our Lord. Amen.

FROM THE SAME PSALM:

The attacks against your faithful, O God our heavenly Father, are not only frequent, but they are constantly being tried and assaulted so that they may fall into complete destruction. Nothing is more desirable to the devil and the hostile powers than turning aside your image from its predestined end. Accordingly, we cry unto you, who possess infinite mercy joined together with supreme justice, that out of the goodness and charity which you bestow upon us, that you snap the ropes of temptation and grind up the snares of those lurking in ambush. That way the enemies of our salvation will be put to shame, as they rightly deserve, and all people may understand that your justice does not allow their tricks and traps to go unpunished forever. [*159r*] Thereby the blessing which you have destined for your elect will not be hindered, and the salvation which we, relying on your promises, have been looking forward to will not fail due to any power of devilish deceit or machination. Through Jesus Christ, our Lord. Amen.

FROM PSALM 130:

O almighty God, you have been accustomed to afflict your faithful harshly and rather often so that thereby they may return to you with burning and perfect repentance. This is what we are experiencing in the Church now in these trouble-filled times, for we, who hitherto have been ungrateful to you in countless ways and who have everywhere transgressed your commandments and law, have been so harassed innumerable times by fierceness of the devil and his minions that we are forced to cry out to you from the abyss and the deepest depths of our misfortunes lest you were to wish to punish our sins so severely. If you decided, O God, both to examine and to punish our iniquities according to their merits, who of us would be so clean and holy that he would stand before your justice? But because we know that you are noteworthy for your supreme kindness, each morning and evening we look up and [*159v*] wait for your help. So despite the fact that our iniquities are very numerous, may you be pleased to redeem us from them all out of your abundant goodness and mercy so that freed from present dangers and pressing troubles, we may both believe and proclaim that true redemption is found in you alone. Through Jesus Christ, our Lord. Amen.

FROM THE SAME PSALM:

When we are constantly tossed about on the deep sea of temptations, O great and good God, we cannot be equal to the temptations so we beg quite rightly that you mercifully come to redress our situation. For you are both judge and witness of our affairs; if you were to wish to examine all the actions in which we ever sinned and punish then severely, who, I ask, could stand before your tribunal? Since supreme, even infinite kindness is found in you, we beg you that we may rely on that alone for redeeming our iniquities. Every day at every hour we find nourishment in that singular hope; we trust that you will never forget the true Israel, which is your Church. [*160r*] Grant therefore that we may obtain from you the remission of our sins as the lasting and sincere fruit of this trust. Through Jesus Christ, our Lord. Amen.

FROM PSALM 131:
Since we have been most ungrateful to you, O almighty God, for the supreme benefits which you have conferred upon us, and since we have so far led a life far from worthy of your holiness and our vocation, there is no reason for our heart to be elated or for it to walk in wonders. Endow us with your Spirit so that we put aside all haughtiness and arrogance and acknowledge the simple truth: we are sinners. That way we can obtain from you pardon for our sins through true and sincere repentance. Then may we adjust our relations with you so that we may be like a weaned child who is constantly looking to its mother who will feed and hug it. For unless you assist us, what else can we or should we think about our powers, except that they will get us in trouble? Because the Church has no one except you for her refuge and is completely stripped of human [*160v*] help, she now looks to you like a child and prays that you do not desert her but so rescue her out of your goodness that she may devote herself to calling upon your name and praising it forever. Through Jesus Christ, our Lord. Amen.

FROM THE SAME PSALM:
O great and good God, who alone has the right to be exalted and excellent, we pray that you do not allow pride to break into our hearts, which are otherwise quite stubborn and rebellious, for all human haughtiness and self-esteem can be nothing except vanity, which has no real or rightful basis. We therefore beg for a humble heart, downcast eyes, and that we may steer clear of projects and endeavors that go beyond the measure and limits of our calling. Grant, we beseech you, that our soul may depend on you just like babies do upon the breasts of their nursemaids. For we see that your Church will never be happy unless she stops hoping in herself and puts all her hope and trust in you alone. Through Jesus Christ, our Lord. Amen.

[*162r*] FROM PSALM 132:

We know very well that you, O great and good God, are not at all unmindful of the covenant in Christ Jesus upon which you have entered with us, but we confess that we ourselves have fallen short of those most holy agreements and commitments. We ought to have lived for you and consecrated all our actions to your name. We did exactly the opposite. We were very cold in our devotion to true and proper piety, nor have we pursued with burning zeal as we should have the reform of your Church. O God, be pleased not to avenge these iniquities of ours. Do not turn away from these prayers of ours because of what we have committed against you. In all our prayers we beseech you that the places in which abides the ark of the covenant, that is, the Church which is your chosen spouse, may at last be able to enjoy a quiet and tranquil peace so that your kingdom may progress in greater happiness and that the glory of your name may be spread more broadly. Make it clear, we beg, that you really abide in your Church, as you promised, by clothing your faithful with holiness and salvation. May the lamp of your people, as your promised, not be extinguished, [*161v*] but may a regal luster and the splendor of majesty shine in her continually. Through Jesus Christ, our Lord. Amen.

FROM THE SAME PSALM:

Since in your immense goodness you have decided, O great and good God, to abide continually in the gathering of the faithful, which is the Church redeemed by Christ's blood, we beseech you that you never forget this promise of your love. We earnestly hope that your resting place may be among us and that you may find in our hearts lodgings made holy and well furnished through faith. Just as we have no doubt but that you want this covenant to remain firm and inviolate, so we ask that you grant us never to leave it but to seek after and carry out the indications of your will, which you have deigned to teach us in your Holy Scriptures, so that the ministers of the sacred rites, the faithful people, and all ranks of the elect may shine resplendent to the honor of your name with true devotion and sincere virtues. Through Jesus Christ, our Lord. Amen.

[*162r*] FROM PSALM 133:

When those who are marked with your name live with one another on the best possible terms and confer together on the best ways of worshiping you, O almighty God, then day by day your Church grows more and more glorious and powerful. Conversely, she is badly fragmented and weakened if those who ought to have dwelt in her like brothers suffer from the ulcer of dissensions and divide themselves into factions. We hope that by your kind gift we may be given peace such that we may join together like members of the same body, which is the Church. But our multitudinous sins stand as an obstacle to such happiness. Can it be that those who differ from you can agree among themselves? We earnestly ask that you cross off the offenses by which we have grievously and repeatedly angered you and that you be pleased to receive us into your grace. Thus embraced by your kindness and mercy, may we cling to you inseparably. That will be the source from which our lasting peace flows, from which the Church is made rich and fertile in good works, from which the hidden and secret [*162v*] treasures of your Spirit reveal themselves and burst forth into sweet fruit, and from which the fragrant smell of justice and godliness shall be wafted across the whole earth. Accordingly, grant those who are humbly beseeching you, good Father, that they may have peace with you within themselves and with all others as far as possible. Then in accord with your promises they may gather in your name, enjoy your presence, experience your richest blessing, and at last attain to life everlasting. Through Jesus Christ, our Lord. Amen.

FROM THE SAME PSALM:

Since by your supreme kindness, O great and good God, you have adopted all of us as your sons through faith in Jesus Christ, it would have been fitting for us to live truly as brothers and not as strangers. There is nothing more desirable or delightful for the devout than getting along harmoniously in the house of God. We therefore suffer no small pain when this fraternal unity, which should be cultivated in a singular way, is being everywhere torn apart and violated. [*163r*] But we confess that we ourselves have provided the obvious cause for this trouble and calamity. We have not been united to you with our whole heart, and we have not obeyed your commandments in all respects, as you require. How can we be good companions and coheirs with our neighbors? We therefore pray you, O God, that you forgive us the sins we have already committed after setting ourselves in opposition to your commandments and law. Join us together to one another by a solid charity into the holy body of your Church so that the sweet perfume of our shared conviction like mutual love may be spread as far as possible and that by the dew of your blessing day by day we may be made more and more fruitful in devout activities. By your kind gift may we attain to not only a peaceful life freed from present evils but a blessed eternal life in the end. Through Jesus Christ, our Lord. Amen.

FROM THE SAME PSALM:

Since you, O great and good God, have adopted all believers as your children because of your kindness, grant that just as we are brothers by a holy birth, [*163v*] so may we be joined together by love, peace, and lasting charity, that while living here we may possess an unmixed pleasure from this special peace, and that we may be a sweet perfume toward life everlasting for all other people who are alienated from you. Your Church, heavenly Father, can be this special example for all mortals to admire. We have really experienced how you are wont to pour forth generous blessings on all who live friendly, cooperative lives in your saving doctrine and worship. We therefore now ask you for this above all riches and other earthly goods. Through Jesus Christ, our Lord. Amen.

FROM PSALM 134:

It would indeed be a pleasant and delightful task, O almighty God, for us to sing your praises constantly and extol your wondrous works ceaselessly. Doing so would require godliness, so that we devote to it not only the day-time but also the hours of the night. Nonetheless our sins and repeated failures urge us rather to tears, groans, and sighs by which we keep [*164r*] saying before you, "O God, we have sinned grievously, and our iniquities are more numerous than the sands of the sea and the stars of the sky, but now we lift up our hands to our holy sanctuary, which is your only Son, Jesus Christ; and we strive to gain by his intercession and grace what we cannot obtain by our own dignity or merits." We urgently ask, good Father, that you at last bless the people who seek refuge in you on Zion, that is, from the hidden treasury of your kindness. Rescue them from their current troubles so that we, whom you deigned to call to a knowledge of your name, may be allowed to voice plentiful thanks and praise with free and joyous hearts to you, who created heaven and earth. Through Jesus Christ, our Lord. Amen.

FROM THE SAME PSALM:

Since you have endowed with an outstanding promise, O almighty God, all who come together to worship you so that you not only want to be there with them but you also are going to set aside special benefits for all who excel in faith and devotion and have been made extremely zealous for your sacred congregation so that they have no desire more earnest [*164v*] and long-standing than that of frequently standing before your face in holy gatherings. But because we take note of how we are defiled with serious sins which weigh so heavily upon us that we cannot dare to glorify and praise you as Christians should, we therefore pray that out of your mercy, goodness, and kindness you deign to grant us pardon so that we may be rescued from the minions and servants of Antichrist, who are doing their best that no place or opportunity be given any longer for your faithful to gather together for your pure and proper worship. Set aside for yourself, we beg, those who so earnestly desire with pure intentions to lift up their hands and direct their prayers toward you. Help, cherish, and defend them from heaven. That won't be at all impossible for your wonderful and invincible power, for it was by your might that the earth and all that is contained in it were not only created but also continue and are preserved. Through Jesus Christ, our Lord. Amen.

[*165r*] FROM THE SAME PSALM:
Your goodness, O great and good God, is so great that it deserves to be glorified forever. We would like to lift up pure hands everywhere to celebrate you and give thanks to your goodness, as is right. Since this ought to be done especially in sacred gatherings, we ask you to be with us there and bestow an abundant blessing on your Israel. Through Jesus Christ, our Lord. Amen.

FROM PSALM 135:
All who prompted by the Holy Spirit come together as one to celebrate your name, O almighty God, have set before them a great mass of blessings, which you have most richly bestowed upon our human race. In heaven and on earth, both of which you created with wondrous wisdom, you continually govern all things according to the decision of your will: you so dispose the clouds, rains, winds, and the other works of nature that [*165v*] they work together most zealously for the advantage of mortals. Since you have put the souls of princes and kings under your dominion, you continually bend them to what is needed for the salvation of your faithful. This is abundantly clear, even more than clear, in the cases of the King or Pharaoh of Egypt and of Sihon and Og, the mighty kings of the land of Canaan.[13] This so strengthens and increases the hope we put in your promises that even though we see the Church greatly oppressed by terrible dangers, we still remain confident that you will help her from the secret and hidden treasures of your mercy so that you may above all forgive our countless and shameful failings by which we have criminally defiled ourselves. That way you will break, overcome, and check the arrogance of the devil and his bodyguards so that we may not be compelled by them to accept once more the worship of idols and adore those

[13]See Ps. 135:9–11; Deut. 2:24–3:13.

statues which cannot speak, hear, and breathe, even though they seem endowed with eyes, ears, hands, and jaws. Grant, we beseech you, good Father, that all may continually praise and glorify your name in the original, or rather the perennial, peace and tranquillity that comes from Zion, that is, from the true Church. Through Jesus Christ, our Lord. Amen.

FROM THE SAME PSALM:
O almighty God, you deserve commendation for many reasons and are to be praised by many names. Firstly, you are good, and your name is pleasant and wonderful. Secondly, you have adopted us as your special people, that is, the true Israel, and you are endowed with so much power that not only is there no other creature but there is not even any other god who can be compared to you. In heaven, on earth, in the sea, and in the abyss it is you alone who does wondrous works. You stir up the lightning, winds, rains, waves, and storms, and you rein them in according to your decisive command. The Egyptians, the Amorites, and the Canaanites felt your power when you were favoring the children of Israel with your kindness, and governing them with indescribable paternal love and mercy. Since you are accustomed to guide the course of nature in such a marvelous way, to judge your people, and at length to comfort your servants, we therefore beseech you to turn your glance, to look and see the afflictions and dangers of your Church. Do not deal with us as our iniquities deserve. We confess with our whole heart that we have lived lives quite unworthy of your name and of our [*166v*] calling, but now when we are so afflicted we do not return to idols, which are the work of human hands and which neither speak, nor see nor understand, even though they have a mouth, eyes and ears. Instead we take refuge in you, our true and only God, so that just as you love the Church and desire to be praised in her, so may you deliver her from threatening evils. Through Jesus Christ, our Lord. Amen.

FROM THE SAME PSALM:
O great and good God, there are two things that ought to stir us especially to praise you. One is that nothing can be found or thought about that is greater than you. The second is that unmixed happiness and solid pleasure are achieved in recounting your praises. On top of that, so great is the number of your benefits that reason for praising you is not only provided everywhere but it almost overwhelms all who think about it with the least attention. Thus without your Spirit they cannot easily [*167r*] find either a beginning or an end to praising your name. When we pay attention to this, we earnestly ask you in our prayers that we may heap praises upon you in a pure faith, especially in

our sacred meetings, give you true worship, and proclaim you by an upright life and holy behavior. Through Jesus Christ, our Lord. Amen.

FROM PSALM 136:

All around your power and supreme goodness are so abundant in serving us, O great and good God, that human thought can never sufficiently compass them. When we examine either how heaven is studded with beautiful and almost countless lights, or how the earth is filled to overflowing and decked with delightful fruits, we always encounter these glorious witnesses of your singular and wonderful kindness toward us. Added to these there are the signs you showed in Egypt when you made clear how you had at heart the liberty of your Israelites by overturning the tyrant with all his goods and then by stripping him of his life. You offered the Israelites no less trustworthy protection in the vast and [*167v*] harsh desert as their most powerful defender when they overran the whole land of Canaan and subjugated its kingdoms to themselves. May you, who are endowed with a goodness, kindness, and mercy so excellent and never ending, look favorably, we pray, upon your Church, which is already undergoing acute and terrible dangers. Do not be turned from your innate kindness by the vile sins by which we have befouled ourselves and your Holy Gospel. We pray that you forgive us for all the sins we have committed against you. Since it is you who give food to all flesh, do not let your faithful be deprived of the sound teaching and the pure and rightful sacraments, which are truly the food of life everlasting. Make every person here understand how good and mighty you are so that you may be feared by everybody, as is fitting, and loved everywhere with fervent enjoyment. Through Jesus Christ, our Lord. Amen.

FROM THE SAME PSALM:

Such is your goodness, O almighty God, that you not only wish to encourage us by it but also (which is no small part of our happiness) you wish that [*168r*] we feel and acknowledge it. To that end you have produced with supreme and wonderful artistry beautiful things both in heaven and also on earth. If we study all these things with a devout heart, we will doubtless find our hearts constantly enkindled and fervent toward you. Moreover, so that you might more powerfully move us and our stony and frozen hearts, you chose for yourself the one people of Israel in which to proclaim how great are the zeal, providence, and the generous benefits which you bestow on those who have once and for all dedicated themselves to your worship and godliness. Finally you have poured forth all the treasures of your goodness in Christ

Jesus, our Lord and your beloved Son, so that you might deliver us from eternal death. Deeply moved by the striking miracles of such great benefits, we give you thanks—not as much as you deserve but as much as we can—and with all our strength we commend the Church to you. Through the same Jesus Christ, our Lord. Amen.

FROM PSALM 137:
All those who take into account godliness and religion, O almighty God, [*168v*] find it extremely painful to see the Church scattered, sound doctrine laughed at, the praise of your divine name put to scorn, and things that belong to religious ceremonies used instead for profane pleasures. Since we see that we are little short of having such things happen to us at this time, we humbly lay before you these daily petitions of ours so that as soon as possible, because of your mercy and holiness, you may be pleased to wipe away all our sins. They are almost infinite and most grave and were not committed only out of weakness and ignorance—very many are those done out of malice and set purpose. Take pity on us and be pleased to remove from us the bitter tricks and attacks of the Antichrist, lest the Church be deprived of all holy joy and spiritual happiness, lest the mouths be shut of those who teach good and saving doctrine, lest your rightful worship be handed over to oblivion, and lest mockers usurp the praises and poems used to glorify you. We beseech you, good Father, for the glory of your name to avert from the Church all the anger and wrath which we have deserved because of the sins we have committed; rather [*169r*] direct them against those who think about nothing in their hostile attacks and embittered hearts except destroying and laying waste your heritage. Through Jesus Christ, our Lord. Amen.

FROM THE SAME PSALM:
Your Church, O almighty God, would have certainly desired to extol joyously your name with psalms and hymns, but until now her oppression and captivity amid the shadows and blind errors of imported superstitions has been very great. Hence it is more appropriate for her in her sorrows to put aside gladsome instruments and devote herself day and night to wailing, weeping, sorrow, prayers of lamentation, and fervent supplications by which she may beg for your help. It were better to forget all delight in the alien tents of this world than have the memory of true godliness seep away from her memory. We therefore beseech you to rescue her immediately from the tyranny of the enemies of godliness, who get more delight out of destroying her than from anything else. We beg that you turn toward them and put a stop

to their mindless attacks, lest [*169v*] they hereafter defile your spouse, the Church, with their errors and depravity. Through Jesus Christ, our Lord. Amen.

FROM PSALM 138:

Your mercy, O almighty God, is so splendid and marvelous that it deserves to be glorified with fitting praise in the assembly of princes and of the mightiest rulers. Because you richly carry through on your promises with utter fidelity, giving salvation everywhere to those who call upon you, the esteem for your name has soared marvelously. Since there exist an infinite number of monuments to your mercy, we pray and beseech you not to hold back your mercy in these wicked times of ours; do not allow yourself to be alienated from us, even though we did not take into account, as was rightful, your laws and your wishes in our actions. We have committed terrible sins against you, we have committed deadly offenses, we have scorned and deserted you. We acknowledge and confess that. But however unworthy we are that you should show favor to us, still it is characteristic of you to grant pardon to those who humbly beseech you with faith. Do not pay attention in this most horrible business [*170r*] to what we deserve but to what befits you. If you now assist those who call upon you, there will be no mortals who will not attend upon you—the common people, the nobles, and even the kings themselves will try to outdo one another in heaping up your praises. You will make your trustworthiness crystal clear: even though you live in heaven, you have a care here for the most lowly and downtrodden, and even though you seem to live as high and far away from us as possible, still you provide examples of justice and goodness so that all may come to understand. We pray that you so strengthen us in hope, O God, that even if we have to walk amid a host of troubles, that we will not fall because your right hand upholds us. Whatever we are of ourselves, remember that we are the work of your hands. Through Jesus Christ, our Lord. Amen.

FROM THE SAME PSALM:

The greatness of your name and the nobility of your words, O almighty God, deserve to be extolled with supreme praise not only among the common and ordinary folk, but also among the famous and distinguished, seeing that you endow all mortals with splendid benefits and have never failed to live up to your promises and your pledges and truth [*170v*]. Indeed, you always hear those who call upon you with a pure faith and sincere heart. Therefore all those who are distinguished and possess nobility and power among mortals praise you, for they recognize the wonderful wisdom of your counsels. While you are yourself most eminent, you do not despise things lowly and down-trodden; from afar you seem to spy out the proud, without giving them the least approval. We therefore ask you to revivify us amidst our troubles. Hold in check the power and hatred of the enemies of godliness so that while you are helping and protecting us, the works of your hands, your mercy may stand resplendent with eternal glory. Through Jesus Christ, our Lord. Amen.

FROM PSALM 139:

So great is your knowledge and providence, O almighty God, that you know completely every single human word, deed, and thought. Even before our souls express their thoughts with the tongue, you know them. Nobody can fully grasp or describe how great is the wisdom you manifest in fashioning and molding our bodies [*171r*]. If we were to equal the coursing sun in quick-ness or outstrip the speed of the dawn, or to wander about climbing to the heavens or plunging down to hell, there is no place where you would not be there to meet us. For right from our first development as an ugly fetus of our body with its parts, none of which were as yet distinct, you already had them present before your eyes and under close scrutiny. Since you are manifest as wonderful in all respects, we pray that you be worshipped and adored, at least in your Church, in accord with your dignity. May the wicked depart along with all who misuse your name contemptuously. Search through your own people, we beg, and examine them so that they may come to know them-selves. Should it be, as happens through human weakness, that they have strayed from the true path which is your goodness, lead them back to the path of everlasting happiness. Through Jesus Christ, our Lord. Amen.

FROM PSALM 140:

O great and good God, we cannot expect from evil and wicked men [*171v*] anything other than evil fruits, for where the heart is wicked, you will never see words and deeds maintaining uprightness. We therefore implore you with all our strength to rescue us from the violence of the wicked and from their evil designs. Many are the snares, traps, and trip wires which the devil and his minions have laid out for the Church. Be yourself her strength and salvation, and bolster her with firm protection in the day when the war of temptations is fought so that the wicked devices with which she is furiously attacked and unluckily oppressed may rebound against their authors. If you do that, you will maintain your long-standing practice of upholding with divine and heavenly protection those who lack human help. Then the just will constantly proclaim your name and enjoy eternal happiness in the favor of your glorious countenance. Through Jesus Christ, our Lord. Amen.

FROM PSALM 141:

We daily implore your protection, O almighty God, and desperately desire it so that our prayers may obtain before you the status of acceptable sacrifices. Because we realize that this is impossible unless we completely divorce our souls from our evil habits, [*172r*] we therefore especially ask you to remove from us all the sins by which we have foully defiled both ourselves and your name. Previously we have not hidden the fact that we have led unworthy and damnable lives. Indeed, we have opened this up before you and made it clear by a common and spontaneous confession. Grant then pardon to your suppliants, and hereafter strip our hearts so completely from the disease of foul vices that we no longer have anything to do with them in thought, word, or deed. May you strengthen the hearts of the devout with such courage and devotion that they do not allow themselves to be enticed by the deceitful allurements and false promises of the wicked. Strike, punish, and correct us, O God, rather than allow us to become soft and listless by the enticements, pleasures, and flatteries of the enemies of godliness. As you see, we have been broken and killed, and final destruction threatens the Church. But we lift up our eyes anxiously to you and beg that you rescue us from the traps and snares of our wicked foes. Since they are now beyond any hope, it were better for them to be caught up in their own snares and evil tricks so that your Church may be granted a way of escaping their criminal hands. Through Jesus Christ, our Lord. Amen.

[*172v*] FROM THE SAME PSALM:

Be pleased, O almighty God, to give us prompt help because of your goodness when we call upon you, lest we be torn away from your word and religion for any reason. May the prayers we pour forth go up to your presence like a pleasant perfume and an acceptable sacrifice, even though our sins do not deserve it. We confess that our hearts have very often inclined toward harmful things and that we have not kept a sufficient watch over our mouth and words to keep us from using that organ in doing wrong, and we have been far too inclined toward and eager for evil activities. That is why we are now being so corrected and punished by you. But out of your mercy and goodness, O God, deign to grant us this: that we may realize that these punishments of yours are pure blessings of your supremely paternal affection for us so that we may deem and evaluate them, when they come forth from your providence, as more helpful than would be our enjoying to the utmost the favor and the pleasures of the world and of the wicked. We have so much trust in you that for us it is an established fact that you make a practice of bringing help to those [*173r*] (provided they call upon you) whose bones have been both so pulled apart and so scattered around that it was almost as if they had already gone down to hell. In accord with your usual practice, do not desert the Church at this time when she is sorely afflicted, but rescue her from the snares, traps, and nets of the wicked. May it be not your people but the wicked themselves who fall into the snares they have fashioned and into ditches they have dug. Through Jesus Christ, our Lord. Amen.

FROM THE SAME PSALM:
Do not delay your help, we beg you, O great and good God, when we cry out for aid from you. This is our daily sacrifice by which we honor and venerate you; as we learn from your Scriptures, it is no less pleasing to you than if we were to bring a sweet odor and pleasant perfume to your altars, as was the custom of the ancients. We therefore pray you to set a trustworthy guard over our tongue and heart that we may not plan, either in word or in the soul's thought, much less in deeds, anything against your law. Keep us from commerce with the ungodly [*173v*] and make us most inclined not only to accept fraternal admonitions and corrections but to ignore praise and flattery. Since there are a thousand traps and snares which our ancient foe has hidden to entrap us, may your favor deliver us in the end from them all. Through Jesus Christ, our Lord. Amen.

FROM PSALM 142:
Every day we lift up our voices before your face, O great and good God, and pour out our prayers and petitions that we may present the sadness and anxiety of our hearts and do it before you, who alone know the path and plan for delivering your people from their terrible afflictions. Our spirit is in constant torment within us when we think about the state of our present affairs. Though we look right and left, we do not see anyone who really wants either to recognize or to take up the cause of your Church. We attribute the evils that have come upon us to our sins, which have so grievously aroused you against us that you stir up such raging and deceitful enemies against your people. Practically everywhere they have set up traps for us, [*174r*] and violence is employed routinely. So take pity on us now, O God our loving Father, when your servants seem to be devoid of all refuge, and nobody is left who might have an interest in saving our souls. May you yourself listen to our shouting

and be a firm fortress for us and our portion among the living. Rescue us from our persecutors, who now seem to have gained the upper hand. If you rescue the Church from this woe, your name will be glorified everywhere, and all peoples will congratulate us when they see how good you have been to us. Through Jesus Christ, our Lord. Amen.

FROM THE SAME PSALM:
Since we are constantly encircled by infinite dangers, O almighty God, our very necessity leads us never to cut short our prayers; indeed, we are always pouring them out, and doing so most fervently, before your face. Is there anyone better than you to whom we should be presenting the woes and crises in which we are caught up every day? You know all things, and the tricks and deceits of the hostile powers are not hidden from you. [*174v*] You alone can be our refuge and help. No trust should be put in human help, for they either do not want to help or cannot do so. We therefore earnestly cry out to you, who are our refuge and our lot in the land of the living, so that you rescue us from the devil, the ancient enemy of the human race, and from his minions. For then our souls will be refreshed and restored and shall confess your name, and all who love justice will join us and glorify your blessings with well deserved praises. Through Jesus Christ, our Lord. Amen.

FROM PSALM 143:
We strongly desire, O great and good God, that you look favorably upon our common petitions and that for the sake of your fidelity and mercy you listen to the prayers we pour forth. We do not deny that the sins, by which we have offended you in the ordinary way, do not deserve this. Were you to wish to try us and exercise severe justice when there is no mortal, or even any creature however pure and holy, who could undergo it, we too would doubt-less lose our case, [*175r*] and would not be able to stand trial before you. Look with your usual kindness and goodness into how the enemy is violently perse-cuting our souls and how we plainly seem to be so crushed and forlorn that our condition seems to differ from the dead by very little. Our spirit is much troubled within us, and our heart is totally numb. Still we retain a vivid memory of your original and ancient mercy, by which you were wont to bring marvelous help to your elect when things seemed hopeless. That is why we now not only lift up our hands to you but our whole chest is panting that you deliver your Church from her enemies. Direct us with your good Spirit so that hereafter by your will and good pleasure we may faithfully carry out whatever

is right and holy, after we have been delivered from our current woe and revivified by your favor and support. Through Jesus Christ, our Lord. Amen.

FROM THE SAME PSALM:

O great and good God, our justice is so weak that those who have been taught by your Spirit [*175v*] know full well that our justice cannot stand up under your judgment. Our spirit is accordingly downcast, and our heart completely fails when we examine our own merits. But we immediately turn to your mercy, and we confess that our justice does not come from us but is your doing. Propped up and encouraged by this faith, we beg for your favor amid the dangers of this life. For if you do not come to our help, we see that there is no hope for our salvation. Show us the path on which we may walk safely and teach us the manner of carrying out you will, and govern all our actions and thoughts by the Holy Spirit, who proceeds from you. Through Jesus Christ, our Lord. Amen.

FROM PSALM 144:

We acknowledge, O great and good God, that all military might and energy come from you alone, who distribute them at your discretion to whomever you wish. When therefore we attribute power and victory to your name, we absolutely take you for our citadel, fortress, rock, and shield. [*176r*] Although we understand that man of his own nature has no grounds why he should be recognized by you and that we have sinned so grievously that we are utterly unworthy of having you pay any attention to us, we still rely on your mercy and dare to ask you that in this difficult and terrible time you manifest your power from heaven to help us and scatter and disperse our enemies. Stretch forth your hand, we beg, and rescue us from the hands of the wicked. It is you who are wont to bring salvation to the kings and princes who trust in you, and you frequently delivered not only David but many others of our fathers from harmful situations and terrible dangers. Since you always heap up innumerable and splendid gifts for your people—not just spiritual gifts but also temporal ones such as numerous children, flocks, riches, and honors—it is thus easy for all the nations to see that the nation is blessed which really has you for its God. Do not now wish to reject your Church: you see indeed her afflictions, dangers, and worries; rush to her help, and do not allow the enemies of your name to lay her waste. Grant [*176v*] that finally rescued from these woes she may sing a new song to you and forever voice her praises to your name. Through Jesus Christ, our Lord. Amen.

FROM THE SAME PSALM:

There is no other force outside your power, O great and good God, in which your people may find a rock, fortress, shield, and refuge prepared for their use. Besides, what account should your goodness make of us, who are worthless dwarfs? Surely both we and all our possessions will pass away like a shadow and mere vanity. Unless you assist us with the mercy with which you are endowed and deliver us from the dangers which endlessly threaten us from all sides, who otherwise could escape from the deceits and subtle wiles by which the enemy of the human race assaults us daily? We therefore pray that you yourself come to our help so that later we may celebrate your praises with new hymns and praises. We do not ask this only so that we may possess the blessings which pertain to this life and worldly prosperity, for [*177r*] although the common folk value these the most, we instead consider the happiest thing would be if you yourself were to manifest yourself as our God, as you are in truth. Through Jesus Christ, your Son, who lives and reigns with you forever and ever. Amen.

FROM PSALM 145:

You are endowed with such singular and outstanding dignity, O almighty God, that our study of it, however insightful, can compass it only to the least degree. But by faith we know this: you are full of mercy, and so full that you are extremely slow to be provoked to wrath. Such is your goodness that nothing can be found, either in the creatures you have made or in the ordering of the world, in which your supreme kindness is not clear. Since we know that the Church, which is your kingdom, is to endure constantly, we ask that you support her constantly when she seems be collapsing and that when she seems completely downcast, you lift her up, nourish in due time all the faithful with your word, and satisfy with your abundant grace all those who trust in you. Do not allow those who call upon you with a pure heart [*177v*] to be denied their petitions. Through Jesus Christ, our Lord. Amen.

FROM PSALM 146:

Worthy are you, O great and good God, that we should constantly glorify you by praises with our whole heart and from a sincere soul. There is nothing more noble or useful that we can accomplish in life. We should trust in you and not in men, regardless of how prominent and powerful they may be, for their bodies easily waste away, their soul is breathed forth, and their designs come to naught. But you, who created the whole world, strengthen your promises with eternal truth while you champion the oppressed, feed the famished, free inmates from chains and prison, give sight the blind, lift up the downtrodden, favor the just, protect pilgrims, orphans, and widows, and parry the tricks, schemes, and deceits of the wicked. All these, which are your wonderful deeds and are constantly on display before us, marvelously increase our faith. Inspired by that faith, we urgently beseech you that [*178r*] you both govern and preserve the Church, which is your kingdom, amidst the tossing waves of the world. Through Jesus Christ, our Lord. Amen.

FROM PSALM 147:

Exceptional praise is owed to your magnificent glory, O almighty God, for we see you restoring the broken, lifting up the meek, and casting the wicked right down into the abyss. There is no force that can be compared to your power. You rule the stars, and they are like your sheep or like servants whom you call by name to do your tasks. You produce the clouds, rainfalls, and hay; you give nourishment to cattle and the young ravens, and you provide a refuge without infantry or cavalry for those who fear you. Look with favor, we pray, upon your Church; fortify her against her enemies and increase the peace of her children. Do not allow her to waste away by a shortage of your word. With your word send her snow, ice, and sleet, and when it shall seem right, instantly calm the blustering winds. Cause the temporary misfortunes, which you use to try her, to vanish suddenly before the favor of your grace. To other [*178v*] mortals you have not acted in this fashion by revealing to them the secrets of your Scriptures, but grant it to us so that we may use them for our salvation. Through Jesus Christ, our Lord. Amen.

FROM PSALM 148:

O almighty God, the monuments to your goodness and power in all the things you have created are famous and glorious far and near. They seem to proclaim your praises in a wonderful and unique way so that were anyone to explore with real thoroughness the heavenly minds, the sun, moon, stars and the system of the heavens, he would not find anything there except an unmixed statement of your charity and wisdom. The clouds, rains, lightning bolts, winds, mountains, plants, animals, and all the works both of nature and of political power by which governments are carried on among men teach us the same lessons. It is surprising how we are so cold about this, for after we have found so much stimulation and excitement from all these things we fall silent and are all but tongue-tied in praising you. What is even worse and harder [*179r*] to accept, instead of the encomiums and praises which we owe you for the great benefits you have conferred on us, we return insults, complaints, and curses. Even when we do not voice these in so many words, we have still dishonored your sacred teaching by so befouling ourselves with the filthy stains of sin. We ourselves do not dare to make statements praising you, and we have held back others from praising your name by our evil examples. It is then hardly undeserved when our troubles grow worse day by day. But, O God, we beg you not to want to back away from the course of goodness and mercy that you have set in this most unhappy time. We know that you can easily overcome any opposition. Your powers remain unshaken—you wanted to conceal them for the moment so that we could rightly understand how great our sin is. Grant now, in accord with your promises, that the Church may obtain and retain all the good things that are suitable for glorifying your name as it deserves. Through Jesus Christ, our Lord. Amen.

[*179v*] FROM THE SAME PSALM:
Your unbounded goodness, power, and wisdom, O almighty God, marvelously manifest themselves in all the things you have created for our sake. It is therefore rightly said that all creatures proclaim you, for they have not come into the light by their own natures. It was you who called them into existence, and later when they had come to exist, they were confirmed in existence by your command and nothing else. They observe the laws you laid down and do not exceed the limits you decreed and fixed for them. While we observe these things each day, it is right that we be stirred to glorify your name, for in them there rises before our eyes and mind the unique craftsmanship of you alone. Having been moved thereby, we now fly to you for refuge, for we have learned that you are the author of so many and such wonderful things. We pray that you deign to raise up the horn of your power on behalf of your people, that is, of your Church, so that she may be able to stand up against all the powers of hell and be more and more united to you everyday. Through Jesus Christ, our Lord. Amen.

[*180r*] FROM PSALM 149:
You are indeed worthy, O almighty God, of having a new hymn continually sung unto you in the Church and of having your praises celebrated in the congregation of the faithful. How could it be that those who are your people should not proclaim you as their maker and their king, and that not just by their hearts and voices but also with all the physical instrument built for that purpose? Since you are to be praised and proclaimed for your nature and goodness and your supreme benefits toward us, do not be so moved by our sins that you chastise us in your anger. Forgive us, we pray, because of your

kindness, when we return to you and beg for your help with continuous prayers. If you take as much pleasure in your people as you have sworn rather often, help them in their great need and bestow on them your resources. Provide us with this theme for extolling your name—may it always be in the mouth of your faithful. We do not doubt that you can extract vengeance from the Gentiles and from the peoples that blaspheme against you and that you can restrain the kings and princes who oppose your worship with leg-irons and chains, laying down [*180v*] severe judgment upon them. We therefore request that you convert even them to you with the double-edged sword of your word, but if that is not quite pleasing, then get them off our necks so that everybody will understand how much you value those who are committed to you and are eager in praising you. Through Jesus Christ, our Lord. Amen.

FROM THE SAME PSALM:

Since you have repeatedly blessed us with new favors, O almighty God, it is needful, unless we were to desire to neglect our duty completely, that we give thanks every day to your holy name with new hymns and songs in the gathering of your faithful people. How can we come to an end of glorifying you when we realize we possess you at every moment and in all things as our creator and our king full of salvation? Certainly when we recognize how much you favor your faithful people and bestow the richest gifts upon the devout, it is right that we should bring forth evidences of our grateful heart in our thought, speech, and behavior, with all the instruments, methods, and arguments that can be so used. In order for us to do that better, put [*181r*] into the hands of our heart the sword of your word so that we may take vengeance upon the flesh, the vices, and the wicked desires which have all but destroyed us. Thereby we can shackle and bind our innate sin so that it may be stripped of the tyranny which it has exercised over the sons of Adam. Through Jesus Christ, our Lord. Amen.

FROM PSALM 150:

When all the things you have made praise you, O almighty God, not only do they do something owed to your dignity and greatness, but they perfect themselves in a rich and wondrous way. There is nothing we can do which is more excellent than glorifying you as the highest and supreme good of all things. Every single day we experience your boundless benefits toward us. Besides, while here the huge weight of our sins rest heavy upon us and because of them we are hard pressed by a tremendous burden of afflictions, we cannot focus very well on your benefits and your infinite goodness. The result is that a person praises badly what he scarcely knows. We pray to you, O God, from the bottom of our heart [*181v*] that the burden of our sins be lifted from us; having put that aside, we do not doubt that you will drive the darkness of present troubles away from the Church. Then she will be able to lift her eyes to you, her maker and redeemer, and she will glorify with the highest praises, as is right, the riches of your goodness and the wonders of your wisdom. But now, we are everywhere confronted with such sad and sorry spectacles that we see nothing but your wrath which threatens us. We do not deny that we have fully merited your wrath; we beg and beseech you that you take it from us so that we may be stirred to the worthy praise of your name not only by words but by every instrument which is suited to lifting up our hearts to you. Through Jesus Christ, our Lord. Amen.

FROM THE SAME PSALM:

O almighty God, the holiness and greatness of your name is celebrated constantly in your glorious sanctuary by the blessed and spiritually minded. They can do this more splendidly [*182r*] to the degree that the secrets of your majesty are seen more closely and clearly. It is also rightful for mortals to devote themselves to praising you always, for they see how the immense treasure of your goodness, power, and wisdom is daily manifested both in the heavens and in all creatures. But we have this task above all others: that enlightened by faith and the Spirit we learn more about your mysteries from the Holy Scriptures than nature can proclaim with all her beauty. We therefore beseech you to stir our hearts so that we may worship you with the purest of praises and prayers. Through Jesus Christ, our Lord. Amen.

[*182v*]

[*182v*]

P RAYER OF DOCTOR PETER MARTYR AGAINST BREADWORSHIP [ἀρτολ–
ατρείαν] AND ALL SUPERSTITION

Assist us now at last, I beg you, heavenly Father, and enlighten the minds and hearts of your Christians with the Spirit of Jesus Christ, your Son, that they may leave behind idols and superstitions and be converted to worshipping, adoring, and calling upon you alone in purity and sincerity. Do not permit any longer that the honor which is owed to you alone be paid wickedly and sinfully to bread, wine, pictures, statues, and the bones of the dead. Your holy name has already been subject to these insults long enough. The purity of your Gospel has already lain in filth long enough. More than long enough have men twisted your Son's institution of the Supper to foul idolatry. At some point put a stop to the fury of men who are mad and bent on hurling themselves to destruction. Keep them from committing shameless and immoral prostitution on every hill, under every tree, and in all the crossroads, [*183r*] streets, temples, and chapels with bread and wine under the name of your Son's sacrament, and keep them from defiling your sacred worship so wickedly and shamefully. Unless you, O great and good God, take away and overturn with your mighty hand this breadworship, it is all over with human salvation and the purification of your Church. Help, O God, help your people whom you have redeemed with the blood of your Son. Do you, Jesus Christ, true and eternal God, solidify this work which you have begun and carry it through to its desired end. But if the sickness be beyond hope of recovery, and there is to be no longer an open and public place for the truth in your Church, come as soon as possible to exercise your judgment. For the glory of your name keep such a terrible reproach away from the sacred Supper, which you have established with unbelievable mercy and singular goodness. For you live and reign with the Father and the Holy Spirit forever and ever. Amen.

THE END

Index to Introduction

Design by Tim Rolands
Cover and title page
by Teresa Wheeler, Northeast Missouri State University designer

Text is set in Galliard,
designed by Matthew Carter
and released in 1978 by Mergenthaler Linotype.
Display is set in Hadfield.

Printed and bound by Edwards Brothers, Ann Arbor, Michigan
Distributed by Thomas Jefferson University Press & and Sixteenth Century Journal Publishers,
Kirksville, Missouri